D0071686

Paul Mazursky

Show Me
the Magic

Simon & Schuster

SIMON & SCHUSTER
Rockefeller Center
1230 Avenue of the Americas
New York, NY 10020
Copyright © 1999 by Tecolote Productions
All rights reserved, including the right of reproduction
in whole or in part in any form.
SIMON & SCHUSTER and colophon are registered trademarks
of Simon & Schuster Inc.
Designed by Karolina Harris
Photo section designed by Liney Li
Manufactured in the United States of America
1 3 5 7 9 10 8 6 4 2
Library of Congress Cataloging-in-Publication Data
Mazursky, Paul.
Show me the magic / Paul Mazursky.
p.   cm.
Includes index.
1. Mazursky, Paul. 2. Motion picture producers and directors —
United States—Biography. I. Title.
PN1998.3.M339A3   1999
791.43'0233'092—dc21   [b]   99-14008 CIP
ISBN 0-684-84735-3
Letters written by Federico Fellini reprinted
with permission of Associazione Fellini.

Photo credits: *Tempest* © 1982 Columbia Pictures, Inc. All Rights Reserved. Courtesy
of Columbia Pictures: 26; *The Pickle* © 1992 Columbia Pictures, Inc. All Rights Reserved. Courtesy of Columbia Pictures: 41; Brian Hamil: 31, 40, 42; Elliot Marks: 27,
28, 29; © 1999 Helen Miljakovich: 4, 9; Photographs by Eric Liebowitz from *Enemies, A Love Story* provided courtesy of Morgan Creek Productions, Inc: 36, 37, 38;
Down and Out in Beverly Hills, from The Everett Collection, and *Scenes from a Mall,* by
Carol McCullough-Wexler © Touchstone Pictures: 34, 35, 39; *Blackboard Jungle* ©
1955 Turner Entertainment Co. All Rights Reserved: 7; *Alex in Wonderland* © 1970
Turner Entertainment Co. All Rights Reserved: 14; *I Love You, Alice B. Toklas* © 1968
Warner Bros.-Seven Arts, Inc. All Rights Reserved: 10, 11.

My thanks to Sam Cohn,
Jeff Berg,
Esther Newberg,
Gina Salerno,
Michael Korda,
and Chuck Adams.

For Betsy

Contents

Introduction

Since I was a little boy, I have loved to make people laugh. I love to tell intricate stories about some of the greats I've worked with. Being something of a performer myself, not only do I tell the tale, I act out the different roles—Peter Sellers' British accent or Fellini's sweet Italian cadence. All of my training as an actor and a comedian comes into play. At last I have some great roles! One day my friend David Freeman, the writer, suggested that I stop telling all these stories. "You've got a book there. Put it down on paper in your own voice." So I stopped yakking and forced myself to keep my mouth shut. The need to get everyone's attention (love) is very strong in me, but the more I withheld, the easier it was to write. Thank you, David.

While writing this book I've wondered if it would mean anything to other people. Jewish boy from Brooklyn moves to Greenwich Village and marries a shiksa. Okay, a nice beginning. Lad gets a part in a Hollywood picture, later becomes a nightclub comic and then a writer for Danny Kaye. Not a bad second act. Then he begins to direct and write his own films and meets along the way a fabulous cast of characters: Peter Sellers, Fellini, Natalie Wood, Isaac Singer, Mel Brooks, Little Richard, Bette Midler, Jeanne Moreau, Richard Dreyfuss, Raul Julia. Not to mention the arrival of two daughters and three granddaughters, and his friends, and his incredible wife, Betsy, who has heard the travails of forty years of showbiz angst.

Would this mean anything to anybody? I've always believed that the power of art is that the more specific it is, the greater chance it has to be universal. The detail is what makes it so human. There is something quite sobering about writing one's memoirs. Not only does it dredge up the past (which I often find myself rewriting), but it reminds you of those places you came from before the show went on the road. My parents and two sets of grandparents, a couple of my devoted teachers at P.S. 144, poor Carl Hutt, a buddy of mine whom I punched in the mouth because he kept stepping on the back of my shoe, my first girlfriend, Gilda, who let me actually touch her massively wired brassiere in the darkness of the Loews Pitkin . . . The past and the recent past begin to merge until we come to *today*. This is not, however, a biography. These are memories, most of them remembered because of the extraordinary men and women I dealt with. I hope these memoirs are like a nice piece of halvah. Once you take a bite, you will want another and another.

Show Me the Magic

1

Fear and Desire

I was born Irwin Lawrence Mazursky on April 25, 1930, at Brooklyn Jewish Hospital. As early as I can remember, I hated the name Irwin. When my mother came out of the apartment on Bergen Street in Brownsville to call me in for dinner, I cringed. "Irwinnnn!" she shouted. "Irwinnnnnn!" Why Irwin? Why not John or Bogie or Errol or maybe Clark? And why did I hate Irwin? I had not yet read *Three Men on a Horse*, where the schnook character is named Irwin. Nobody ever teased me about it. There was just something about the sound of it that I couldn't stand. My grandfather, Sam Gerson (my mother's father, my *zeda*, who jumped off a train in Russia in 1905 and deserted the Russian army to get away from the anti-Semitic cossack goyim and eventually made his way from Hamburg, Germany, to Ellis Island), told me that my Hebrew name was Israel or Yisruel, but those names seemed too un-American to me.

By the time I got to Brooklyn College and started acting in school plays, I began to fool around with other names. Irwin Lawrence as Cassius . . . Lawrence Irwin . . . No. How about Bart Irwin or Bart Lawrence? I liked the name Bart. For some reason Bart sounded strong, ballsy. But then Bart seemed too much of a cowboy name. No. How about Michael Irwin? Again, no logic. Irwin as a last name didn't bother me; anything seemed fine as long as it wasn't Irwin Mazursky. I was getting desperate.

Since I knew I was destined to star on Broadway as soon as I graduated, I had to have a name. How about Michael Barrymore? Or Barry Michaelmore? With every school play I used a different name. In my senior year I coproduced an off-Broadway production of *He Who Gets Slapped* by Leonid Andreyev. We did it at the Masters Institute on Riverside Drive for $200. Bob Weinstein, my coproducer and fellow student, put up a hundred, and I put up the rest. Bob directed and I starred. But I used the name Irwin Mazursky.

About a week after our final performance I got a phone call at home. (This in itself was a major event. In those days you just didn't get phone calls unless someone died. The phone was to be used only in emergencies. My parents, who hated each other, never used the phone. When I used it, which was rarely, I would close the door so no one could hear me.)

"Hello? Irwin Mazursky?" "Yes. This is me." "My name is Howard Sackler. I saw you in *He Who Gets Slapped*. You were quite good. I've written a screenplay, and I think you're perfect for the role of Sydney."

My first thought was that it was a put-on by one of my friends. But there was something about the way he said "quite good" that made me think otherwise. My heart was pounding. Screenplay! The role of Sydney! "Sure," I said. "I'd be interested in the role of Sydney. What do I do?"

Sackler (who later wrote *The Great White Hope* for Broadway) gave me an address on Sixteenth Street. Sackler also arranged for me to read the script first. (Sackler, a golden-haired boy wonder and later one of my best friends; Sackler, who cuckolded me with my girlfriend Naomi in Mexico City; Sackler, the inspiration for the role Chris Walken played in *Next Stop, Greenwich Village*, the poet about whom Larry Lapinsky says, "Underneath the pose is more pose.")

The script was *Fear and Desire*, about four soldiers caught behind the enemy lines . . . somewhere . . . in some war. When they spy on the enemy through binoculars, we see that they themselves are the enemy. Very avant-garde. Sydney is the rookie G.I. He has a nervous breakdown and gets to rape a woman while she's tied to a tree. What a part! I smell Oscar.

The next day I take the subway up to Fourteenth Street. I'm a little early and don't know where to go. I look around and see a church and go in. I ask God to help me get this part. I've never been in a church before. I don't believe in God, but this seemed the right thing to do. Finally, I go to the apartment. I ring the bell, and a female voice tells me to walk up the three flights. A bell! An intercom! A female voice! I was in a strange new world. The door opens, and there is an intense dark-haired girl about my age. She's wearing leotards. And to make matters even more exotic, there is a black dog standing next to her. The dog looks as if he'll attack at any moment.

"Irwin Mazursky?" she asks.

"Yes, that's me!"

"I'm Toba, Stanley's wife. Come in." She closes the door, and I see an apartment, very simple and modern, with almost no furniture. There are, however, a couple of expensive-looking cameras lying on a table.

A rumpled young man with black hair and intense eyes is standing in the corner. He's in his early twenties. "Hi. I'm Stanley Kubrick. Would you please read for me?"

No small talk, barely a handshake, and before I know it, I'm reading with this Kubrick guy. He's not much of an actor, but his eyes are blazing right through me. I lose myself in the part. I figure things must be going well since we're reading the entire script.

I don't try anything fancy, just a very emotional, borderline psycho performance, complete with hysterical laughter.

"Very good," says Kubrick. "You have the part. We leave Monday for California. I'm shooting this in the San Gabriel Mountains."

I silently thank the Christian God I had prayed to in the church. My life in art is suddenly validated! But then I realize what Kubrick has said. "Monday? But I have school on Monday. I go to Brooklyn College. I'm a senior."

"So take a few weeks off. Four weeks. That's all."

I breathe deeply. "I'll ask the dean for permission tomorrow. Can you wait till tomorrow?"

Kubrick nods. "Yeah, but I have to know right away. Oh, it's a hundred dollars a week and room and board. And we pay for the airplane ticket."

"Round trip?" I ask him.

For the first time Kubrick smiles. "Yeah. Round trip. But it's a nonscheduled flight out of Newark." Toba smiles, too. Even the dog seems happier.

"By the way," I ask Kubrick, "have I ever seen any of your pictures?"

"I made a couple of shorts. Let me know tomorrow, okay?"

I'd never met a guy like this Kubrick. He seemed so mature, so determined. A man who knows what he wants and will probably get it. He reminded me of John Garfield in *Humoresque*.

The next day the dean gave me a four-week leave of absence. "Quite an opportunity, starring in a film in Hollywood. Good luck, Mr. Mazursky." The corridors of the Brooklyn College drama department were burning with the news that Mazursky was off to make a film.

"What name are you going to use?" asked Bob Weinstein. "I don't know. As long as it's not Irwin Mazursky. What do you think of Gary Lawrence?" I asked. "I hate it," said Weinstein.

A few days later I am waiting in the rain at Newark Airport with Frank Silvera, my costar in *Fear and Desire*. I had never flown before and was more than a little nervous. I had seen Frank play

"Nat Turner" in the theater so I knew what a great actor he was. He was the first black actor I had ever met. He was a handsome man in his mid-thirties with a deep, gruff voice. His skin was the color of bronze. (He later often played Indians and Latinos in the movies.) For some reason Frank took to calling me either "kid" or "Sydney." "Don't worry, kid. I've flown a lot." "But did you ever fly nonscheduled?" I asked him. "What do you think of Kubrick?" said Frank. "I know he's a great photographer, but I don't know what he knows about acting." "You're right, kid. But I can help with the acting." Frank told me about his work with the Actor's Studio, the Method, Strasberg, Kazan. My head was spinning. I was on the way to everything I'd ever dreamed of. Frank told me about the political climate, the horrors of red-baiting.

By the time we were in the air I was too interested in Frank Silvera's stories to be nervous. He was going to play a part in a new film by Elia Kazan as soon as we finished *Fear and Desire*. "What's it called?" I asked him. "*Viva Zapata!*," Frank said. "With Brando and Tony Quinn. I'd like it if you help me run lines." "Now?" I gulped. Frank laughed, "No, kid. Not now. Once we get to L.A. and settle in."

Suddenly the plane lurched and dipped. Food trays slid forward. I felt as if I were on the Cyclone in Coney Island. (The Cyclone was the most vicious loop-de-loop ride. Satisfied customers often threw up as they got off the ride.) Rain pelted the windows of the plane. I heard thunder. I saw lightning. I was scared shitless, but Frank didn't seem to notice the life-threatening storm raging around us. "Yeah, kid, I play General Huerta in this *Zapata* thing. You can be very helpful." "Great, Frank." "Sure thing, kid." And Frank fell asleep.

Stanley Kubrick got the money for *Fear and Desire* from an uncle of his named Martin Perveller who owned a drugstore in San Gabriel. He was a little man who always carried an adding machine. He had a Doberman pinscher that had epilepsy. Perveller warned us that the dog might throw a fit. The budget of the movie was about $20,000, a lot of money for a small-town druggist, but Stanley was very persuasive.

At the end of four weeks we were still shooting. (I was positive that I wouldn't graduate, but Kubrick assured me we'd finish in two more weeks—and we did.) Stanley told the cast he had to drive down the mountain and try to get a few thousand more from his uncle. Frank Silvera and I went with Stanley. This was a chance to get away from the intensity of the location, plus we might find something decent to eat at Perveller's house. The food on location (a Boy Scout camp in the San Gabriel Mountains; we ate and slept in log cabins and shot in the nearby woods) was pretty bad, and Silvera had worked up an enormous appetite.

Stanley drove the car down the mountain with his usual intensity. "I'll get the money out of that cheap bastard!" He actually spat on the window to emphasize his point. He was livid. It was Humphrey Bogart driving with Ida Lupino in *High Sierra*. I knew Stanley was determined since we had already shot for a month. Conditions were never easy. The crew consisted of four Mexicans who moved the equipment and did a little building; Steve Hahn, a friend of Stanley's who recorded the dialogue (no sync sound); Bob Dierkes, a former coworker with Kubrick at *Look* magazine who handled follow-focus on the Mitchell camera; Skippy Adelman, the still photographer; and Toba Kubrick, who served as the script supervisor. There was no dolly track, just a baby carriage to move the camera. Stanley did all the shooting. No matter what the problem, Kubrick always seemed to have an answer. To me there was never a question that Stanley was already master of his universe.

By the time we reached the Perveller house, I, too, was starving. We nodded hello to Martin, who had already set up the adding machine on a small table in the living room. Frank and I made our way to the kitchen and made ourselves a couple of ham sandwiches. We could hear Stanley shouting at Perveller: "I only need another five thousand to finish, Uncle Martin!" Perveller sounded very upset: "Five thousand? Do you know how many aspirins I have to sell to make five thousand dollars?"

Frank and I wolfed down our sandwiches. Through the sliding doors I saw the Doberman standing next to the swimming pool. He seemed tense, either because of the shouting match or, I thought, maybe he was going to have an epileptic fit. Frank and I made ourselves extra sandwiches to take back just in case Perveller turned Stanley down. We could see Martin pecking away at the adding machine, trying to figure out just how much his nephew really needed to finish this movie.

A half hour later a triumphant Kubrick drove us back up the mountain. "Congratulations, Stanley," said Frank, "you did it." Kubrick nodded as he took a curve. "Yeah. I just hope it's enough to finish. I'll never get another cent out of him."

Two weeks later we finally wrapped *Fear and Desire*, and I flew back to New York just in time to graduate from Brooklyn College. I was by now a legend in the theater department. Not only had I starred in a film, but it had gone two weeks over. But I was still Irwin Mazursky.

*

About two years passed. I found myself waiting tables at the Sunrise Manor in the Catskills. A lot had happened. I had looped my entire performance as Sydney in *Fear and Desire*. (I was now positive that I would win an Oscar). The film was scheduled to be released. I had moved to 205 West Tenth Street in Greenwich Village where the rent was $55 a month, and I was reading Céline and Faulkner and Anaïs Nin. I had ended an affair and lost a best friend . . . and I had fallen in love with Betsy Purdy. One Sunday I took a walk with my friend Frank, a premed student at NYU. We found ourselves listening to the folksingers in the circle under the arch at Washington Square Park.

"You want to pick up a couple of girls, Frank?"

"Sure," he said.

I'd never done anything like this, but there was something in the air. I looked around. The circle was mobbed. My eyes stopped at an adorable blonde wearing a purple skirt and super-hip Allen Block sandals.

"I'm going for the blonde," I said. "I'm going for the

brunette," said Frank, pointing to another cute girl. I made my way to the other side of the circle and got close to the blonde. She had great goyish cheekbones and perfect suntanned legs. I super-casually found a seat next to her. She was alone, and she was read-ing the Sunday *New York Times*. I was carrying a copy of *Neurotica* magazine (published by my friend Jay Landesman), probably the first "Beat" journal. Since there were only a hundred or so copies of *Neurotica* floating around New York, I felt pretty hip. I smiled at the blonde, but she paid no attention. Finally I broke the ice. "Ex-cuse me, I wonder if I could borrow the drama section for a sec-ond. I'm looking for a movie." The blonde looked at me for the first time, her head tilted slightly to the side. She had blue eyes. Without a word she handed me the drama section. "Here," I said, "you might want to look at this." I handed her *Neurotica*. "Thank you," she answered. Her accent was definitely not Brooklyn or Bronx. She sounded more like Grace Kelly. I looked through the drama section, faking interest, hoping that the blonde would say something about *Neurotica*. At this moment a young G.I. in uni-form appeared at her shoulder. "Excuse me, ma'am, but I'm from out of town, and I'm looking for a dance hall or someplace to have a good time." This was either a pure rube or a great actor trying to make time with the blonde. "Well," she said, very friendly, "I'm not really sure where you can go."

"Hey, soldier," I said, "there's a great bar just around the cor-ner." I pointed toward MacDougal Street. "They have a show in the daytime, and it's always packed. It's called Tony Pastor's." The G.I. grinned and said, "Hey, thank you, sir." "Tony Pastor's," I re-peated. "Yes, sir."

As soon as the G.I. left, the blonde said to me, "That wasn't a very nice thing to do. Tony Pastor's is a gay bar." "I know," I an-swered. "I just wanted to get rid of him." For the first time the blonde smiled at me. "It still wasn't a nice thing to do." And that's how I met Betsy Purdy.

About three months after that I got a job for the summer waiting tables at Sunrise Manor. I was broke, and this job would enable me to save about a thousand dollars, enough to live on for about half a year. Betsy and I had had a few dates, but nothing much came of them. Then one day I met her in the park, and she asked me if I wanted to go out for the day on her friend's father's yacht. Maybe it was the salt air, but we both knew that we had fallen in love. We began to see each other every day. Betsy now knew the story of my life, including the saga of *Fear and Desire* which was due out that fall and would probably make me a star. I'd introduced Betsy to Kubrick, and she would be the go-between if he had to reach me while I was at Sunrise Manor. Every three days or so I called her from a pay phone.

One day she immediately told me she was glad I'd called. "Why?" I asked her. "Stanley Kubrick says he has to know what name you're going to use. They're ready to print the credits. Do you want to use Irwin Mazursky?" "Stanley called you?" "No," said Betsy. "He came over to the apartment."

"Really?" I could hear something tense in her voice. "Yes." "What happened?" "Well . . ."

"Well, what?" Betsy sighed. "He sort of made a pass. But nothing happened." "That son of a bitch! Did he kiss you?" "No. He tried to, but I didn't let him. I told him he was a married man." "Fuck him!" I shouted into the pay phone in the Catskills. "He knows you're my girlfriend! What do you mean he tried to?" "He just leaned toward me on the couch, but nothing happened. Do you want to use Irwin Mazursky?" "No. I hate Irwin Mazursky! What was he doing on the couch?" "Just sitting. What name do you want to use?" We'd been through the name bit many times. "What about Irwin Purdy?" "I don't know," said Betsy. "I thought you didn't like Irwin."

"What about Bill Purdy?" "That's my father's name. I don't think it's a good idea." "What about Bill Mazursky?" I was getting desperate. Betsy said, "I don't think you're a Bill. What about Paul?" "I like Paul. It's strong. Paul Purdy. Paul Purdy in *Fear and Desire*."

Suddenly the operator chimed in. "Your three minutes are up." "Paul Mazursky!" I shouted. "I want to keep Mazursky!" "Okay, honey," I heard Betsy say. "Paul Mazursky. I'll call Stanley Kubrick right now." And the phone went dead.

2

Dr. Strangelove

Los Angeles, 1962. Larry Tucker and I took over the original Chicago company of *Second City* after it played in Los Angeles and eventually turned it into *Third City*. Our approach was a bit less cerebral than the Chicago troupe (which included Alan Arkin, Barbara Harris, and Severn Darden). We wanted more laughs. We fashioned original sketches about a fallout shelter salesman, Peace Corps applicants, and the saga of a showbiz impresario named Abe Tijuana who discovers a brilliant flamenco dancer, El Animal. Larry Tucker weighed about four hundred pounds in those days, and when he rolled up his waiter's red apron and turned it into a cummerbund as he stomped the flamenco, audiences went berserk with laughter. There were nights when I broke up onstage and had to make my exit before I peed in my pants. Larry was hilarious.

Third City led to a four-week tryout stint writing for the new Danny Kaye variety show on CBS television. The four weeks turned into four years, and somehow I'd made the transition from being a mostly out-of-work actor to a hot comedy writer. But I was far from satisfied. Here I was writing sketch comedy for TV while the silver screen was staring me in the face. By 1964, our second season with Danny, I was complaining to a shrink, Dr. Donald F. Muhich (more about Muhich later, including his role as Dyan Cannon's psychiatrist in *Bob & Carol & Ted & Alice*). In 1965, Larry and I wrote a very black comedy called *H-Bomb Beach Party*, a story about an American H-bomb lost off the coast of Spain and the ensuing hijinks in the search for the bomb. The movie almost got made—but "almost" really doesn't count. The swimming pools of Hollywood are strewn with scripts of "almost got made" movies.

By 1966 *The Danny Kaye Show* was in its fourth and final season. Anxious to get started on something of our own, Larry and I rented an office on Sunset Boulevard near Larrabee. The rent was cheap, and we could watch the strolling parade of hippies and hipsters from our front window. For good luck I tacked up a large poster of Lenny Bruce over my desk. We wrote *I Love You, Alice B. Toklas* in about two months. The plan was for Larry to produce and for me to direct. We figured we could do it for about $250,000. The script was about a middle-class Jewish lawyer who is about to get married. His domineering mother insists that his younger brother attend the wedding. The brother has dropped out and become a hippie. Lawyer finds hippie living in a pad in Venice, California, lawyer meets beautiful hippie girl, lawyer gets turned on by Alice B. Toklas marijuana brownies, and has unforgettable sex with hippie girl. Lawyer runs out on his own wedding, drops out, and becomes a hippie. Our plan was to shoot it in real locations around L.A. By now, Larry and I were both represented by CMA (today known as ICM). One day our agent, Perry Leff, called us. "This is a very funny script," he said. "Do you mind if I show it to Freddie Fields?" Freddie Fields was already a legend, one of those agents with real power. Larry and I had never met Freddie or his partner, David Begelman. "Well," I said, "sure you can show it to Freddie, but remember, Perry, I direct and Larry produces." "Of course," said Perry. "I just think it's good for Freddie to read what you boys have written." From then on, Larry and I were almost always called "the boys."

The next day, Fields himself called us. "Let me tell you boys something. This is the funniest script I've ever read. I think Sellers would love it."

"Sellers?" asked Larry.

"As in Peter Sellers," said Freddie.

"But he's English," I said.

"Peter Sellers can do anything. Did you see *Dr. Strangelove?* Is it okay with you boys if I give the script to Sellers?"

"Yes, sir," Larry and I said simultaneously. "But I want to direct," I quickly added.

"Sure thing, pal. But one step at a time. If his lordship likes it, then we'll worry about you directing."

Twenty-four hours later Freddie Fields called me at home. "He loves it. He wants to do it as his next project. I can set this up at Warners today. You boys will get two hundred for the script plus a fee to exec produce, plus points."

The enormity of it all filled me with joy and a certain amount of terror. This was the big time and everything I'd ever dreamed about. Paul Mazursky directs Peter Sellers in *I Love You, Alice B. Toklas!* I knew I could direct even though I hadn't the foggiest idea of where to point the camera.

"That sounds great, Freddie" (I was already calling him Freddie). "But I get to direct, right?"

"Sure, pal," Freddie assured me, "but first you and Tucker have to go to the Beverly Wilshire Hotel and see Sellers."

"What's it about?" I asked.

"He wants to meet the two of you and talk about the script. Don't worry, he loves it." Freddie gave me the time for the meeting but warned me that I shouldn't open up the directing stuff. "Not yet, pal. Let him get around to that. Let it be his idea. Trust me on this one."

I was beginning to sense that there was something odd about Sellers. Freddie talked about him as if he was a bit eccentric. But what the hell, Peter Sellers was a genius, and geniuses have the right to be eccentric.

"What's he doing at the Beverly Wilshire, Freddie?" I asked.

"He lives there, pal. He's making *The Party* for Blake Edwards as we speak."

"Wow! Blake Edwards. That sounds great."

"Yeah, pal. Good luck. No directing stuff. Okay, pal?"

At eleven the following morning Larry and I took the elevator up to the penthouse of the Beverly Wilshire. We had rehearsed our basic moves—no mention of me directing and we agreed that if he was really eccentric, we wouldn't look at each other for fear of breaking up. We knew we didn't stand a chance if we made eye contact. (We had already had a terrible incident with Danny Kaye. More about that later.)

We checked ourselves just before we rang the bell to the suite. We were wearing Nehru jackets. I was slim as a reed. Larry weighed in at about 350, so we made a curious pair. We smiled grimly at each other, almost like two pilots going off on a dangerous mission. Many of Sellers' performances passed through my mind: *Dr. Strangelove* (I'd have to call Stanley Kubrick for the lowdown); *I'm All Right, Jack*; *Lolita* (Kubrick again; they must get along). We were off to the races. Fame and fortune. I rang the bell. In a matter of seconds the door opened wide. I had expected a maid or a valet, but there was the great Peter Sellers himself. "Hello, boys. Right on time. I like that. I love your script." He was shorter than I expected, very trim, and would you believe it, he looked Jewish. Before we knew what had happened, Larry and I were having fun. This guy was great. There was nothing eccentric about him. He was very smart and super-hip. Larry and I exchanged glances, safe with the knowledge that we would not break up.

"What I need, boys, is a voice. The voice of Harold Fine," said Sellers. Harold Fine was his character in *Toklas*. Sellers had boundless energy and enthusiasm. "I often like to start with a voice."

"I know a lawyer named Bernie Petrusky. His voice might be

perfect," I said. "He's about thirty-five. He lives on my block."

"Bernie Petrusky," said Sellers. "Sounds perfect."

"If you like his voice, Peter," I added, "I'm sure Bernie would be happy to spend some time with you."

Sellers looked at me strangely. "Oh, I don't want to spend time with Petrusky. Just his voice, thank you."

I decided not to look at Larry, just to be on the safe side. There was something slightly odd about the way Sellers said, "Just his voice, thank you."

We discussed the script, and Peter truly loved it. We talked about casting and agreed that we would surround Sellers with mostly unknowns. This would be authentic and funny.

"I'll take the Petrusky tapes back to London and get the voice down, and we're off to the races, gentlemen." He hadn't heard them yet, but they were already known as "the Petrusky tapes." "If you boys are free this Monday, perhaps you can come over to Goldwyn and we'll talk about directors."

"That would be great, Peter," said Larry, looking at me to make sure I didn't open my mouth. A few minutes later we all hugged each other in the doorway. Sellers loved us, and we loved Sellers!

By the time we hit the lobby, we were on the phone with Freddie. "He's great, Freddie. He loved us! And we loved him! We're going to get him the Petrusky tapes," I almost shouted into the pay phone.

"What the fuck are the Petrusky tapes?" asked Freddie. I explained. "Oh, yeah. He loves voices. You didn't say anything about directing, did you?"

"No," I assured Freddie. "He wants us to meet him at Goldwyn Studios Monday to talk about directors."

"That's great, boys."

"Maybe I can talk to Blake Edwards," I said. "Sure, pal," said Freddie, "but don't be surprised when you get on the set. They don't talk to each other."

I lit a cigarette. "How do they communicate then?"

"With great difficulty," chuckled Freddie. "No, they talk

through the assistant director. You'll see. Good luck, boys. Oh, it's a done deal. Two hundred for the script and seventy-five to exec produce. Congratulations."

Larry drove us back to the office on Sunset. We were elated. In less than six months we'd written a script and gotten Peter Sellers to star in it. Fairy tale stuff!

"You think he's a little nuts?" I asked Larry. "I mean, he doesn't talk to Blake Edwards." "As long as he talks to us," Larry said. But it's a good thing you didn't look at me when he said he didn't want to meet Bernie Petrusky."

"The Petrusky tapes," I said. We both lost it and laughed until the tears came.

The next day we went to Goldwyn to have our meeting. The set for *The Party* was amazing. The interior of a fancy modern home complete with swimming pool. Lots of extras standing around in exotic party gear—turbans, tuxedos, bathing suits, low-cut evening gowns. Directing was going to be fun. We saw them shoot a scene, and, sure enough, Blake Edwards gave Peter his instructions through the assistant director. "Ask Mr. Sellers if he's comfortable crossing to the phone while he's doing the dialogue." "Yes, sir," said the A.D. Sellers practiced walking to the phone and talking. "Tell Mr. Edwards I'm very comfortable. Very comfortable indeed." Larry and I looked at each other as if to check our sanity. Why the hell didn't the two of them just talk to each other? An hour later, after our first director's meeting, we understood why. Peter Sellers was more than eccentric, he was nuts.

After they did four or five takes, all of which Sellers did brilliantly, Blake Edwards called a wrap for lunch. Larry and I followed Peter to his bungalow. Bert, a tall, very self-contained Brit, served Peter a light lunch. Bert had been Peter's batman in the British army in India, a sort of aide-de-camp, valet, and all-purpose fellow. Peter totally trusted Bert, and his faith was justified. If ever Bert thought his boss was off his rocker, he never showed it. By the same token, he was always very polite but never deferential.

"Bert, see if the boys want a bite to eat."

"Well," I began.

Larry quickly jumped in: "I could handle a chicken sandwich."

"Make it two," I added.

"Certainly," said Bert. "Care for anything to drink, gentle-men?"

We asked for some sodas, and Bert was off to the commissary.

"Well," said Peter, "I've been mulling over the idea of Fellini."

"Fellini?" Larry and I said simultaneously.

"Yes. Federico Fellini. He's the perfect man to direct *Toklas*."

I dared not look at Larry. I knew we were in deep shit.

"I love Fellini," I said. "He's the greatest filmmaker in the world. I loved *I Vittelloni*. I loved *Dolce Vita*. But I don't know if he's right for this, Peter. I mean it's such an L.A. story."

Sellers smiled at me as if I were a child. "Fellini's a genius. A genius can do anything!"

"Fellini's a great idea," said Larry. "But doesn't he only do his own thing?"

"Boys," Peter said with a smile, "there's only one way to find out, isn't there? I'm having *Toklas* sent off to the Maestro right this second." With that, Peter quickly dialed a number. "This is Peter Sellers. Let me speak to Freddie, please."

While Peter busied himself on the phone, I sneaked a glance at Larry. His eyes rolled heavenward. But I was too nervous to laugh. This was serious stuff. Our star wanted Federico Fellini to direct our little comedy about a Jewish-American lawyer dropping out and becoming a hippie. Why not Ingmar Bergman?

"Hello, Freddie. I'm here with the boys, and we all agree that our first choice is Fellini. . . . Yes, yes, Fellini. And if the Maestro is too busy, let's move on to Ingmar Bergman."

Larry quickly turned his back to me, avoiding any eye con-tact. Was this guy truly mad? Fellini, Bergman?

As soon as we left the bungalow, we called Freddie to find out what he thought of Sellers' ideas. Freddie assured us that this was nothing new and that it would quickly pass. "I'll just tell him they're both busy but they'd love to work with him," said Freddie. "Just come up with some more names for the next meeting."

"What about me?" I asked. "No way, pal. It's too soon." We had another meeting at the end of the week. It was exciting to see Blake Edwards at work. Now the guard at the gate at Goldwyn Studios looked at us differently. "Go right in, boys," he said. Even he called us "boys."

"Too bad about Fellini," said Peter.

"Yeah," I lied. "He would have been great."

"I'm equally disappointed about Bergman," said Sellers.

"That's really a drag," said Larry.

"Well, any ideas, boys?"

"What about George Roy Hill?" I asked. "We loved *The World of Henry Orient.*"

Sellers snapped at us: "There's no way I would ever work with that man again! Absolutely out of the question!"

To this day I don't know why. George was a fine director. I had acted in a couple of TV shows for him. He was urbane, very intelligent, and actually helped actors. *Henry Orient* was a delicious film. But Peter didn't want him, and he never got the offer. Instead, Mr. Hill went on to direct *Butch Cassidy and the Sundance Kid.*

I then proposed the newly hot Mike Nichols, but Sellers found him not to his liking. Of course, the more directors he turned down, the better chance I had to be named, so I was in a paradoxical dilemma.

A few days later we suggested the British actor/director Jonathan Miller. We'd seen a BBC production of *Alice in Wonderland* that Miller had done and really liked it. Sellers smiled as only he could, happy, relaxed, and beaming.

"That's a wonderful idea, boys. Johnny Miller's a genius." With that, Peter reached for the phone in the bungalow and called Freddie Fields. As usual he got right through. "Freddie, the boys have just come up with a perfect notion. Jonathan Miller to direct *Toklas.* See that he gets the script through the pouch and is put on the next plane out from London. Thank you!"

Larry and I breathed sighs of relief. It looked as if we were home free. And even though I had mixed feelings because I wouldn't be directing, I really liked the idea of Miller.

Two days later we were informed that Jonathan Miller would be arriving at LAX that afternoon. Larry and I decided to meet him ourselves so that we could at least have an hour alone with him before he met Peter.

We took an instant liking to Jonathan. He was a droll-looking man with sandy-colored hair, and looked something like a character from *Alice in Wonderland*. He was witty and full of enthusiasm about the script. We told him we'd take him to a lot of hippie pads and help with the casting, locations, and so forth.

"Have you ever actually met Peter?" I asked, a bit gingerly.

"Yes," said Jonathan, "but we've never really talked. I loved *The Goon Show* and *Strangelove* and lots of other things he's done. I have heard he's a bit odd."

Larry and I looked at each other and decided to plunge right in. "He's unpredictable," said Larry. "He's nuts and sometimes nuttier."

"You have to be careful what you say," I said.

Miller looked at us. "Oh, I'm used to dealing with all sorts of characters, but I'm not very good at censoring my ideas." We assured Jonathan that he could say whatever he wanted. By now we had reached Goldwyn Studios, and this pleased Jonathan no end. I don't think he'd ever seen a Hollywood studio before, and he was amazed at the number of palm trees he'd seen on the drive there.

When Sellers met Miller, he immediately embraced him as if he were a long-lost friend. "I'm so happy you're here, Johnny," said Peter. "You know the boys?" "Yes," said Jonathan. "They picked me up at the airport." "Splendid." Peter smiled. "I love the script," said Jonathan. "Yes," said Peter. "And the boys have gotten me the Petrusky tapes, so I'll get onto the voice of Mr. Harold Fine posthaste." We explained what the tapes were. "Jolly good idea," said Jonathan. (By now Larry and I had adopted slight British accents as well.) Miller talked about casting, locations, meeting real hippies. Sellers was all happy nods and agreements. Finally, the logjam was broken! *Toklas* was on its way!

Then Jonathan said something about music. I never quite understood what it was he said. It was just an idea, a notion. Peter turned pale and his body stiffened. "I don't think this is going to fly, Johnny. No. Not at all. Bert." He turned to his batman. "See that Mr. Miller gets on the next plane back to London. Thank you so much for coming, Johnny."

With that, Sellers walked out of the bungalow. We had no idea what had happened. Bert was already busy on the phone. Larry and I took Jonathan outside and apologized. We spent a few minutes trying to put the pieces together.

"I said something or other about music," said Jonathan. "He's off his rocker," I said. "Quite," said Jonathan. "Oh, well. Perhaps I can use this experience in some other life." We laughed, but it was a grim moment for all of us. Larry and I didn't know what to do.

The next day Peter proposed that I direct the film.

"It's been staring me in the face all this time," said Peter. "You obviously know the script, and you have a marvelous handle on the acting side of things."

I looked at Larry. He shrugged, as if to say, "Let's go for it."

"Are you sure, Peter?" I asked. "I mean, I'd love to direct this film, but I don't want you to think I'm pushing for it."

"We'll get Freddie Francis to shoot it and Johnny Jymson to do the editing," said Peter, his mind already made up. I had no idea who Freddie Francis and Johnny Jymson were.

"That sounds great, Peter," I said. "Freddie Francis and Johnny Jymson! Wow!" "And I'll be there to help with the staging," added Peter with great excitement. "This is going to be good stuff." I felt like crying with joy. I absolutely believed everything would work out. No matter what I'd thought up to now, Peter didn't seem the least bit crazy. If anything, he made good sense. Support me with a top cameraman and an ace editor and know I'd have Peter himself to help stage the film. Perfectly logical.

As soon as we got back to our office, we called Freddie to give him the good news. "He'll eat you alive," said Freddie. "He's got too much time to turn the thing around." "You don't understand, Freddie," I said. "This was his idea. I didn't push him into it. He really likes me and he really respects me. Besides, what's the worst that can happen?" I could hear Freddie chuckle. "Kid, you don't know this guy like I do. But what's done is done. Let's make the best of it." Larry and I assured Freddie we'd walk on eggshells around Sellers. "Egg shells," said Freddie grimly. "It's a fucking minefield."

I now walked around like a director. There was a new zip to my step, not to mention a certain suaveness. The only person not to get too excited was my wife, Betsy. "That's great, honey," she said. "Just don't work too hard." But my head was spinning with ideas: shots, camera angles, casting prospects, mise-en-scène. Fellini, Truffaut, Sturges, Lubitsch. Billy Wilder, Mazursky! Mazursky!—I was ready to join the pantheon and I hadn't even said "Action!" yet.

A few days later I came up with the idea of getting Haskell Wexler to shoot the film. He had a great reputation, and I thought it would be better if an American did the movie. He'd know the hippie scene and be familiar with L.A. I sent the script to Boston where Wexler was shooting a film. In less than a week I got a letter from Wexler stating that while he had a few script reservations, he'd love to do the movie. I called Peter, who seemed quite elated at this good news. "I hear Wexler is top-notch," he said. "Why don't you pop over to the house tomorrow since it's the fourth of July. We're not filming. We can have a little chat." "I'd love to, Peter. Would it be okay if I bring my daughter, Meg? She could swim." I knew Peter had a pool. "By all means," he said. "Britt's younger brother is here for a visit from Sweden. He's about ten." I called Larry to advise him of the meeting. "Have a great time," said Larry. "Remember what Freddie said about the minefield."

Little did I know. The next afternoon my ten-year-old daughter, Meg, and I arrived at the house. The door was opened by Britt Ekland Sellers. She was wearing a bikini and was probably the most beautiful woman I'd ever seen—a perfect body, huge blue eyes, and full pink lips. Britt was also very gracious. She took us to the backyard area so that Meg could swim with her brother. I forget the boy's name, but he was as handsome as Britt was beautiful. Peter was delighted to see me, and I must admit I was very happy to be there. Peter suggested that the two of us retire to his den for our "chat."

"What do you think of my last few films, Paul?" said Peter. I decided to be totally honest. I knew that crazy people could tell when you're faking it.

"I think you're the greatest comic actor in the world. *Strangelove; Lolita; I'm All Right, Jack*—all masterpieces," I said.

"Thank you," Peter said.

"But I don't think the last few things have been great. I think the scripts were not as good." I looked at Sellers, trying to see if he was offended. He seemed quite cheerful.

"I appreciate your candor. Scripts not as good. Yes. Quite," he said.

"I mean, you were good. You were funny. But the films weren't really great. And you're a great artist, Peter. You deserve better than *The Bobo*," I said. (*The Bobo* was a real turkey that Sellers had made recently in Spain.)

He seemed content. We discussed the Haskell Wexler situation, and that satisfied him. At this point Peter announced that he was off to his bedroom for his afternoon "kip." A "kip" was a nap. Peter explained that since the heart attack he'd suffered a couple of years ago, he always had a nap in the afternoon. "You and Meg stay as long as you wish. Britt will entertain you."

Peter smiled and then was gone. Out by the pool, Britt was supervising the kids who were laughing and splashing. The sun was shining and life was good. I sat down next to Britt, and she confessed that she was worried about a role she was about to play in a new film, *The Night They Raided Minsky's*. Bill Friedkin was the director, and Britt was going to play an Amish woman. I suggested she do some research on the Amish or, even better, go to Pennsylvania and meet a real Amish woman. She liked the idea but was dubious about going. I was now into my "directing" mode, and I insisted that she make the effort. She sighed, and the top of her bikini stretched to its limit. She was stunning. Peter was a lucky man. About a half hour later, Meg and I left. Britt thanked me for helping her. I pecked her on the cheek, and she did the same to me.

The next morning I walked into our office on Sunset Boulevard. Larry Tucker was already there, clearly very depressed. "What's the matter?" I asked him. "Why'd you do it?" said Larry. "Do what?" I said. "Fuck Britt. Freddie just called. He said that Peter is suing for divorce and naming you as the corespondent." I started to laugh. "Come on. I wouldn't mind fucking her, but the closest I got was a peck on the cheek." "Freddie says you're out. Sellers thinks you're the devil." I realized this wasn't a joke. "What are you talking about? This is crazy! I swear I didn't do anything. Meg was with me. Britt's kid brother was there all the time!" The more I protested, the guiltier I sounded. "I'm calling Freddie!" I shouted.

Freddie was put right through to me. "Why'd you do it, pal?" "I didn't do anything, Freddie. I swear." "Was she great? I mean she is a great piece of ass." "The closest I got to her was my shoulder touched hers," I explained. "What was she wearing?" asked Freddie skeptically. "A bikini." "You shouldn't have done it, pal." "Freddie, I swear to you on the life of my daughter who was with me all the time, I didn't fuck Britt Ekland!" "I mean," sighed Freddie, "I'd understand it if you did. She's gorgeous." "But I didn't! The only thing I did was tell Peter *The Bobo* stank!" "That's almost as bad as telling Sellers you fucked his wife," said Freddie. "He practically directed *The Bobo*." I told Freddie I was going right over to Goldwyn to confront Sellers. "Don't do it, pal. That'll be the end of *Toklas*," warned Freddie. "But this is insane! I'm being named as a corespondent! My wife will kill me." "Yeah, but you're clean," said Freddie. "She'll understand. The thing now is for you to lay low. It could blow over."

"What about me?" asked Larry. "Should I still meet with him?" "Absolutely," said Freddie. "Peter loves you." Freddie chuckled. "Let's face it, you didn't fuck Britt."

They were laughing at me even though I was about to make headlines as a corespondent. Somehow Freddie calmed me down, and I agreed to say nothing for a few days. All I knew was that Peter had summoned his lawyer from England. I was very worried. More than that, I was depressed. I was no longer going to direct, and I was truly innocent of all charges. Sellers was paranoid. Perhaps he smelled my lust, but nothing ever happened.

By Friday, everything turned around. When Peter's lawyer arrived at the airport, he was immediately sent home. Sellers had changed his mind and would not sue for divorce. I was relieved. But I was still out as the director; Peter had chosen Hy Averback. Averback was an experienced television director. He had a good sense of humor and knew that he had fallen into this job. I liked Hy. He was more than kind to me. He assured me in that deep, soothing voice of his that I could contribute behind the scenes. That was nice of him, but I still felt down and kind of lost.

In the following weeks the film was cast. Sellers returned to England with the Petrusky tapes, and Larry, Hy, and I were free to work. We found Leigh Taylor-Young and cast her as the hippie girl with the butterfly tattoo on her thigh. Leigh was married to Ryan O'Neal and was utterly beautiful. Joyce Van Patten, an old pal of ours, was set to play Peter's desperately adoring bride-to-be. And the great Jo Van Fleet was cast as Harold Fine's demanding mother who is accidentally turned on by Alice B. Toklas marijuana brownies. We had assembled a great cast. The only problem was that I had to hide during the shooting. Sellers was not to see me. "He could flip, pal," said Freddie. "You gotta lay low."

The first day of shooting was in Venice. The art director was Pato Guzman, later to become my production designer and co-producer on most of my films. Pato was Chilean and had a unique eye for Americana, not to mention a delicious sense of humor. (We worked together for twenty-five years).

Warner Brothers spared no expense. There were large trucks, dozens of crew members, and a huge trailer for Peter. Everyone was excited about the film. The only problem was that I was parked two blocks away. The plan was for Larry to join me every now and then to give me a progress report. It was very frustrating. About two hours after shooting had begun that first day, Bert came hurrying up to my car. "Mr. Sellers wants to see you in his trailer," he said. I was shocked. What was this about? Wasn't I the devil? "What's happening, Bert?" I asked. By now we were walking to the set at a rapid pace. "Don't know, sir. All his nibs said was that he wanted to see you." I went through a dozen scenarios. We reached the trailer, and Bert opened the door for me. There stood Peter, looking every bit like my fantasy of Harold Fine. He avoided any eye contact with me. I looked around and saw Larry Tucker, Hy Averback, and Charley Maguire, the line producer, all standing together in the front of the long trailer. There was a small television set in the trailer. He already had a version of video playback. "Please play take one back for Mr. Mazursky," said Peter. I looked at the three conspirators for some hint of what was going on. Larry had a small smile, Charley was sweating, and Hy seemed to be mouthing to me silently, "Say what you want." Bert hit the controls, and there was a brief scene of Peter walking with his hippie kid brother, played by David Arkin, a nephew of Alan Arkin. I watched the scene intently. What a thrill to see our words on screen! "Ask Mr. Mazursky what he thinks of the take," said Peter to no one in particular. Was this the Blake Edwards communication bit? Hy mouthed his words again, "Say what you want." "Tell Mr. Sellers," I said, "that it's an excellent take. Very good. Perhaps if he had a slight hesitation in his walk, it might be amusing."

The trio turned to Peter for his reaction. Without a moment's hesitation he said, "Let's go for another take. I want to try this hesitation bit." And with that Peter strode out of the trailer. Hy quickly whispered that it was a good idea. I breathed a sigh of relief and followed the group out to the set. "What do I do?" I asked Larry. "Stay and watch or go back to the car and wait for another call?" "Stay," Larry said, smiling. "I think His Holiness liked what you said."

This routine went on for two days. Sellers would ask for me to come into the trailer. The whole time I was there, he said not one word directly to me. I'd give my opinion, and they would go for another take. I was concerned that this would unsettle Hy Averback, but he was splendid. Hy saw the film as a stepping-stone in his career and seemed to really understand the mechanics of Sellers' bizarre head-trip. Larry and I were so relaxed we began to laugh again. Then on the third night of shooting, Bert called me at home and told me that Peter wanted to see me. "Will you be there, Bert? What's it about?" "Don't know, sir. But I won't be there." "What about Britt?" I asked nervously. "Oh, she lives there, sir." Nothing could ruffle Bert. Now what? I wondered. Was this going to be about me as the corespondent? Was it about the film? As I drove to Sellers' house in Beverly Hills, I tried slow, deep breathing to calm myself.

The door was opened by Britt. I forget what she was wearing, but it wasn't a lot. She seemed even more desirable than before, and although I was innocent, I felt guilty. "Oh, hi, Paul," Britt said with a big smile. "Peter is expecting you." She seemed totally relaxed.

I followed her into the living room. There was Peter. He smiled at me. "Thank you, Britt," he said, and she left the room. "Hi, Peter," I said. "Hello, Paul."

He looked at me with great intensity. Was he going to shoot me? Hit me? No. He suddenly rushed forward and put his arms around me. I didn't know what to do, so I put my arms around him. "The ship is sinking, Paul. Sinking, I tell you," and with that he began to sob. What the fuck is going on? I wondered. Here I was holding up a sobbing Peter Sellers. "Sinking, Paul. We need a captain. You've got to take the helm! I've made a terrible mistake!" Did he mean mistake about Britt or about *Alice B. Toklas?* For a moment I thought he would collapse in my arms. "I think Hy is doing a great job, Peter." "You've got to take the helm, Paul," Peter insisted. "Let me be the first mate," I improvised. "Hy is the captain, but I'll be there to help steer the ship." Sellers broke free and looked at me. He smiled and wiped the tears from his eyes. "Yes, Paul," he said with sudden enthusiasm. "You'll be the first mate!" As Freddie had predicted, things could always turn around with Peter Sellers.

For the next month the ship sailed smoothly. Larry and I had found a novel by Michael Frayn called *The Russian Interpreter* that we wanted to turn into a movie. It was about a British publisher who goes to a book fair in Moscow and is approached by a dissident Russian poet who asks him to smuggle his work to the West.

Peter loved the idea and decided we'd call our new company "Peter, Paul and Larry Productions." He summoned David Begelman from New York and Sandy Lieberson, a CMA agent, from London. Freddie would join us for a meeting in Sellers' home in two days. Sure enough, two nights later we all met at Peter's home. Freddie was his usual lively self. Begelman, whom I'd never met, wore a black suit, probably a British cut, a very expensive cream-colored shirt, and a black tie. He was very suave and full of smiles with Peter. Sandy Lieberson seemed very young and likable, a man with no pretense. He was clearly jet-lagged.

Peter was full of enthusiasm. "I love *Interpreter!* This will be the first film that truly explores the Russian coldwar dilemma. It's a perfect role for me, and the boys have come up with some wonderful notions."

Fields, Begelman, and Lieberson nodded enthusiastically. "Sounds great, Peter." "Fabulous, Peter." "It's a wonderful idea. Wonderful, Peter."

"Yes," Peter said, pacing back and forth. "And we're going to call it Peter, Paul and Larry Productions!"

Begelman smiled. "I love it, Peter." Freddie and Sandy nodded approvals.

"And we're going to split the profits equally," said Peter. "One-third, one-third, and one-third. Equal portions for me and the boys."

The agents tried to hide their disbelief. Larry and I smiled modestly, not daring to look at each other. After a moment, Freddie spoke. "Jesus, Peter, I know you love the boys and so do I, but *Interpreter* will be only their second movie. I was thinking more along the lines of fifty percent for you, and the boys split the other half." I admired the way Freddie was so open about his opinion of the deal.

But Peter would have none of it: "Out of the question, Freddie. It's going to be an equal share all around the table!"

"Then that's the way it'll be," said David Begelman. Larry and I quickly exchanged glances. It was clear that our agents knew when the discussion with Sellers was over.

"Wonderful," said Peter. "Let's drink to *The Russian Interpreter* and to Peter, Paul and Larry Productions." We all stood up and toasted. Peter smiled at me, and even though I knew he could turn on me again, this time I was positive that nothing could go wrong. Freddie gave me the quickest glance possible that said to me, "Your troubles are just beginning, pal," but nothing could bring me down.

"Thank you so much for flying in, David and Sandy," said Peter, all smiles. "Well, it's off to bed for me. I'm shooting a film, you know. Have a safe journey home, gents." With that, Peter strode out of the room, a happy man.

About two weeks later the shit hit the fan again. Peter had confessed to Larry and me that while he liked Los Angeles, there was nothing stimulating to do in the evening. He proposed a "cinema club." "We'll show a different film once a week and serve the food of the country the film is set in. I was thinking of Tuesday evenings at 8:30 at the Charles Aidikoff Studios. It's a delightful little screening room. I thought we'd start with *Pather Panchali* by Satyajit Ray, and I would serve curried lamb and the usual condiments."

"That's a great idea, Peter," said Larry. "I loved *Pather Panchali*," I added. "I can't wait to see it again." And I meant it. This was the side of Sellers that was so attractive. It would be fun to see a fine film once a week and talk about it. I began to think of what film I would suggest.

"Good," said Peter. "And Bruce and Thea will bring some hash brownies, and we can get a bit of a buzz on." Bruce and Thea were Bruce McBroom, the still photographer on *Toklas*, and his girlfriend, the great Theadora Van Runkle, who did the costumes for our movie. "So it'll be Bruce and Thea, Paul and Betsy, Larry and Marlene. Of course, Myrna will be there." (Myrna was Peter's secretary.) "And I thought I'd invite Leigh-Taylor," sighed Peter. There was no mention of Britt. By now we knew that Peter had fallen badly for Leigh Taylor-Young, whose husband, Ryan O'Neal, was out of town shooting a movie. As usual, as soon as Peter left, Larry and I had a huge laugh. This was going to be fun!

Pather Panchali, curried lamb, hash brownies—how could we get through the night without losing it?

Came Tuesday night and the first screening, and things went smoothly. *Pather Panchali* was very powerful, the curry was delicious, and the brownies were very potent. Peter sat in the back of the small screening room holding hands with the exquisite Leigh-Taylor. It was fun.

"What shall we see next week?" asked Peter.

"How about *Vittelloni?*" I said.

"*Vittelloni?*" said Peter. "I don't think I know it."

"Fellini's *I Vittelloni*. It's one of his first films. It's really great, Peter."

"Wonderful, Paul! I can't wait for Tuesday!" said Peter.

"I'll bring some hors d'oeuvres from La Scala," I threw in.

"And I'll make some pasta," added Betsy.

"And we'll bring the brownies," said Theadora.

"Fellini's *Vittelloni*, pasta, and hash brownies—sounds like a great mix," said a happy Peter Sellers.

Truthfully, I couldn't wait for next week myself. I loved *Vittelloni* and wanted to see what effect it would have on the crowd. I had first seen it in the fifties at the Eighth Street Playhouse in Greenwich Village. I remembered coming out of the afternoon screening into the summer sunlight, tears in my eyes. Who was this Fellini who told us the story of four bored young men in a small town in postwar Italy and made us feel we knew them like brothers?

Toklas was going very well. Peter had Harold Fine down perfectly. The scenes were funny and sometimes touching. He was truly a genius. Everybody seemed happy. "It's almost Tuesday night," chuckled Peter.

My wife, Betsy, prepared a large pot of spaghetti Bolognese, and I bought a delicious trayful of goodies from La Scala. By the time we got to the Aidikoff screening room, all the others were already there nibbling on their hash brownies. This was a happy crowd. People dug into the salami and cheese and peppers.

"I love these anchovies," said Larry. "As a matter of fact, I also love the peppers and the cheese and the bread, and I also love you, Alice B. Toklas!" Laughter filled the air!

"Well," said Peter. "Shall we get to the film?" Peter leaned over and hit the controls of the squawk box. "All right, Charles, we're ready for the *Vittelloni*."

A few seconds went by, then the heavily New York–accented voice of Charles Aidikoff spoke: "Ready for the what, Mr. Sellers?"

"*Vittelloni*," said Peter. "Federico Fellini's *Vittelloni*. It's his masterpiece."

"Sorry, Mr. S.," answered Aidikoff. "I ain't got no *Vittelloni*."

A stab of fear coursed through my veins. I realized that I had not ordered the film. "Oh, Peter," I said in despair. "I thought Myrna was ordering the films."

"Nobody told me to order anything," Myrna threw in quickly.

"I'm not blaming you, Myrna. It's my fault," I told her. I could see that the others were coming down off their highs very fast.

"You mean," said a very distraught Sellers, "we don't have Fellini's *Vittelloni?*"

"No," I said. "No, *Vittelloni*."

"Does anybody want some spaghetti?" asked Betsy, lifting the lid off the large black pot of pasta.

"I don't want spaghetti, and I don't want *Vittelloni!*" Sellers shouted hysterically.

"Well," said the ever calm Betsy, "I'm hungry." And she began to serve herself. I could see Larry Tucker fighting off massive tears of laughter, but I was pissed.

"I don't ever want *Vittelloni*. Never, ever, never!" shrieked Sellers.

"Fuck you, Peter!" I lost my self-control. "My wife offered you a plate of spaghetti. Who the fuck are you to be rude? I made a mistake. Okay? It's my fault. But fuck you! I'm only human!" I was shaking.

Dead silence in the room. Everyone waited to see the next move. Then from out of the squawk box we heard the marvelously unpretentious voice of Charles Aidikoff: "I ain't got no *Vittelloni*, Mr. Sellers, but I could show you something else. I'm not supposed to show it, but what the hell. Nobody's seen it yet. It's a movie by this guy Mel Brooks. *The Producers*."

"Run it, Charles! Whatever it's called, run it! As long as it's not *Vittelloni!*"

The room went dark. For the next two hours, in spite of the anger and craziness, we all laughed helplessly. We were seeing a comic masterpiece. When the lights went on, Peter dialed a number on the telephone. "Hello, Joe. This is Peter Sellers. Sorry to call you so late. . . . Yes, I know, Joe. It's two A.M. for you in New York, but I had to call and tell you I've just seen the greatest comic film of our time, *The Producers*. It's a masterpiece, Joe. Greater even than Fellini's *Vittelloni*. And I'm taking out a full-page ad to that effect in tomorrow's trade papers." Sellers hung up, a happy camper. He turned to us, completely calm. "That was Joseph E. Levine, the producer. Good night, all."

For reasons that I still do not understand, the *Vittelloni* incident was soon forgotten by Peter. I expected him to carry his rage into the next days, and I couldn't believe he would ever forgive me for standing up to him. Not only did he not mention it, he was even nicer to me. He once woke me up at 2 A.M. and played a record. "Listen, Paul. It's Don Ellis and the Big Band. Absolutely perfect for *Toklas*." I could feel Betsy stirring in bed next to me. "Sounds wonderful, Peter," I said with a yawn. "Yes," he chuckled. "I'm sending Bert over with the disc this very moment." It was useless to argue. Half an hour later Bert delivered the LP as if it were a perfectly normal thing to be doing at 2:30 in the A.M.

Then there was the fabulous evening at the Sellers' home with a concert by Ravi Shankar and his great tabla player. Peter did a perfect imitation of Shankar's Indian accent. After the concert we got to meet Shankar and hear Peter do the accent to his face. Ravi laughed and so did we. These were exciting times. And although we were always slightly nervous that Peter would suddenly lose it, nothing happened. His work on the film was impeccable. He was prompt, fully prepared, and very generous to his fellow actors.

Then came three looney episodes in a row.

It was Peter's routine every morning when he showed up on the set to greet everyone by their first name. "Morning, Hy. Hello, Larry. Good morning, Paul. Morning, Jo. Joyce, my dear . . ." Suddenly Peter turned pale. He hurried into his trailer, visibly shaken. Larry and I raced after him, almost like the Marx brothers swooping along. We knew something was wrong, but what?

"You okay, Peter?" asked Larry.

"June Sampson is wearing purple," said Peter between clenched teeth. June Sampson was the script girl on the film. It was her job to keep a record of all the shots made, the lenses that were used, and the camera angles chosen. The script girl is the watchdog on a film, and June was very good at her job. She was British, always cheerful, and knew Peter. "Purple is death," said Peter, the color all gone from his face. Larry and I peeked out of the trailer. Sure enough, June was wearing a purple cashmere sweater. Larry and I shook our heads in disbelief, as if to say how could she be so stupid as to wear purple.

"Purple is death?" asked Larry.

"Yes," said Peter. "Sophia told me that. You never wear purple on a set. Never! Purple is death!"

We knew that Sophia was Sophia Loren. We also knew we'd better hustle if we wanted any work out of Sellers. We hurried over to June who was chatting happily with someone. I took her aside and told her what had happened. "You have to get a sweater from wardrobe, June." June burst into tears. "Me mum knit this sweater for me. I love . . . this . . . sweater. "June," I whispered, "he's nuts. He thinks purple is death."

We looked over at Sellers' trailer and saw Peter peeking out the door. Larry helped the sobbing June over to a wardrobe woman, and I went back to the trailer.

"She's changing into something else, Peter," I assured him. Sellers nodded, but he was still nervous. "Good, good," he said.

Then Larry joined us. "Take a look, Peter," Larry said. Sellers looked out. He was immediately as happy as a lark, a man who had been reprieved from sudden death. As Peter strode out of the trailer, I saw that June had changed into a vivid yellow sweater. She was still sobbing, but it only took a word or two from Peter to calm her down. He was happy and wanted her to be happy, too. After all, he was saved from death. I looked at Larry.

"Didn't she know that purple is death? Every good script girl should know that," said Larry. We had to close the trailer door to keep our laughter a secret.

The next episode was much worse. Everyone had shown up a few minutes early. The actors were studying their lines; the crew was hard at work. Hy Averback was almost done with his first pack of Marlboros. Larry and I were nervous with expectation. We were finally going to shoot the scene where Harold Fine's mother and father accidentally get turned on by marijuana brownies. Joyce Van Patten, a marvelous comedienne, was smiling into her script. Salem Ludwig, an old Actor's Studio pro who played Harold's father, was relaxing. And Jo Van Fleet, who had done brilliantly as James Dean's mother in *East of Eden*, was studying her lines. Jo had won an Oscar for best supporting actress in *East of Eden*. She, too, was a Studio member. Her performance was meticulous—funny, acerbic, domineering, but never the cliché Jewish mother. We all turned as we heard Peter's voice.

"Good morning, everybody. I slept like a baby lamb. Wonderful kip!"

"Good morning, Peter," said everyone.

I began to relax. He seemed very happy, almost manic.

"Good morning, Hy."

"Morning, Peter," Hy said from inside a big smile.

"Hello, Larry and Paul! How are the boys today?"

"Feeling good, Peter," I said.

"Never been better," said Larry.

Now Peter turned to his fellow actors. "Good morning, Joyce."

Joyce beamed at Peter, almost as adoring as the character she played in the film. "Good morning, Peter."

"Hello, Salem. I trust you slept well."

Salem nodded. "Just fine, Peter."

"Good morning, Jo." Jo Van Fleet, her reading glasses perched on her nose, her face buried in her script, muttered, "Good morning, Peter."

Without any warning, Sellers turned on his heels and stared at Jo, a look of sheer disgust on his face. "Good morning, Peter?" he said, imitating Jo. "I don't call that a really nice 'good morning,' do you?"

We all stared at him, not yet sure whether or not this was some sort of joke on Sellers' part. Jo Van Fleet had done absolutely nothing except say, "Good morning, Peter." True, she hadn't really looked up at him when she said it, but no one could be nuts enough to take umbrage at that! In a matter of seconds we knew that that was enough to do the trick.

Jo's lips were quivering with fear. "But Peter, I was studying my sides. . . . I did mean it as a nice good morning."

Peter turned to all of us for affirmation. "Well, I still don't call that a really nice good morning! Anything but! You're playing my mother in this film, and I should think a mother would have a better good morning than that for her son!"

In the most shameful day of my life, I found myself nodding to Peter. So were Hy and Larry. We were humoring this madman at the expense of a now sobbing woman. We were afraid to tell him to go to hell. If we did, the picture would certainly go down the drain.

"But Peter," wailed Jo, "I love my son! Aaaaahhhhh!"

Then the magnificent Salem Ludwig stood up. He was a short man, but he seemed seven feet tall. "Mr. Sellers," he said calmly, "I think you are being most unfair to Miss Van Fleet. She was studying her lines. She meant no disrespect. Moreover, what you're doing is very cruel and uncalled for."

I wanted to shout, "Bravo!" but of course I didn't.

Peter looked at Salem. He smiled. "I quite appreciate what you're doing, Salem. Quite. That took a lot of courage on your part. But, nevertheless, that was not a nice good morning."

With that, Peter turned and walked out of the soundstage. Hy and Charley Maguire sped after Sellers. Larry Tucker and I lifted Jo up and half-dragged her to her dressing room. "He's crazy, Jo. He can't help himself. You're innocent! That *was* a nice good morning." But all poor Jo could manage was deep racking sobs.

We got her into her small trailer, and she immediately dialed a NY phone number. Nothing we could say calmed her down. Salem came into the trailer, and we told him what a stand-up guy he was. Then we realized that Jo had called her psychoanalyst in New York and was tearfully telling him what had happened. "He said I wasn't a good mother," Jo sobbed into the phone as Salem patted her on the back.

Larry and I raced out of the trailer and trotted to Peter's bungalow. In addition to his trailer, Sellers had a large and comfortable bungalow. By the time we got there, Peter was methodically handing shirts, socks, and underwear to Bert, who transferred them into a beautiful brown leather suitcase on the bed.

"I do think, Bert," said Peter, quite relaxed, "that an earlier flight to London would be preferable." "I'll do what I can, sir," said the implacable Bert. *Toklas* was in ruins. Kenny Hyman, the head of the studio, joined us. Hyman told Peter in no uncertain terms that he had to finish the film, but Sellers seemed not to even hear Hyman. He handed a pair of felt slippers to Bert. "We don't want to forget these, do we, Bert?" "No, sir," said Bert, neatly packing the slippers.

I was desperate. "Peter," I said, "you do realize she's a sick woman. She's calling her analyst in New York right now." Peter looked at me. "Her analyst?"

"Yes," I leaped in. "She's obviously got severe problems."

"Big problems!" added Larry.

"Big problems?" said Peter.

He was on the edge. I said, "Peter, I think Jo is so into playing your mother that she flipped. She got confused. She didn't know what she was doing, so she behaved rudely!"

Larry and Hy Averback nodded their agreement. Everybody was nodding. I was disgusted with myself. Could I sink any lower? Then Peter began to unpack the clothes that Bert had just packed.

He put his socks and underwear back into their drawers. My God, he was changing his mind. Just for good measure, I sank even lower. "Peter," I said, "it would take a great man to forgive Jo Van Fleet." Peter looked at me understandingly. Then he looked at his wrist watch.

"It's getting on to lunch. I'd like a small bite, a bit of a kip, and then let's get on with our work."

We practically fled the bungalow. "I was bad!" I said. "Very bad."

"He's certifiable!" shrieked Larry.

That afternoon, Peter Sellers, Jo Van Fleet, Joyce Van Patten, and Salem Ludwig made us laugh until tears ran. The love between Peter and Jo as Harold Fine and his mother was more than abundant. They had an eerie camaraderie that could not be explained except to say they were both geniuses . . . or was it necessary for all actors to go through the hell of that morning to get these results! Was this "the Method" taken to the extreme?

About two weeks later we were in the home stretch of the movie. As good as things had gone before, we now faced a new and very dangerous problem. Peter's real feelings for Leigh Taylor-Young were seriously interfering with his "reel" feelings for the character in *Toklas*. At this point in the movie, all of the hippies were moving into Harold Fine's apartment, making him very uptight. They were even sleeping in his bathtub. Harold had to get tough with his hippie girlfriend. Instead, Peter doted on Leigh-Taylor, his shiny eyes filled with love instead of anger. Nobody seemed to be able to do anything about this. I asked Hy if he would mind if I spoke with Peter. "Be my guest," said Hy, and he meant it. In spite of everything that had happened so far—the "Britt corespondent" incident, the *Vittelloni* debacle, the Jo Van Fleet travesty—in spite of all these things, I still believed I could reach Peter Sellers when it really counted. I was different.

"Peter," I said. "I think this is going to be a great film." We were on the set of Harold's living room, a dozen hippie types

lolling around. "I quite agree with you, Paul. This is a good one,"
Peter said with a nod. "Can I be totally honest with you, Peter?" I
asked. "Of course. I would expect nothing less," answered Peter. I
could already see the slightest glimmer of doubt in his eyes. Perhaps it was his paranoia. I've always felt that paranoid people really
suspect the truth. They may be nuts, but they are also keenly
aware of real feelings. (My mother, who was quite paranoid, always accused me of not wanting her in L.A. when she came out for
a visit. "You wish I would go back to New York, don't you, my
wonderful son?" I always pleaded innocent on all counts, but the
truth was, I did want her to go home. I was afraid of her.) "Well,
Peter," I said, "I think you've got to be tougher with Leigh-Taylor
in this scene. Much tougher." "I don't follow you," said Peter, his
eyes getting blank now. I decided to leap right in. "I think you're
letting your real feelings for Leigh creep into the scene." Peter
looked at me as if I were a snail. "You're giving me very bad vibrations, Paul. Very bad." I felt a combination of fear and determination. "Nevertheless, Peter, you're hurting the movie." Sellers
stood up, livid with anger. "Very, very bad vibrations indeed!" I
lost it. "I don't care what kind of vibrations I'm giving you! You're
fucking up the movie!" Peter pointed at me and said, "Very, very
bad vibrations!" "Fuck you and fuck your vibrations!" I shouted,
then turned and headed for our trailer.

Larry had obviously heard me shouting. "What happened?"
he asked. "Is he coming this way?" I said. "Yeah . . ." "Then I'm a
goner!"

Peter leaned into our trailer and pointed at me, "Very bad vibrations! I don't want to see you here ever again!" He turned and
left. I was back where I started, an outcast on my first film. For the
next few days I was back to hiding and sneaking into dailies. But
somehow Peter's work had changed subtly. He was tougher with
Leigh, and the scenes went well. At the wrap party, Peter stu-
diously avoided me. It was a strange ending, but Freddie Fields
had predicted everything.

Ten years later I was staying at the Beverly Hills Hotel for all
the Academy Award hoopla. *An Unmarried Woman* was up for best

picture, best screenplay for me, and best actress for Jill Clayburgh. I was shooting *Willie and Phil* in New York and was back in Los Angeles for the awards ceremony. I returned from an interview and was about to walk into the hotel lobby. There was Peter Sellers. We hadn't seen or spoken to each other in all these years. I felt all the old emotions, a dizzy combination of fear, adulation, laughter, and downright wonder at this amazing man. Was he really Chauncy the gardener from the brilliant *Being There?*

"Hello, Paul." "Hello, Peter." He took my arm and said, "You've done very well. I've seen all your films. Very well indeed." "Thank you, Peter." For some reason I felt like crying. "I was wrong, Paul. Will you ever forgive me?" "There's nothing to forgive. We were all very emotional." "Be well, Paul." "You, too, Peter." He went for his car, and I walked into the lobby.

3

Bubbe and Zeda

I loved my grandparents unconditionally. They owned a candy store in Brownsville, which meant that sweets were always available. Delicious pieces of milk chocolate were broken off into big chunks. Chocolate was sold in pieces in those days. In fact, almost everything was available by the piece. There was very little that you couldn't buy one of for a penny: one Lucky Strike or one Camel or a single long pretzel that you could dip into your vanilla malted milk—or "maltie," as we called it. Licorice came by the piece, even marshmallows. Kids would come into the store and say, "Gimme one Lucky Strike for my mother and a penny's worth of chocolate." To this day I have an appetite for all these sweets that are no good for me. As a late-onset diabetic I know I shouldn't eat licorice or chocolate or ice-cream or halvah (the killer of them all; halvah is made from sesame seeds and is the Middle East's gift to the sweet buds), but all too often I'll secretly buy a goodie and say to myself, "It's only this once, it's not going to kill me, and besides, if I die I may as well die with the taste of chocolate on my lips."

My grandparents had come to the United States in 1905. Sam Gerson was from Kiev, Russia. He served in the Russian army as a scribe. He had beautiful handwriting. But the hardships of anti-Semitism became too much for him so he deserted the army. My short, prematurely bald *zeda* jumped off a train and made his way to Hamburg, Germany. To me, he was a great adventurer, a Jewish Errol Flynn. My grandmother, Ida, my *bubbe*, was about four feet ten inches tall. I never heard her complain about anything even though she obviously had had a life of great hardships. At the age of twenty she escaped from Poland, from the Pale of Settlement, and made her way across the border into Germany. She hid in a wagon filled with sacks of potatoes, and at the border crossing the guards thrust bayonets into the sacks barely missing Ida. (I used this story in *Next Stop, Greenwich Village*. Shelley Winters tells her son, who is about to go to Hollywood, that he "should never forget where he came from. Your grandmother hid in a sack of potatoes to escape the Cossacks.") Sam and Ida both made it to a ship that sailed to America, and it was on the ship that they met and fell in love. (What a movie that would make! But who the hell would do it? Can you imagine me pitching this to the boys at Disney? These two little Jews meet and fall in love on a ship going to America in 1905! We could get a young Ron Silver and a young Barbra Streisand. Wait a second, they say, what about Brad Pitt and Winona Ryder? Brad Pitt as my *zeda*? You've got to be kidding. Now Winona Ryder . . . hmmmm. . . . maybe.) Sam and Ida married in New York and joined thousands of poor Jews and Italians and Irish in the struggle to make a life. Sam got a job making cigars. Ida kept house. Soon they had two children, and it was then that tragedy struck. A large truck ran wild onto a sidewalk and hit my grandfather, destroying the better part of one of his legs. He was crippled for the rest of his life. But he, too, never complained. (I still don't understand how *I* can complain so much about the trivia of showbiz ups and downs, while my grandparents just went on with their lives. Don't I come from the same stock?) There was no such thing as insurance then, and so the best they could manage was a little candy store in Brownsville, Brooklyn. By the time I was six years old, in 1936, I would come home from school and go right to the candy store. I loved it!

My grandfather often told me stories about his life in Kiev. I would sit at the kitchen table with Zeda, as I called him (Yiddish for grandpa), sipping hot tea from a saucer and sucking on a cube of sugar. When the saucer was drained, Zeda would pour more hot tea from a glass. He told me stories about Peter the Great, about Ivan the Terrible, about blinding snowstorms with great black bears wandering through the forests, about the savage pogroms and cossacks on horseback whipping Jews. I could almost see the scenes he painted. Sam had read all of Tolstoy, Dostoyevsky, and Pushkin, Lermontov, and his favorite, Turgenev. (After he came to America and learned English, he reread all those books. "They're better in Russian," he told me.) My grandfather played the fiddle and would often heighten the drama of a story with a few strokes on the violin. He made me laugh with his violin imitation of a squeaky door or a cat or a seesaw that needed oiling or a baby crying "Mama." He created homemade scrapbooks. He cut out articles and photos from the Jewish newspaper *Forward* or from *Life* magazine or the *Reader's Digest*. Anything that interested him would be pasted into the scrapbook. You'd find there Albert Einstein, Karl Marx, F.D.R. and his black Scottie, Fala. Somehow, Greta Garbo and Charlie Chaplin made their way into Sam's book. Babe Ruth was plastered on a page right under a photo of Maurice Schwartz, the great star of the Yiddish theater. Anything that Sam thought was deserving went into his books. To add to my delight, my grandfather drew delightful pictures of red birds, musical notes that danced, blue and yellow flowers and brown camels and monkeys with long tails. (Years later, when reexamining the scrapbooks, the drawings seemed amateurish to me, but when I was six, they were works of art.) What they represented was the need of this man to express his feelings about the world he lived in. The scrapbooks were his art. The scrapbooks were Zeda's movies. I suppose that's where I inherited my need to create.

When it came to God, even my grandparents confused me. My parents, Dave and Jean, were holiday Jews. They observed Passover—or Pesach, as we called it. My mother actually went to the trouble of keeping special plates and silverware for Pesach. Then there was Rosh Hashanah, the New Year, which was always celebrated. The Jewish kids in the neighborhood had an edge over the Christian kids. We didn't have to go to school on Easter, but we also got Passover and other Jewish holidays off. And finally and most important came Yom Kippur, the Day of Atonement, the day you asked God to forgive you for all your sins that year, the day you fasted to prove your devotion to God. I never remember my parents fasting. My mother always had some great excuse. "I tried, but I got dizzy," she'd tell me. My father didn't even offer an excuse. My grandmother fasted for twenty-four hours, spending the day in the synagogue praying to her god. The day before, Bubbe prepared a meal that needed only to be heated to be then devoured by the starving Jews: roast chicken, home-baked challah bread, chicken soup with noodles, chopped liver, chicken fat to dip the challah in, homemade apple strudel. I smell it now! I would walk around the corner to the synagogue and wait to hear the sound of the shofar, the ram's horn, being blown, signifying the end of the day. Then I would race into the shul to greet my starving *bubbe*. But what about Zeda? How did he handle the Day of Atonement? One Yom Kippur when I was six or seven, I went into my grandparent's apartment. I was trying to fast and was desperately thirsty. All my friends bragged that they had not had a thing to eat or a drop to drink. "I don't even have any saliva," my friend Pinny told me. As I went into the kitchen, I looked at Zeda with disbelief. He was cutting himself a piece of pickled herring to go with his bread and hot tea. "Zeda!" I shouted. "You're eating. You're eating on Yom Kippur, the holiest day of the year." "Yes, Yisruel," he said, patting me on the head, "I'm eating." "But Zeda, Bubbe is in shul fasting!" "I know, sweetheart," he said to me. "I don't understand, Zeda. Why is Bubbe fasting and you're eating?" My grandfather smiled. "I'm eating because I'm hungry," he said. "But what will God say?" I asked. "Who knows for sure what God will say," said Zeda, "but I think even God would enjoy your *bubbe's* pickled herring."

4

Git Gat Giddle

Danny Kaye and I had two things in common. We both grew up in Brownsville, Brooklyn, and we both went to Thomas Jefferson High School. Danny was seventeen years older but we both had experienced the streets of Brownsville: the crowded markets filled with pushcarts crammed with fruits and vegetables, sour pickles in wooden vats, underwear and socks, washboards, chunks of dark brown soap; the peddlers shouting out the prices, and the buyers, mostly women, examining the goods with knowing eyes and hands before making a purchase; tomatoes and oranges being squeezed; women sniffing the fish and the farmer cheese. (To this day I love to go to exotic bazaars. I've been to Egypt, the Amazon, Turkey, Iran, Jerusalem, Mexico City, Bangkok—all fabulous but none more fabulous than the market on Prospect Place in Brownsville.)

I was positive that Danny Kaye and I would have a lot to talk about when I got the job as one of the writers for the Danny Kaye variety show on CBS in 1963. I wondered if Danny had known any of the Murder, Incorporated mob in Brownsville. I couldn't wait to tell him about my friend Butch whose father gave everybody in the building on Bergen Street a free bag of Passover foods every year. Butch's dad, a tall, redhaired man who always wore a suit and tie, was a polite and kind fellow. It came as a shock to all of us when we found out that he was a gangster!

And then there were the *yentas* who lived on our block—old ladies who leaned out second-floor windows watching the action below. Yentas knew everything that went on in the neighborhood. They even knew what had just happened in your own apartment. They had great hearing and perfect eyesight. A top-flight yenta could smell you before you turned the corner and then shout down to you where you had just come from. When I think of my favorite yenta today, I smile, but in those days she was a royal pain in the ass. I was positive Danny would get a kick out of my yenta stories, and I couldn't wait to hear his tales.

Danny was fifty in 1963, a major Hollywood star. His fast-talking "git gat giddle" songs, written by his wife, Sylvia Fine, were tour-de-force pieces. Danny could sing, dance, and do inspired physical comedy. And, he was an attractive man. His wavy red-gold hair topped a delightful smile and a trim figure. Danny Kaye was not a schlumpy comedian. Even though he cut his eye-teeth in the Catskills, the Borscht Belt, Danny did not come across as Jewish. He could *tummel* with the best of them, but there was something Waspish about him, which I think helped him achieve great success in films. I'm not sure why Danny went from movies to the strain of a weekly television variety show, but probably his movie career had hit a bump in the road and CBS had made him an offer he couldn't refuse. Only after I wrote for the show week-in, week-out for four years did I realize how much energy was needed just to show up every Monday. Being funny was another matter.

Very few people in the humor business agree on what is funny. That's because they take so many different approaches to humor. Second, professional humorists don't laugh. They want to make you laugh. So even though you may think you've come up with something funny, only the audience makes the final judgment. Third, some comedians can take a piece of material that is not really very funny and make it funny with their performance, or ruin a funny piece of material with the wrong delivery. The problem we faced with Danny Kaye was that while he was a great performer, he wasn't really very funny. He was amusing. He was talented. But not deeply funny, not ironic. He had a great "sneeze" that you could always count on for a laugh. Danny would start to sneeze, then just before actually sneezing, he would catch himself and calm down, and then a second or two later he would sneeze so big you'd have to hold the table.

Danny was an expert in catching his fingers in a drawer, closing the drawer and then howling in silent pain. He could trip, stumble, twirl, and fall with the best of them. He had a very fine double take or stare, especially when a joke didn't work. But funny? No. Sid Caesar was funny; Jackie Gleason was funny; Jack Benny was very funny. Danny Kaye was endearing, delightful, entertaining, tasteful, but he wasn't really funny. The first time I got wind of this was when I worked up the courage, after about four weeks on the writing staff, to tell Danny that we both came from Brownsville. I knew that by now Danny was aware of me because he called me "Paul," not "kid." He definitely knew that Larry Tucker and I were writing partners. I found a moment alone with Danny on the set one afternoon.

"You know, Danny," I said tentatively, "I graduated from Thomas Jefferson High." Danny looked at me, and I could see a venetian blind coming down over his eyes. Like an idiot, I continued. "Yeah, I grew up in Brownsville. Remember the Loew's Pitkin? The movie theater on Pitkin Avenue? . . . And what about Murder, Incorporated?" Danny showed no sign of recognition— not even a nod or an "Oh, yeah." Nothing. Like a complete fool, I went on. "I still go back once in a while . . . when I'm in New York. Obviously. As a matter of fact, my grandparents still live there. They like it!" Danny turned and walked away. No anger, no impa-

tience. Just a total disregard for the Brownsville question. I had expected a joke, a shtick, a move, an imitation of a yenta. But no.
Nothing.

What does Danny's failure to react to Brownsville have to do
with being funny? I think a funnier person would have let me off
the hook with some sort of witticism, any small attempt at humor
that would have told me to shut up about Brownsville, something
that would have said to me: "I'm not at all interested in talking
about pushcarts and pickles. Don't you know who I am? I'm
Danny Kaye. I entertain the royal family. I'm buddies with the
great Dodger left-hander Sandy Koufax. I fly a Lear jet, for
Christ's sake!" If only Danny could have said that to me.

By the same token, let me make it clear that Danny treated
the writers with respect, something almost unheard of in Hollywood. Danny knew he needed the best and always made us feel
comfortable, even when we ran into problems, like a sketch bomb-
ing at dress rehearsal. The writers included Mel Tolkin and Shelley Keller, two funnymen who had written for the Sid Caesar *Show
of Shows*; Herbie Baker, a longtime friend of Danny's, who wrote
special musical numbers; Ernie Chambers and Saul Ilson, tasty
fellows who specialized in writing connective chatter for Danny;
Gary Belkin, a man with bushy dark eyebrows who would lie on a
couch in the writers' room and hold his paycheck up to the light so
he could read it, thus driving Mel Tolkin crazy. "What in God's
name are you reading, sir?" shouted Tolkin. "Just my check, Mel."
"Put it away, sir! I can't stand it!" "Why? I'm not bothering anyone," said Gary. "You're bothering me! Me, sir. Me, Mel Tilkin."
"That's Tolkin," said Gary. "Talkin," stuttered Mel. "I mean
Tolkin. . . . Yes, Mel Tolkin!"

Shelley Keller and Mel were co–head writers, although they
didn't have an official title. But they argued a lot.

"We did that on *Caesar*, Mel," Shelley said with a frown.

"That's patently ridiculous," said Mel, obviously pissed, his
Russian accent getting thicker. "Ve did a sketch about cowboys,
not astronauts."

"But it's the same premise, Mel!"

Mel filled his pipe with tobacco. "Who cares about premises, sir! Ve have a sketch here!"

Ernie Chambers would chime in. "I doubt if Danny ever saw the Caesar show. Why don't we try it, Shelley?"

Shelley, a chubby, side-burned man with the sad eyes of a basset hound, sat at the lone typewriter in the room. It was Shelley's job to type anything he heard pitched that might work, might be funny, in Shelley's opinion.

"So type!" Mel said to Shelley, lighting match after match in an attempt to get his pipe lit.

"Be careful you don't start a fire," said Shelley, pecking away at his typewriter.

Mel put his pipe down in disgust and snipped off the tip of an expensive cigar. I'd look over at Larry Tucker to see his reaction. I knew that Larry knew we were in some kind of nuthouse and had better keep our mouths closed.

Larry and I were hired originally on a four-week trial basis at $350 a week each. Larry was one of the great funny people. I had first met him in New York in the fifties when I auditioned for him. He was running a small nightclub called Down in the Depths and was beginning to make a reputation for himself. I had a partner named Herb Hartig, and we had written a comedy act. Larry Tucker didn't think we were ready for his room and turned us down. Several years later I moved to Los Angeles and for a while did the comedy act as a single. I had pretty much lost my appetite for nightclubs because of the drunks and the gangsters and the sometimes very square audiences. In New York I had played the Village Vanguard, the Reuban Bleu, and One Fifth Avenue, all sophisticated places that understood satire. I'd played Storeyville in Boston (square) and The Gate of Horn in Chicago (hip). I had a successful four weeks in San Francisco at the hungry i. I thought I had it made as a stand-up comic, but then came the Interlude in Los Angeles (I followed Lenny Bruce) where the laughs were very sporadic and, finally, a disastrous booking at the Statler-Hilton in Dallas, Texas. I was onstage for forty minutes and got not one laugh.

Except for occasional weekend gigs at the more sophisticated coffeehouses in L.A., I was now back to acting. And since there was very little acting coming my way, and I had the added pressure of supporting our one-year-old daughter Meg, I was forced to take a job as a messenger boy for Red Arrow. By then I had acted in Kubrick's *Fear and Desire* and Richard Brooks' *Blackboard Jungle*; I had enjoyed some solid parts on live TV in New York, and I had had varied success as a nightclub comic. But now, in 1960, I had reached rock bottom. At thirty I was delivering scripts, messages, memos, packages, what-have-you in my constantly overheating '53 Studebaker. To make matters worse, I had to wear a Red Arrow uniform with a lightning bolt on the sleeve.

It was at this point that I heard from Larry Tucker. "Hello, is this Paul Mazursky?" "Yeah," I answered. "Who's this?" "Larry. Larry Tucker." "Hey, Larry. I didn't know you were out here." "Yeah," said Larry in his reedy high-pitched voice. "I've decided to go into acting." "Really?" I said. Sure, I thought, you fucked up the nightclub business by not hiring me, and now you want to become an actor. "Yeah . . . and I was wondering if you could help me get an agent." "Sure," I said. "You represent me and I'll represent you." "Is it that tough?" asked Larry. "I'm a delivery boy." I told Larry about Red Arrow. "Jeez," he said sympathetically. "Well, let's get together anyway." What did I have to lose?

From the very first moment, Larry made me laugh. We were on the same wavelength even though I regarded myself as a Greenwich Village hipster, an intellectual comedian, an actor capable of playing Hamlet or the Fool in *King Lear*. Larry was more of a funnyman. Of course he got a lot of laughs on fat jokes, but his humor ran much deeper than that. He had a great heart and a wonderful sense of the absurd. He told me about the time he'd gone into White Castle, a cheap New York hamburger joint that specialized in tiny, delicious burgers. Larry asked the counterman for a dozen burgers. "Is that to go, sir?" asked the counterman. "No," answered Larry, "I'll eat them here."

By some great stroke of good fortune, Larry and I were asked to take over the Los Angeles production of Chicago's *Second City*.

The show still worked, but we wanted to add new material. We began to improvise, and slowly but surely we came up with several very funny new pieces. I was the straight man, and Larry was the funny guy. One of the people who saw us perform was Perry Lafferty, who had directed me in some good parts on live TV in New York. Now he was the producer of the new Danny Kaye show. Larry was a friend of Ernie Chambers, one of the writers. Between Lafferty and Chambers a strange offer came our way. "Do you and Tucker think you can write comedy for Danny Kaye?" It was Perry Lafferty on the phone. Without dropping a beat we told Perry that we certainly could. They offered us a four-week trial at $350 a week each. This was $300 a week more than I was making with *Second City*. In less than a week Tucker and Mazursky showed up at CBS on Fairfax Avenue to meet the rest of the staff. Essentially, we had replaced the great Larry Gelbart who had signed on to write only the first show.

Four years later we were the only surviving writers, the deans of the staff. We had become fairly adroit at turning out sketches for Danny. We had introduced Harvey Korman and Joyce Van Patten to Danny, and they had become his second bananas. I had made the transition from being an actor to being a writer. As much as I complained about the pressure of coming up with something every week, I had also learned how to write to a deadline. And along the way I had met and worked with some extraordinary people: Tolkin, Keller, Chambers and Ilson, the outrageous Pat Mc-Cormick, Ron Clark, Norman Barasch, and Carrol Moore. There was Bobby Sheerer, the director, who later became the producer when Perry Lafferty became the head of CBS. Bobby had a contagious joy.

Larry and I had begun to write screenplays. All of this because of Danny Kaye. Make no mistake about it, Danny was a great star, a dynamo, a man who took chances. But to this day he remains a sphinx to me. And I still think that this great performer's lack of irony is the answer to the riddle. Two incidents tell the story.

We were in our third year. We had reached the point where we were now pitching ideas to Danny at the weekly meeting, ideas in-spired by sketches we had already done in the first two seasons. The show was a hit, but we were always in danger of running out of gas. Tolkin and Keller had aged considerably in the past three years. Ron Clark and Pat McCormick had brought new energy to the writing staff, but Danny never "got" Pat's humor—it was raunchy and sur-real, two qualities that were not in the Kaye lexicon.

"Say, Danny," offered Pat one pitch day, a huge Churchill cigar in his mouth, "what about a sketch about a nervous collie that pees on fire hydrants?" Danny stared open-jawed at Pat. The rest of us were equally dumbfounded, but I figured maybe there was more to it. "You'd play the collie," chuckled Pat. "Of course you fake peeing, but I think there are a lot of laughs there." (Pat later ended up writing some of Johnny Carson's best jokes.)

Larry and I had reached the point where we were always in danger of breaking up and laughing at the wrong time, particu-larly in front of Danny. We were silly and childish, qualities you shouldn't have when you're making a hundred thousand dollars a year. But only with this schoolboy behavior could we get through yet another season. And Pat didn't help. He wanted us to lose it in front of Danny. Pat McCormick was the original wild and crazy guy. Pat's pranks included dropping his pants as he walked down the aisle in a crowded airplane and pretending to be shocked at the sight of his boxer shorts decorated with red and blue polka dots. At six-feet-four he made a hilarious figure. Dropping his pants in public was standard fare for Pat. He dropped his pants at his mother's funeral. He dropped his pants in Westminster Abbey in London. He was determined to make Larry and me break up in front of Danny Kaye.

Every Monday morning the writers, the producer, the direc-tor, and Herb Bonis, Danny's right-hand man, would meet to hear the new show read by Shelley Keller (or sung by Herbie Baker), and then to pitch ideas for the next week's show to Danny. All of this was preceded by general chitchat about the previous week's show and by Danny telling a story or two. The trouble was that af-ter three seasons we knew all the stories. They almost always involved a celebrity that Danny knew well, such as Princess Margaret or Sandy Koufax, or was about flying his beloved Lear jet.

"All right, fellows," said Pat McCormick to Larry and me. "I'll bet you five dollars that as soon as Danny mentions a celebrity, you'll break up." We decided to take the bet. "Bullshit," said Larry. "We won't laugh."

Danny came into the room, and we said our hellos. The show that Saturday had been a good one, and we were all happy.

"Have a nice weekend, boys?" asked Danny.

All the writers lied and told Danny they had enjoyed wonderful weekends. Pat looked at Larry, who sat next to him, and then at me, across the long table. Pat rolled his eyes like a pinball machine. Not funny. We didn't even smile. Then Danny spoke. He wore a baseball cap and funny-looking space shoes, his feet lounging casually on the table.

"I was up in the Lear yesterday—took Sandy Koufax out for a spin . . . and I told him about Princess Margaret." For the first time Danny mentioned three things in one sentence. Pat rolled his eyes again, this time crossing them. Larry lost it. He began to heave his shoulders, great gasps of laughter roaring out of his mouth. Then I went, too. Soon we were both laughing uncontrollably. Somehow Pat retained his composure, still twirling his eyes in cartoon comic circles. Danny looked at us and took his feet off the table. You could tell that he was not happy. This made it even funnier. I ducked behind Mel Tolkin, who was sitting next to me. I didn't want Danny to see me, but how could he miss it? We were shrieking with laughter.

"What the hell is so funny?" demanded Danny, rising to his feet. "*What the hell is so funny?*" Danny exited the room, slamming the door behind him, his face white with anger.

"That's five bucks each, fellows," said Pat.

"Well," said Herbie Bonis, "that's the end of the season for you boys." Herbie had lost an eye in World War II, and whenever there was a problem, he would take the glass eye out of the socket and clean it with a fresh white handkerchief. As he did it now, Larry and I laughed even harder.

"Are you boys masochists?" asked Perry Lafferty.

"Fools! Self-destructive foolishness! *Kinderspeil!*" sputtered Mel Tolkin.

"What are you guys, out of your fucking minds?" asked Shelley Keller.

By now the enormity of what had happened dawned on both of us, and we stopped laughing. Then the phone rang. Bobby Sheerer picked it up.

"Hello? . . . Yes, Danny. He's right here."

Sheerer pointed at Larry and handed him the phone.

"Hello, Danny. This is Larry. I want to apologize"—all this in his most contrite voice. "I really don't know why we broke up, Danny. But Paul and I used to break up in *Second City*, and we just— Oh, thank you, Danny. I can't thank you enough. . . . I assure you it had nothing to do with you personally. . . . Thank you, Danny. . . . Yes, I'll tell Paul."

Larry hung up, a devilish smile on his cherubic face. "He wants to see you down in the bungalow." He pointed at me.

"What did he say?" I asked.

"He forgives me. He just wants to talk to you."

We both started to laugh again. Now Pat whooped with laughter. Perry Lafferty warned, "You had best hurry down to the bungalow, Paul."

I ran into the men's room and washed my face with cold water. I combed my hair. I didn't want Danny to see me in disarray. I looked at myself in the mirror and began to improvise a subtext like a method actor. "You just found out you have cancer," I told myself. "This is the worst day of your life." Then I went down to the bungalow, repeating the cancer mantra to myself.

Danny's secretary, Becky, whom I usually adored, looked at me with scorn. "You can go right on in, Paul. Mr. Kaye's expecting you." Her southern accent dripped with venom. I guessed that Danny had told her the awful story of the breakup.

I knocked at the door and heard Danny say, "Come on in, Paul." Danny sat a table, his back to the window. Slants of bright sunlight slithered through the venetian blinds backlighting

Danny. As usual, his feet were up on the table, next to a pot of coffee and a couple of cups. Danny looked very, very sad. I figured this was it, the end of the line.

"Danny," I began, "you have every right to fire me. I'm ashamed of myself. I still don't know why I laughed, but I know it made you feel bad. I can only say I apologize from the bottom of my heart. I just lost it. Maybe Larry and I are both crazy. Maybe we're worn out. We're always breaking up."

I looked at him. Of course I was telling a half-truth. Yes, we were worn to a frazzle, but we had laughed at the three-name combo. Nevertheless, Danny smiled for the first time.

"Hey, Paul. That took a lot of guts for you to say. Don't you think I've ever broken up?" I didn't know what to say. "I broke up onstage many times. Sometimes it's just something silly, something foolish that sets you off." "Right," I said. "Sit down," said Danny. I sat. "Thank you." "Would you like a cup of coffee?" he asked me. "That would be very nice." I felt the blood surging again through my veins. I was practically off the hook. Danny poured me a cup of coffee. "Cream and sugar?" he asked me. "I'll help myself. Thanks, Danny." Danny smiled. He was his old self again. "You know, Paul, I was up in the Lear jet yesterday taking Sandy Koufax out for a spin, and I told him about Princess Margaret." I bit my tongue to keep from laughing. I could taste the blood in my mouth, so I sipped the hot coffee. I suddenly had the idea that maybe Danny was testing me, that he knew why we had laughed before. But no, I could see that wasn't in the realm of possibility. Danny just went on and on about Sandy Koufax and the Princess, and I just kept on biting my tongue and sipping the coffee, nodding happily all the while. Not only didn't he know why we had broken up, he was doing it all over again.

About seven years later, long after the Danny Kaye show had gone off the air, I found myself desperate to find the money to make *Harry and Tonto*. I had already made *Bob & Carol & Ted & Alice* and *Alex in Wonderland*, the first a huge hit, the other a giant bomb. Now I wanted to make a film about an old man and his cat. I had written the script with Josh Greenfeld, an old pal from my

Greenwich Village days. It was a funny and touching story about a seventy-year-old widower looking for a place to live. I loved the script, but nobody wanted to finance a film about old age. Then I thought of Danny. He was now about sixty. He wasn't doing anything beyond his wonderful UNICEF trips to visit children all over the world and occasionally conducting an orchestra in comic fashion. Danny Kaye as "Harry"? It seemed possible. Also, I knew that Danny could actually finance the film himself. I sent the script to Herb Bonis and got a call within a few days.

"It's a beautiful script," said Herb. "I think Danny would be perfect." I was excited. "Danny wants to meet with you. He loved *Bob & Carol*." "Does Danny like the script?" "Yes," said Herb. "That's why he wants to meet with you."

We set a date to meet at Danny's home. At least half a dozen times when I had been there in the old writer days, Danny had cooked Chinese or Italian for us. He was a great cook and really enjoyed our pleasure when we ate one of his exotic dishes.

Herb Bonis opened the door and welcomed me with a big hug. Herb was a very decent man who never lied and had Danny's trust. But I knew that nobody made decisions for Danny. "We're really proud of you," said Herb. "You've made such great progress." I was touched. Then I saw Sylvia Fine Kaye coming down the stairs. To me she was still a legend. "I like your script very much," said Sylvia. I was relieved. If anyone could influence Danny, it was Sylvia. Maybe he'd put up the money and star. I started dreaming of the cross-country locations we needed. Then Danny, looking chipper and relaxed, came downstairs. "Hello, Paul." We hugged. All my old feelings came back. My confusion about Danny's humor, my admiration for his great talent, my gratitude for his trust in my talent before anyone else. I knew that my four years as a writer on the Kaye show had been the bridge to my career as a writer/director. It was an emotional moment. I looked at Danny, trying to figure out if he could play the age. Absolutely, I said to myself.

"Don't you think I'm a little young for this part?" asked Danny.

"It's a movie, Danny," said Sylvia. "Of course you can play seventy."

"See, she thinks I look seventy," said Danny, obviously kidding.

"There are things we can do, Danny," I said. "Whiten your hair, the way you'd walk, maybe a mustache—"

"But my real problem is that I think it needs a few more jokes," said Danny.

I suddenly saw the project jump out the window. Jokes! I didn't want jokes in *Harry and Tonto*. Humor, yes. Jokes, no.

"What kind of jokes, Danny?" I ventured.

"Oh, I don't know, Paul—some more physical stuff. Why can't this old codger bump into things? You know what I mean."

I felt like throwing up. Then Sylvia tried to come to the rescue. "Danny, this is not sketch humor. This is a story about an old man looking to live his life out with some dignity. No pratfalls." She was very firm. I wanted to kiss her. I could see Herb Bonis take his glass eye out for a cleaning, and I knew it was curtains.

"I think there is a lot of humor already, Danny," I said. "Once we get into it, into the situations, you'll see the humor. After all, the man talks to his pussycat. He walks his cat on a leash."

Danny smiled. "I know, I know. That could be funny."

I don't remember what else was said. There were lots of compliments about my career, my script, about how great the Kaye show had been, but I knew that *Harry and Tonto* was a dead issue. Once again it was clear that as brilliant a talent as Danny Kaye was, he had no irony.

Two years later Art Carney won the Academy Award for his devastatingly simple-looking portrait of "Harry."

5

Gypsy Jean

My grandparents called my mother Jennie. It was more Yiddish that way, I guess. But my father, Dave, called her Jean, as did her friends. As far back as I can remember, she and my father never got along. For starters, they had nothing in common. My father, who was the eldest son in a family of seven, never finished high school. The eldest son often paid the price: He had to go to work. Dave was a sweet man who wanted nothing more than to read the obituaries in the *Daily News* and see a double feature on Sunday. He lived a life of desperation from the day I was born until 1939 when sounds of World War II could be heard and jobs opened up. For many years he lived on what he got from the WPA—$13 a week. He sold apples on street corners, and he probably tried other tricks to make a buck. Jean, on the other hand, typed over a hundred words a minute, played the piano, and was a prodigious reader. She brought home some money typing and playing piano for a dance school. When I was about eight years old, they offered to teach me ballet for nothing, but I would have none of that sissy stuff. (Years later, when I was an actor, I studied ballet with Paul Godkin in New York.)

Jean totally dominated the household, and since I was the only child, all the pressures of her own frustrations fell on me. Her fantasy life was rich. Her instincts for beauty were strangely touching. Every week she took me to see at least one double feature. Sometimes she even told me to cut school so I could go with her. "I'll write you a note and tell them you had a cold." She'd load us down with milk chocolate, licorice, and halvah. I saw Humphrey Bogart and Errol Flynn, Carole Lombard and Clark Gable, Bette Davis, Joan Crawford and John Garfield. There was Edward G. Robinson, Walter Brennan, John Wayne, Cary Grant, Gary Cooper and Marlene Dietrich, the Marx brothers and the Ritz brothers, W. C. Fields and Charlie Chaplin, Irene Dunne and David Niven, Ronald Colman, Peter Lorre and S. Z. "Cuddles" Sakall. And little Irwin learned to do imitations of almost all of them. From the beginning I was a funny kid. When my parents argued, I tried to break up the fights with humor. A joke, an imitation—anything that would put a stop to the ceaseless bickering. "I'm little Caesar, see you guys." I'd do my Edward G. Robinson, forcing my lower lip to bend à la Robinson. "Judy, Judy, Judy!" I'd do my British-accented version of Cary Grant. (Years later when I worked in the Catskills as a weekend comedian, I'd do the same imitations, but this time with Yiddish accents. "Can I have a nice piece of boiled beef, please, Mrs. Silverman?" I'd recite in the nasal tones of Peter Lorre. The audience loved it.)

But what strange force led my mother to take me to see the great foreign films of the day? To the opera? To the Apollo Theater up in Harlem for the Wednesday night amateur hour? She would drag me uptown on the subway to the Thalia Theater to see such foreign screen stars as Louis Jouvet and Michel Simon, Arletty, Harry Bauer, Jean-Louis Barrault in *Children of Paradise*, Jean Gabin and Michelle Morgan. By the time I was twelve years old I even knew the names of some of the great foreign directors.

"I think Jean Renoir is a genius," my mother announced after we saw *Grande Illusion*.

I was familiar as well with the great Swedish tenor Jussi Bjoerling, Jean's favorite. We'd get into the Metropolitan Opera for a dollar, the price of a seat in the highest balcony, and Jean would weep when Jussi hit the high C. So would I. I didn't understand it, but it moved me. Poor Dave had to suffer Jean's recriminations when he failed to jump for joy at her account of what we had seen.

"He hit the high C! It was like going to heaven!" said Jean, tears in her eyes.

"Good, good," Dave said, yawning. "What's for supper?"

"I'm talking about a great artist, and he's talking about supper. Go to hell!"

"But I'm starving," my father said.

"He's starving! You hear? He's starving!" My mother looked at me for approval. I felt a nasty brawl coming on.

"I worked like a dog today. Sure I'm hungry."

"A dog has more appreciation of Jussi Bjoerling than you do!" shouted my mother.

"A dog eats better than me."

"*In dred zel a vein!*" ("Go to hell" in Yiddish.) When my mother spoke in Yiddish, it usually meant that the argument was about to spin out of control. Poor Dave didn't know what hit him. All he wanted was some meat loaf, mashed potatoes, and green peas.

Why did Jean take me up to the Apollo? It was an hour's trip on the subway. It meant going to Harlem at night. We were usually among a very small number of whites in the audience. (The truth of the matter is that Harlem in the thirties and forties was not at all dangerous. It's a lot more dangerous today in Beverly Hills.) It can only be because Jean had an instinctive love for the talent of the great black artists. There was Peg-Leg Bates who danced on a wooden leg. Great singers like Billie Holiday and Dinah Washington, Billy Eckstine, Cab Calloway doing his inimitable version of "Minnie the Moocher." We saw Count Basie and his orchestra; Chick Webb, the hunchbacked drummer par excellence; Lester Young; and many other jazz greats. By the time I was fourteen I had already seen many of the supreme black performers. But the truth is that I didn't really appreciate it. It was fun, I liked the adventure, but I didn't understand the significance of what I was seeing. Today, fifty or so years later, I still remember some of those great evenings, and somehow I now understand what all this meant to me. My mother, Jennie Gerson Mazursky, was a hipster, a gypsy, a beatnik, a hippie. She almost always went against the grain. Although she lived in a lower-class, mostly Jewish ghetto, she listened only to her own drummer. She wore exotic turbans and scarfs; she was dramatic, larger than life, a Yiddish Gloria Swanson. She was trying in the only way she could to tell her son how beautiful the world could be.

By then her black moods had already begun. She would sometimes fall into a deep depression. The older I got, the more severe her mood changes became. It was almost as if she knew that someday I was going to leave. "Take me away from him," she often begged me. She was talking about my father. "Where do you want me to take you?" I asked her skeptically. "Anywhere, as long as it's away from him." I explained that this was neurotic (I was now seventeen), that she was laying a massive Oedipus trip on me. "Don't hand me that crap!" she told me. My life was like a play by Clifford Odets with a lot of Freud thrown in.

When I told my mother that I was about to leave for Los Angeles to be in a movie, she said, "Don't let it go to your head." But I knew she was thrilled. Three years later, when I went to Hollywood to act in *Blackboard Jungle*, she told me to "say hello to Clark Gable if you see him. Tell him your mother loves him." And she meant it.

When I finally moved from Brownsville to Greenwich Village, my mother reacted by banging her head against the kitchen wall. I walked out of the apartment gripping my two suitcases, afraid to look back. I heard her wailing, and that was more than enough for me. Once a week Jean and Dave would visit me in my one-room apartment on West Tenth Street. The first thing Jean would do was look around disdainfully and ask, "How can you live in such a dump?" Dave said nothing, but I think he wished that he could live there, too. Then my mother would plop down her shopping bag and take out her goods: chopped liver, corn bread, lox, and cream cheese, sometimes a chicken. She'd hand the goods to Dave. "Put it in the icebox before it goes rotten!" she'd tell him. Then Jean would take out the neatly folded laundry that she did for me. The more stuff she brought, the more anxious I became. It was as if all my friends were in the room laughing at me. (Years later I showed all this in *Next Stop, Greenwich Village.* Shelley Winters played Jean, and I think Jean would have approved.)

Back in Brooklyn, she would sometimes sit in her room in total darkness. She refused to talk about it; if I pressed her, she became angry. I begged her to see a doctor and get a tranquilizer. She told me to "go to hell." I think Prozac would have changed her life.

By now I was dating Betsy, my shiksa girlfriend, and I decided to test the waters and introduce Betsy to Jean. I arranged a meeting on a Sunday afternoon in Washington Square Park. I warned Betsy that my mother was not likely to be too friendly. After all, Betsy was about to steal me away. Betsy, always sanguine, just smiled. She was adorable.

As we approached the park bench, I prayed there wouldn't be a scene. Sometimes Jean would get pissed at something and explode—anywhere, anyplace. One afternoon a woman with a large head of hair sat in front of her at a movie. "Just my luck," my mother said loud enough for the entire theater to hear. "I have to sit behind a giant!" "Please, Ma," I whispered. "What am I saying," Jean yelled at me. "I'm sitting behind a head like a horse." The poor woman turned around. She was not particularly large, but her hair was rather full. "If you don't like my hair, lady, you can just move," said the woman. "Why don't you move?" my mother said. "I like my seat," said the woman. My father and I quickly shifted two seats to the left. "Here, Jean," said my father, patting the new seat next to him. "No. No way will I change seats!" The audience began to shush my mother. "Please, lady, we're trying to see the movie." "You can all go to hell," shouted Jean. "Is it my fault I'm sitting behind a giant?" I tried to shrink down in my seat and become invisible. Finally, my mother moved. I forget the name of the movie.

"There she is," I whispered to Betsy. My parents were sitting on a bench. I could see my mother's shopping bag at her feet. She was knitting. When Jean saw Betsy, she just smirked. I took a deep breath.

"Mom, Pop. This is Betsy Purdy, my girlfriend."

"Hello," said Betsy. "I've heard a lot about you."

"I'll bet you have," sneered Jean. "Oh, big shot, I'm knitting you a sweater. I need a measurement."

"Ma," I whined. "Not now. Not here in the park."

"Hello," my father finally said to Betsy. I was grateful for that. I could tell that Dave thought she was beautiful.

"Why can't I take a measurement in the park?" demanded my mother, rising up, She now had a tape measure in her hand. What could I do? I put my hands over my head as my mother put her arms around my chest to measure me. I could see Betsy smiling. I wished that I could magically be somewhere else. Of course nobody really looked at me, but it felt to me as if the entire park was staring at this little boy named Irwin whose mommy was measuring him for a sweater.

Jean never really approved of Betsy, but then I doubt if she would have given the okay to any woman. A few days later, when we were alone, she said to me, "Why does my son have to pick out a shiksa? There's a million nice Jewish girls in the world. My wonderful son has to stab me in the heart and pick a goy!" I knew there was no sense in arguing with her, but I couldn't control myself. "Why do you care if she's Jewish or not? You're not a good Jew anyhow!" I told her. "Look who's talking! How dare you call me a bad Jew? And by the way, big shot, I'm a Jewess, not a Jew!" "Ma, she's a wonderful girl. I love her." "What do you know about love? You're just a little *pisher.*" (*Pisher* is a Yiddish term for little squirt, a small-timer, one who doesn't pee a lot.) "Well, I'm going to marry her," I said. "You hear, Dave?" Jean turned to my father for help. "You hear how he talks to his mother?"

Dave shrugged. "I like her," he said.

With that, Jean exploded. "If you like her so much, then you marry the shiksa, too!"

A few weeks later I brought Betsy to Brownsville to meet my grandparents. I didn't think they had ever met a Christian woman. My *bubbe* baked her special rugelach, delicious sweet things made with raisins and cheese and chocolate. She served hot tea. She was very friendly. Sam, my *zeda*, showed Betsy his scrapbooks, and then he played the violin for her. Later, as I prepared to leave, my grandmother whispered to me, "Such a wonderful girl. You'd never know she isn't Jewish!"

In 1957, Betsy and I had our first child, Meg. My mother fell in love with Meg the moment she saw her. She knitted little booties and angora caps with cat ears, tiny sweaters, even baby gloves. I knew Jean still had her mood swings, but I thought Meg might bring her out of it.

By 1959 my career in New York was at a standstill, so I decided to move to California, to Hollywood. Television work was drying up in New York, and I was starting to get nightclub jobs out west.

I was also into my second year of therapy. It seemed all I talked about was my mother. I loved her, I hated her, I was afraid of her, I wasn't afraid of her. There was no doubt in my mind that in my mother's presence I often became infantile. Never was I more so than the day I told her I was moving. I understood her despair, but I saw no way out of it. As much as I felt fear and dread, I also felt a certain elation at the thought that maybe finally I would be free. But even three thousand miles didn't do the trick. As broke as we were, I'd call my mother three times a week.

"Ma, it's Paul." "My son's name is Irwin, not Paul." "How's the weather in the Apple?" I said, trying to change the subject. "The weather is rotten. How's Meg? How is my darling grandchild who I'll never see again?" "Stop it, Ma. You'll see her soon. You'll come out for a visit." "Sure. Where will I stay? In a cemetery? Your shiksa wife doesn't want me." "She does. Betsy likes you, you know that." "She likes me more than you do. That much

I'm sure of." "Ma, I didn't call to argue." "Tex is fine." "Good. He's so cute," I said. Tex was a red Manx cat that Betsy and I had given to Jean. She often walked the cat on a leash in Washington Square Park. Tex was the inspiration for "Tonto" in *Harry and Tonto*.

When Jean finally did begin her yearly visits out west, I tried my best to make peace. But as soon as I saw her, the same powerful dynamics of love and hate took over. I was getting more and more successful, but in her eyes I was moving further and further away from her. She accused me of not really wanting her out here, and in my heart I knew she was right. I was still afraid of her.

By now I was on my second therapist, and I at least had the insight to understand my fears. I just didn't seem to be able to do anything about them. The therapist pointed out that some love is better than none, and there was no doubt in his mind that my mother loved me desperately. And somehow I had come out whole. I functioned very well and had a good marriage. "It's time to stop blaming your mother," Dr. Muhich said to me.

Finally, in desperation, I decided to try to get Jean to see Muhich for one visit so that he could meet this person that I talked about so much. Maybe Jean would get some insight herself. Dr. Muhich thought this was a good idea. Jean didn't, but she agreed to go.

"What does he charge, this shrink of yours?" "Fifty dollars an hour." "I guarantee you he's full of shit," my mother said. "Why don't you just give me the fifty bucks?"

But she went. I took her to Muhich's office on Camden Drive in Beverly Hills and introduced them. Muhich was a smallish man with very intense eyes and sandy-colored hair. (He later played Dyan Cannon's therapist in *Bob & Carol* . . . and Mike the dog's therapist in *Down and Out*.) Muhich smiled politely at my mother. She rolled her eyes at me as if to say, "Are you kidding?" I fled the premises, promising to return in fifty minutes. I came back just in time to see the door to Muhich's office open. My mother exited triumphantly. Dr. Muhich was pale. She had clearly put him through the ringer.

The next day when I saw him, he told me that I was a living miracle. "It's a wonder you're so healthy," he sighed. "She's one tough cookie." "You see?" I said. "I told you." "She's very bright," he said. "You're telling me." "And she loves you." "I know." "But she thinks you're an infant. You're still her baby, her tiny baby." "What else is new?" I said. No amount of so-called insight ever seemed to give me any real freedom from the fear that I always felt with Jean.

In 1971, Betsy and I and our two daughters, Meg now fourteen years old and Jill, six years old, moved to Europe for half a year. I wanted to live in Rome to see what life was like surrounded by all that beauty. No sooner had we arrived than we heard about an earthquake in Los Angeles. Jean had come out to say good-bye to us and then decided to stay on in L.A. for another week or so with some friends of ours. I called her.

"Ma, are you okay? What happened?" "Sure. You leave me here in this godforsaken city so I can die in an earthquake!" "I didn't know there was going to be an earthquake." I was right back into her rhythm. "I was lying on the couch, and boom I fell off! I thought I was dreaming. I hate this city! I want to go back to New York where people take subways and walk and they don't have earthquakes!"

I told her how beautiful Rome was, that the girls were fine, and that they sent her their love and kisses.

"How's Fellini?" she asked me. She knew that I knew him because he had acted in *Alex in Wonderland*. "He's great, Ma. He's a beautiful man." "Well, tell him your mother who almost died in an earthquake loved *La Strada*. "I'll tell him, Ma." "And tell him I love Giulietta Masina."

Five months later I got a call in London, where we had moved. It was from Chris, a Danish friend of Jean's. He was crying. He told me Jean had died in his apartment. "She just stopped breathing," he said, weeping.

I flew back to New York and went to the morgue to identify her body. Although I was terribly sad, I felt a strange elation. It was a guilty feeling. Jean's death had finally released me from my fear. When her body came up on the morgue elevator, the attendant asked me if I wanted to be alone. I nodded. I looked at Jean, at Jennie. She was only sixty-one. She had lived long enough to see her little boy become famous. She had succumbed, and I knew that she was finally free of the terrible black moods, the despair. Maybe I was free, too. I began to weep. I loved her. I knew it.

There was one final surprise. I arranged for her funeral and invited everyone I could think of. My father had died ten years earlier. His brothers and their wives were invited to the funeral, and so were a few of Jean's friends. I told the rabbi to please not talk about show business. Then I saw the crowd arriving. Who were these people? I recognized my relatives, and I knew Chris, her gay Danish friend, but the others? There was a gay policeman, a sailor, a dozen others. They were weeping. They loved Jean. They were friends from her other life. She'd met many of them at Jones Beach where she often went in the summertime. They shook my hand and gave me their sympathy. They were part of her gypsy life. I suddenly felt that I had never really understood her. Then the rabbi began his speech. "This wonderful woman, Jean Gerson Mazursky, mother of Paul Mazursky, the noted director of such films as *Bob & Carol* . . ." I shrunk into my seat, cursing the rabbi under my breath, but then I realized that Jean would have gotten a big kick out of all this.". . . *& Ted & Alice* and *Alex in Wonderland* . . . and the coauthor of *I Love You, Alice B. Toklas*. Paul also appeared in *Blackboard Jungle* and . . ."

6

Maestro

Alex in Wonderland was a movie about a film director who had just come off a smash hit and didn't know what to do next. It was precisely the position I was in after *Bob & Carol & Ted & Alice*. The success of that film had made Tucker and Mazursky the flavor of the month in Hollywood. But after several months of stops and starts, Larry and I had no follow-up project. We were both blocked. That's when the idea came: Let's do a movie about a blocked director. Not only is "Alex" blocked, but he dreams in the style of other directors, including the incomparable Federico Fellini. Of course, Fellini's *8½* was by now world famous as a movie about a blocked director.

The script fell into place quickly, and Mike Frankovich, who had produced *Bob & Carol* . . . , told us he wanted to do *Alex in Wonderland*. Mike was a formidable figure in Hollywood. He had been a star football player at UCLA, had moved on to the movie business, and had worked himself up from being a guard at the gate to an assistant film editor and, finally, somehow, producer. By the time I met him, Mike had already been the head of Columbia Pictures in Europe and was now producing four films a year in his own special unit. He had worked with filmmakers David Lean, Carol Reed, and Sam Spiegel, as well as just about every movie star in the business. He was a man of great generosity and large appetites.

When I'd gone to him with *Bob & Carol* . . . , Mike said, "I like the script. Who do you see directing it?" I told him it had to be me. "What the hell have you ever directed?" Frankovich asked me. I told him I'd been an actor and that I'd directed in the theater, that I'd made a twelve-minute short called *Last Year at Malibu*, but, even more important, that I wouldn't sell *Bob & Carol* . . . unless I got to direct it. Larry Tucker was totally supportive.

Frankovich was a large, burly man with white hair. He loved big Churchill cigars. He looked across his desk at me and frowned. "I'll call you tomorrow around noon," he barked. I left his office positive that I had blown it, but the next day precisely at noon Mike called to tell me I was the director. "We'll surround you with top-notch pros for camera and editing and get you a great first A.D." And that was that. I don't think there are any Mike Frankoviches out there today.

When we got together for our casting ideas for *Alex in Wonderland*, Mike asked us who we saw playing Fellini. There was a brief scene where Alex accidentally meets the great Fellini. For some reason Anthony Quinn happened to be in Frankovich's office. Mike knew Quinn very well, and he often had a visiting star with him when we chatted. "Why don't we try to get Fellini himself?" I said. Quinn volunteered that he had Fellini's address. "Send him a telegram," he suggested. Quinn had starred in *La Strada* and knew Fellini well. "Do you think he'd do it, Mr. Quinn?" I asked. "Probably not," said Quinn, "but you never know. And if he doesn't want to do it, I'll play Fellini."

Larry and I were thrilled. We sent off a telegram telling

Fellini that I had just done *Bob & Carol . . .* and asking if he would act in my new film for just one day—in Rome. Two days later we received a telegram from the Maestro saying that he absolutely did not want to act in my film and, moreover, he didn't even know who I was. "P.S.," he added. "If you ever come to Roma, please call me." Mike Frankovich didn't hesitate for a second. "You boys get the hell on a plane to Rome tomorrow morning. He wants you to chase him."

There was no talk about the expense of two round-trip tickets and the hotel. This was the old Hollywood. The next day Tucker and Mazursky were on a plane to the Holy City. As soon as we got to our hotel (the Excelsior—nothing but the best), we called Mario Longardi, Fellini's right-hand man.

"But, please, who are you?" asked Longardi. "Does the maestro know you?" "He told us to call him if we ever came to Rome. So here we are." We explained the telegram. Now Longardi remembered. He obviously had sent the telegram for Fellini. "I will call you back soon," he told us. We were dying to run out to the streets and see *la dolce vita.* Neither of us had ever been to Rome, but we had seen Fellini's version of it in *La Dolce Vita:* Marcello Mastroianni cruising down the Via Veneto in his convertible, dozens of sexy Italian gals promenading their wares.

But we had to sit and wait for the phone call. In less than an hour Longardi called us and said that Fellini would meet us the following evening in the lobby of the Grand Hotel. "Eight o'clock sharp, if you please, gentlemen." The next twenty-four hours seemed to take forever. We soaked up this fabulous city by night, sipping cappuccinos, flirting with every girl that passed our table. We walked to the Trevi fountain hoping by some miracle to see Anita Ekberg and Mastroianni hip-deep in the water. We drove by the Colosseum and the Forum, and the next day we did it all over again. Rome was thrilling! Life was beautiful! Soon I was going to meet my idol, the great Fellini. As the time neared eight, I began to worry. He'd see that *Alex* was my attempt at an *8½.* Come on, kiddo! A film director is blocked and ends up making a movie about it? Would he scoff? Would he be angry? At 7:45 Larry and I planted ourselves in the lobby of the Grand Hotel. We tried to be casual, but we kept turning to the revolving doors. I don't remember what we wore, but with Larry's girth and my thinness then, we must have looked like Laurel and Hardy.

At exactly 8:00 P.M., we saw the great man coming through the revolving doors. He wore his signature upturned black fedora and had a black coat tossed over his shoulders. He was a tall man, much taller than I had imagined. He was accompanied by a much smaller man with a sweet smile on his face. I thought I heard the music of Nino Rota playing in the background. Larry and I stood up. My knees were shaking slightly.

"Mr. Mazursky and Mr. Tucker?" said the other man.

"Yes, that's us," I said.

"I am Mario Longardi."

"And I am Federico Fellini. Perhaps you have heard of me." Fellini was smiling. He looked at us with great curiosity. He shook hands first with Larry. "So you are Mazursky?"

"No, sir. I'm Larry Tucker."

"Then only you can be Mazursky," said Fellini. He started to laugh. I wanted to cry with joy. "But why you are here?" he asked me. His voice was pitched higher than his size would seem to indicate.

"You told us to call you if we ever came to Rome," I said. "So we're here."

Fellini shook his head in disbelief. "But you are *pazzo*," he said, looking over to Longardi for help.

"Signor Fellini says you are crazy," Longardi said with a smile.

The ice had been broken. Fellini said something in Italian to Longardi. Then he turned to us and said, "My English is very terrible. But I think we can understand each other. Come, let's find a place to eat." We said good night to Longardi and were now alone with Fellini.

Who can explain why anything happens? Fellini had not yet seen *Bob & Carol* . . . , so he didn't have any idea of what my work was like. It's true he was fond of freaks, of giants and dwarfs, of hermaphrodites and clowns. Maybe Tucker and Mazursky seemed like a new oddity. We were both funny and Fellini loved a joke, so maybe that explains it. In any case, we spent the next four days and nights hanging out with Federico Fellini. We had brought along a print of *Bob & Carol . . .* , and one night we showed it to Fellini and Longardi. Larry and I sat in the back of a small screening room, worried to death that he would not "get" the film. There were not yet any subtitles. But every now and then, always at the appropriate moments, Fellini chuckled or laughed. Once or twice he leaned over to Longardi and asked him to translate a word or two. Finally, when the lights came up, Fellini turned to me. "But this is so sweet, so funny, so . . . American. It is very beautiful."

It didn't take long to feel comfortable with Fellini. He seemed more like an older brother to me than some great icon. His warmth was genuine, and his humor was irrepressible. He wanted to understand Americans—why we were still so naive, so childish, and yet so powerful. He loved food, and we found ourselves in the best Roman restaurants. Caesarina's was a particular favorite of Fellini's. Later I found out that Caesarina was a woman from Bologna whom Fellini had backed in this restaurant. She was famous for her Bolognese treats. Then there was Gigi Fazzi Restaurant, where the crowd stopped eating when a celebrity entered. Their knives and forks would be suspended in midair as they stared at the latest star. As soon as they knew who you were, the noise resumed. When Tucker and Mazursky entered with Fellini, there was complete, eerie silence for about thirty seconds. Fellini found this very amusing. "They are going crazy to try to guess who you are," he said with a chuckle. Larry and I were thrilled to be with Fellini, but we had not yet convinced him to act in our movie. "You don't need me," he cautioned us. "Use a puppet or a dwarf. But not the real Fellini. This is your character's fantasy." I told Fellini I disagreed with him. "It's more interesting if Alex meets the real Fellini." Fellini smiled. "I have met myself many times. I don't find me very interesting. In fact, sometimes it is depressing." We laughed. "But Alex idolizes Fellini. He doesn't idolize a puppet." "Perhaps he could meet a giant, a seven-foot-tall Fellini. Or is that too phallic?" Federico asked.

No matter how much I pleaded my case, Fellini remained elusive. I worried. Sure we were having a great time driving around Rome with the world's greatest director, but we couldn't nail him down to a commitment. Finally, the last night of our stay, after Fellini had driven us back to the Excelsior, we embraced in an emotional farewell in front of the hotel. Then Fellini said, "You really want this, *caro* Paolino? You truly want me to be in your film? You must have it?" I nodded. "I must have it, Federico." "All right," he said, "I will do it." We embraced again. Our four days had been a fantasy right out of a Fellini film.

The next few months went by quickly. Donald Sutherland was a very believable "Alex." Donald is a superb actor and a man of great charm and devilish humor. I loved him. Ellen Burstyn played his wife. She found her inspiration from my wife, Betsy. I don't think Betsy was thrilled with the idea of my making a "home movie" about our lives. My daughter Meg played one of Alex's daughters. She was twelve, wore braces, and was very convincing. Viola Spolin, the mother of improvisational techniques in the American theater, played Alex's mother, who was clearly based on my mother, Jean. (When my mother saw the completed film, she threatened to picket in front of the theater in New York. "How dare you show me like that?" she shouted on the telephone. "But, Ma—" "Don't 'Ma' me, you ingrate! The least you could have done was get Bette Davis to play me! Who the hell is this Viola Spolin?")

And then there was the incomparable Jeanne Moreau who played herself. Moreau is a woman of great beauty, immense talent, and no bullshit. She does what she wants because she wants to do it. Period. When we decided it might be interesting for her to sing in Alex's fantasy, Ms. Moreau wrote lyrics to George Delarue's theme music from *Jules and Jim*. I will never forget the sight of Moreau singing as she walked down Hollywood Boulevard arm in arm with Sutherland.

We had a week to go on the film. I was home in bed on a Sat-

urday night when the phone rang. It was the long-distance operator. She had a call for me from Rome, from Mario Longardi. I
could tell immediately from the tone of Longardi's voice that
there was trouble. "I am sorry to inform you, Paul, that Fellini will
not be able to appear in your film. He has changed his mind." I
was too shocked to say anything coherent, to even try arguing. I
said good-bye to Longardi and hung up. I called Larry Tucker,
and we made a bold decision. We would not tell the studio what
had happened. I would go to Rome with Sutherland and my cameraman, Laszlo Kovacs, as planned. I would try to convince
Fellini; if all else failed, I would hire some Italian actor to play
Fellini, and we'd still shoot one day in Cinecittà.

As soon as I got to Rome, I called Longardi. "Hello, Mario.
It's Paul Mazursky. We're here in Rome ready to shoot."

I could hear the disbelief in Longardi's voice. "But, Paul,
didn't you understand my phone call? The Maestro does not agree
to appear in your film."

"No," I lied, "I thought you said he will be in the film. We
must have had a bad connection, Mario." I'm sure Mario, gentle
and trusting as he was, understood my duplicity.

"I will not call Federico. If you want to talk to him yourself,
he is having dinner right this moment in Caesarina's."

I raced downstairs and took a taxi to the restaurant. I knew I
had taken things too far, but I was desperate. As I walked into the
restaurant, Caesarina herself recognized me. She smiled and
pointed out Fellini's table. I felt that all eyes were on me as I approached the great man. He had a large swirl of pasta wrapped
around a fork and was lifting it to his mouth as I stepped up to the
table. He had not yet seen me.

"Federico," I said, "I'm here. I'm in Rome with Donald
Sutherland. We want to shoot the scene tomorrow."

Fellini looked up, the spaghetti close to his lips. He looked at
me as if it were perfectly normal that I was in Rome. Then with a
shrug he said, "All right. I will do it."

Soon, I was digging into my own plate of pasta, and Fellini
was telling me he'd bring his real editor, Norma, to Cinecittà for

the scene tomorrow. Not a word about Longardi's phone call. Fellini smiled at me. "So you think you are great enough, Paolino, to direct Federico Fellini?" "No," I said. "You can do whatever you want." "But I insist," said Fellini. "You are obliged to help me." I smiled. I was very happy. Mike Frankovich was right. If you wanted Fellini, you had to chase him.

The shooting went very well. Fellini improvised a line or two, each time asking my permission. "Please, Paolino, may I say so and so here? It will not disturb you, Maestro?" He had taken to calling me Maestro, knowing that it made me laugh. When the work was finished, I told him that I had three days left before I flew back to Los Angeles. "Should I go to Florence or Venice?" I asked him. "That depends on you. Do you want marijuana or LSD?" Fellini asked me. "Firenze is like marijuana. You will be very happy there. Venezia is not like any place you have ever experienced. She is like an acid trip." "I think I'll take Venice," I said quickly. "A happy choice," said Fellini. He immediately got on the phone and called the Danielli Hotel in Venice. He spoke to the concierge and told him to take care of "Mazursky."

When I got to Venice, I immediately went out to the Piazza San Marco. The music of Rossini filled the plaza. Lovers of all ages strolled hand in hand. Something about it made you want to cry. I hurried back to the hotel; I wanted to call Betsy and share my feelings. As soon as I stepped into the room, the phone rang. It was Fellini. "So, Paolino? You are 'high'?" "You were right, Federico. It's so beautiful. Thank you." "*Ciao*," said Fellini. "Send me a note now and then, dear Paolino."

About a year afterward I moved to Rome with my wife and two children. *Alex in Wonderland* had laid a colossal egg, and I was reeling from this failure. I liked many things in the film and couldn't understand the terrible hostility toward the picture. But that's show business, folks. I decided to move to Europe to at least try it out, to live among the great beauty of an older civilization where they understood artists. It didn't take long for me to learn how naive I was, how romantic I was, how full of shit I was. I had only to talk to Fellini to hear his complaints about the endless crap he had to go through to know that I was dreaming. To make matters worse, Betsy hated Rome. She spoke not one word of Italian, which made shopping difficult. Also, in 1971, there were endless *scioperos*, hiccup strikes that might last only as long as a hiccup or perhaps all winter. One week the postal workers would strike, another week the hotel workers, the barbers, the garbage men, the museum employees. It was impossible to know how long a strike would last. Poor Betsy got more and more depressed. I was not too supportive. "We have a great apartment. The kids are in a good school. We have plenty of money. What the hell is your problem?" I shouted. "I can't even buy a chicken," said Betsy, close to tears but also angry. "If I want a lightbulb, I can't find the store. The Italians are rude. They push and shove." "Shove them back!" I shouted.

We got more and more tense. Fellini knew about all this. I had told him that I was having troubles, that my wife did not like Rome. He was aghast. How could anyone not like his beloved Roma? So each week he would take us to another restaurant. "When she tastes Caesarina's cooking, dear Betsy will love Roma." At the restaurant, Fellini would pick up a luscious Bolognese treat and actually lift it to Betsy's mouth. "Please, *carina*, taste this." Betsy would dutifully swallow the goodie. "Now," said a confident Fellini, "now do you like Roma?" Without missing a beat, Betsy shook her head. "Nope," she said. I wanted to pour ice water over her head.

I often went to dinner with Fellini alone. He introduced me to a great assortment of types. A lion tamer—I had never met a lion tamer. There was a strange fellow who lived in a candlelit basement. He arranged metal objects on the floor and then predicted the future. There were exotic women who dined with us. Lots of flirting, but that was all. Fellini's driver had helped me buy a secondhand Peugeot, so I usually did the driving. Often, when we went out to eat, Federico would make me stop the car so that he could run inside a cafe and telephone ahead to see who was at a certain restaurant. One night we stopped in front of a place so that Fellini could check inside. He came rushing out. "Ekberg is in there. Let's go to Fregene." Fregene was where he had a summer home. It was near the water and about an hour from Rome. Fellini knew all the restaurants and particularly loved their cheeses.

Some days Fellini would call me and ask if I'd like to spend the day with him while he ran some errands. I'd meet him in front of the Canova cafe in the Piazza del Popolo. Fellini would drive me in his chocolate brown Mercedes. He lived nearby, at 110 Margutta, a cozy block full of art galleries. I lived four blocks away, so it was very convenient. He would drive to his attorney's office. Sometimes I would wait outside, sometimes I would sit in the office while Fellini chatted it up. Then we'd go to his beloved Cinecittà. Fellini was preparing *Roma*. He'd make a few phone calls, crack jokes with his staff, meet with his production designer, Danillo Donatello, and then we'd go to lunch, usually at the Nuevo Fico, a charming country-style restaurant fifteen minutes from the studio. "Do you think Betsy would change her mind about Rome if she ate here, Paolino?" I decided not to risk it.

Some mornings when I'd drop my daughters off in front of the Canova where they caught their school bus, I would walk a few paces away and hide until the bus came. The girls wanted to be more grown-up and wait by themselves. They were six and thirteen years old.

One morning I stepped away, and lo and behold, there was Fellini having a quick cappuccino. He didn't see me. He happened to be standing right next to Jill, my six-year-old. I knew that he loved children. He could see Jill staring at a delicious pastry on the counter right above her head. He bought it for her. This happened several times. One day I told Federico I'd seen him buy Jill sweets. He was delighted at the coincidence.

"Has Giulietta [his name for Jill] seen my film *The Clowns*? he asked me. I told him no. He decided to arrange a special early screening for her. A few nights later, Betsy, Jill, Meg, and I went to a screening room. It was only six-thirty. Fellini spoke to my daughters, but particularly to Jill. "This is my film about clowns. They are funny men, these clowns. I hope you will enjoy yourself." Jill smiled shyly at Fellini. The room darkened and the film

began. In about five minutes Jill began to snore loudly. She was
sound asleep. Fellini spoke in the darkness. "Thank you, Paolino,
for bringing your child to the work of my life's blood so that she
can snore at it." We couldn't stop laughing.

One late afternoon Fellini called and asked if I would like to
join him for dinner. I arranged to pick him up at 8:00 P.M. in front
of the Bernini fountain. It was drizzling when I got there. I saw
Fellini standing with a woman under her flowered umbrella. I
lowered my car window and called out to him. He smiled and
quickly came over to the car. I got out and shook hands with the
woman. Her name, I think, was Maria. She was dark, moderately
attractive, and about thirty-five. Federico suggested that we drive
Maria home and then we two go out to eat. Of course, I agreed.
They got into the backseat of the Peugeot. Fellini gave me direc-
tions, and in about ten minutes we stopped in front of an apartment building. "*Momento*, Paolino," said Fellini, getting out of the
car with Maria. I said good night to her. Federico took her to the
doorway of the old building and kissed her on both cheeks. I didn't
know if that meant pure friendliness or something more sexual.
Italians were constantly kissing each other on both cheeks, sometimes three kisses. Fellini got back into the car, not a word about
Maria. We eventually found a restaurant and had dinner. I don't
remember what we talked about, but I was hoping Fellini would
bring up Maria. Nothing. Finally I drove him home to 110
Margutta and then drove to my apartment at Passegietta di
Ripetta. The old Italian man who "watched" cars on the street—I
think his name was Luigi—tipped his cap to me and wished me a
good night. As I got out of the car, I saw Maria's pink-and-yellow-
flowered umbrella lying on the backseat. I took it out. What to do
with it? Luigi gave me a knowing smile. I opened the trunk of the
car and tossed the umbrella in. On second thought, I shoved it way
back in the trunk where no one could see it.

The next day when Betsy was out trying to buy milk and
bread, I called Fellini. "Federico, that Maria left her umbrella in
the car." Fellini responded quickly. "I do not remember any umbrella." "Sure," I told him. "It's pink and yellow. A ladies umbrella.

I'm sure she'll miss it." "Who will miss what?" said the Maestro. I didn't know if he was breaking my balls or what. "Maria will miss her umbrella. Her pink and yellow umbrella," I insisted. "Paolino," explained Fellini, "let me make myself clear. If there is an umbrella, regardless of color, I, Federico Fellini, do not want this umbrella. Why don't you give it your wife, to Betsy. Then perhaps she will love Roma." "No way, Federico," I said. "I'll just throw the umbrella in the garbage. We don't need any more umbrellas." "Good," said Fellini. "Then that settles the question of the umbrella?" I told him yes. I figured that he did not want to see Maria again.

But somehow I found it impossible to throw the umbrella away. I even began to dream up a film about an umbrella. It would go from person to person, and we'd see three or four different stories. Maybe it would be my next film. (I've never written that movie. My next film was *Blume in Love*, which was clearly inspired by my days in Venice.) Fellini never brought up the subject of the umbrella again.

About four months later Betsy and I decided to move to England for a few months before returning to the United States. Our European adventure was winding down. I sold the Peugeot to an Israeli medical student. The day came to hand over the car to him, in front of my building. Luigi, the car watcher, was there. I gave him a big tip, and we said an emotional good-bye. Then I opened the trunk of the car to show the Israeli the spare tire and the jack. Betsy was there, too. She was very happy. Her ordeal in Rome was almost over. In fact, now that we were about to leave, she had begun to like the Eternal City. She probed around in the trunk to see if she had left anything there. Suddenly I remembered the umbrella. Too late, Betsy plucked it out. "What's this?" she asked, a queer look on her face. The Israeli smiled. So did Luigi. "That's Fellini's umbrella," I blurted. "Fellini's?" asked Betsy. "But it's a ladies' umbrella." "Yes," I said. "It's Maria's." "Who's Maria?" Betsy asked. I decided to tell the truth. After all, what had happened? Fellini had a lady friend who had left her umbrella in my car. Nothing more. "Maria is a friend of Fellini's. We went to dinner one night—" Betsy interrupted. "Who went to dinner? You and Maria?" "No, no, no," I said. "Federico and I went to dinner. But first I drove Maria home." I could see that Betsy was skeptical. The Israeli and Luigi turned away to give us some privacy. "Okay. But why didn't you give Fellini back the umbrella so he could return it to what's-her-name?" "Maria," I said. "I offered to give it to him, but he didn't want it back." Betsy smiled at me. I don't think she believed a word I said. She turned to the medical student. "Would you like this umbrella? It rains a lot in Rome." "Sure," said the Israeli. "I can always use a good umbrella."

Over the next twenty-two years I managed to get to Rome about twenty times—sometimes to promote a film, sometimes to shoot a film (*Tempest* with John Cassavetes; a month at Cinecittà), but many times just to enjoy my favorite city. I would always spend time with my great friend Emi De Sica, the daughter of the sublime Vittorio. She had been very kind to Betsy and me when we lived there. Her daughter Eleonora had played with my daughters.

I saw Fellini whenever I could. He came to the States several times, and we renewed our friendship in New York and Los Angeles ("But how can you live there, Paolino? I cannot find this city . . ."). We wrote to each other several times a year. Fellini's productivity never waned. He was always either shooting or preparing, but he was also having more trouble finding the money to make his films. One evening after shooting a tough scene for *Tempest* in the water tank at Cinecittà, I had dinner with Federico. About ten years had passed since the time I had lived in Rome. Out of the blue I brought up the pink and yellow umbrella. Federico remembered everything. I told him what had happened to the umbrella. "Perhaps now she is in New York City, this umbrella, and you must do a film about her." "And Maria?" I said. Fellini took me by the shoulders and looked deep into my eyes. "You must know this, Paolino?" "Yes," I answered, smiling, "I must know." "A woman," said Fellini, "is like a house. When you first meet her, she is a beautiful house with so many charming rooms. When you look in her eyes, you can even see the furniture, the paintings on the walls, the flowers. The possibilities of happiness are enormous. You love this house, this woman. But then one day while you are looking at this beautiful woman, you look over her shoulder, just a few inches to the right, and there is another woman. And her house is even more beautiful. Soon you are moving out of the first house and into the second."

Sometimes Fellini wrote to me in Italian. But his best letters were in English. Some of them were handwritten, some were dictated.

> Dear Paolino,
> I finally received one of your little letters. It made me very happy dear friend. But what made me even more happy was to read that your last film is a big success. I had already been informed of this by a young american director who came to see me here in Rome (I can't remember his name, but I know he has just made a film for television called "DUEL" based on a science fiction book). This director* told me about you and about your film. He said that the film has received good reviews and is a box office hit. Good!
> I am finishing up the dubbing of "Amarcord", which should be completed in a couple of months. It's been a hard film but I had fun doing it anyway, like always. And now what? Now I am preparing another film. I don't know if I'll come to New York. I don't think I will. Will you come to Rome for a little while? Not even you know.
> Let's write each other more often dear Paolo, even if we have nothing more to say than that we are finishing a movie or that we are starting a movie.
> Do you need anything from Rome? From me? Just ask me, I will always be happy to be useful to you. Well, I will hug you now. I hope to see you sooner or later. Send my regards to whoever you want. Be well.

*The director is Steven Spielberg—P.M.

Paul Mazursky
449 North Las Palmas
Los Angeles, California
90004

Dear Paul,

Thank you for your wishes for a "happy new year" . . . I too send you my much delayed wishes.

For now I'm planning on staying in Italy. If you come to Rome I'll be happy to see you.

I'm glad to know that everything is going well with your film "Harry & Tonto". I will start shooting "Casanova" next summer.

Giulietta is well. I send you my phone number (but don't give it to anybody). You can call me every morning before 9. Having made no progress with my English, I prefer writing you in Italian.

I hug you with affection dear Paul.

(Federico Fellini)
Dimenticavo l'indirizzo di Peppino Rotunno
Via V. Tiberio 14, Roma.

Dear Paul

I'm happy to read that you are making a new picture in New York so full of memories and old dreams for you. That's already a very good starting. Harry and Tonto was a very "Mazurskian sweet, funny touching picture" Dear Paul and I loved it because it was like you are. I saw it in Paris months ago in a little theatre full of young students and the picture gave me the feeling of our friendship: a real friendship between two students. I'm now in trouble with my new one picture like always after all. It's now one year that I'm breaking my balls with that damn project. I hope to see you (when? how? where?) but it will happen anyway.

Good luck to you Paul

Love to Betsy. Kisses to you

White space (?) to correct all the mistakes of my english

16 July 1977

Paul Mazursky
Twentieth Century Fox Film
Corporation
Box 900
Beverly Hills
California 90213
U. S. A.

Caro Paolino:

Finally I hear from you! But why don't you send me your home address instead of making me write to Fox? I often thought of you, confusing you though sometimes with Frank Capra. What to do? I am getting old. I forget names. I can't even remember when I made my last film because there must have been a last film since I haven't done anything for two years.

I am seized by a desire to do nothing. Here in Italy we've been living for a long time waiting for something to end and something else to begin. The problem is nothing ends and nothing begins. I have a contract with Guccione I signed two years ago and then I have never heard from him, so I signed another contract for my next film with an American producer called De Laurentiis. I also signed other deals with NBC, with ORTF and a couple of editors. At a certain point, I ask myself how am I going to do all this with the feeling of fatigue and listlesness gripping me?

Do you think you will come to Rome? Dear Paolino, I would like to write you at length but the American lady I am dictating to is about to have a baby so we must stop. If it's a boy, we'll let you know.

Auguri. Ti abbraccio. Un abbraccio also to everyone.

Rome; 18 september 1979

Dear Paul,
I've just received your letter and I am glad to know you have nearly finished your new film and that you are coming to Rome. I will see you with joy as always, dear Paul.
When you will be in Rome you can find me in Cinecittà—Studio 5—at this number: 74.64.330.
I am here looking forward the end of this film "La città delle donne" because I am really exhausted and disgusted as never before. I think I will do something else in the next future, can you suggest anything?

Best wishes,

Roma, 26.4.1979

Dear Paul,

I received your letter with great pleasure. I still cannot accept that my friend Nino Rota has gone. I should have chosen another composer more than two weeks ago, but something within me seems to stop me from doing so.

I still can't believe that it's happened. In this "soul's state" I have begun to shoot the movie ten days ago. I work from one day to another, feeling as through I have been working on an interminable film for thirty years.

I'm becoming sentimental and literary, but you can under-stand all this.

I kiss you dear Paul. Even though I don't see you often, you know that we are both sitting on the same school-benk, with a little difference that I am younger that you, and that for eight years, you are still in the same class because of a lack of good school-marks.

I kiss you and wish you all the best with your work.

Rome, Nov 19, 84

Dear Paul,

I'm dictating this letter over the phone to Fiammetta, for she tells me you sent me a wonderful T shirt with Ginger and Fred on it, and I won't be back in Rome until the end of next week.

Thank you, dear Paul. I'm waiting for more consistent presents, and if you haven't got the time to go around in shops, art galleries and jewellers you can send the equivalent amount in checks.

I was in Los Angeles, but of course I didn't dream of calling you. I'm kidding, of course: I looked for you but without success. Maybe you weren't there at the time, in any case I only stayed three days.

A big hug, my dear friend, and best of luck for your work,

Federico

Rome, March 2nd, 1987

Dear Paul,

the gentleman who brings you this letter is Ibrahim Moussa, the producer of my latest film, which I believe aroused the interest of an American distribution Company, maybe Columbia. In any case, Ibrahim will be able to tell you how things stand.

Now, with brutal sincerity, I must tell you that when I was asked if I could take care of the English version of this film, my answer was no. I've had too many bitter experiences to get involved once again in these criminal enterprises, the only purpose of which is to destroy your work, your efforts, and anything good you might have come up with.

There were only two occasions in which I was in part satisfied: Satyricon, because Peter Brook had accepted to take care of the Eng-

lish dubbing; and the French version of Casanova, because it was done by a colleague whom I like and estimate, Patrice Chereau.

All the other times, including Casanova in English, were absolute disasters. Since then, I put as a condition to the producers who try to get me involved in the foreign versions of my film, the fact that I agree to look into them only if there is a colleague whom I trust, who with talent, experience and a bit of affection, will accept the responsibility of the translation of my picture.

I was asked to suggest some names, and even though I knew I was going to give you trouble, problems and nuisance I mumbled your name. It was greeted by applause, by Columbia, by the producer, by Fiammetta who happened to be there at the moment, and by two extras who were passing by, but who knows what they understood. The only one who made problems, right after pronouncing your name, was myself, because I know that even though you have a great friendship for me you probably have no intention of going crazy in the attempt to give a more profound meaning to this little mess I made.

Well, that is all, dear Paul, see what you can do according to your availability, your willingness and your interest. Let me just add one little thing, so that all is clear: I would like 85% of the sum you will ask. In fact, do you think you could give Moussa a little advance payment for me?

A warm hug, my dear friend, and excuse me, sincerely,

Rome, Oct 19, 87

Dear Paul,

thank you for your affectionate note, even if I'm a bit sur-prised at your enthousiasm for the women of Rio. What do you mean, at your age you didn't know they were like this? What had you been doing all this time? How could you live? I was seven, I was in nun's boarding school in Rimini, and the Mother Superior was Brazilian. What emotions, Paul! What a 'BUNDA'! After that, all the maids, governesses who accompanied my childhood and ado-lescence up to University, were chosen by my Father who made them all come from Brazil. How odd that we never spoke about it. And Norma, Fiammetta, where did you think they came from? Sao Paulo, Rio, Bundoya, Brasilia. Marcello is also very involved with Brazil. That's why I often call him in my pictures.

I must interrupt this letter and run to the Grand Hotel, where 24 dancers from the OBA-OBA Company are impatiently waiting for me. Well, I'm happy for you, better late than never (but maybe it's a bit too late).

I hug you, Paulito, evviva la bunda! Yours

Federicão

Agosto 1997

My dear Paul
for me too was very simpatico to meet you again. Simpatico and like always very natural, normal, and daily (it is correct?)
I hope that your feeling about the negative conclusion with that strange guy who you met and who calls himself V. C. Gori, will bring you luck in any case. When we will stay again at FICO's restaurant totally relaxed and irresponsible.
Love caro amico.
Stay well and work soon very very soon.

Dearest Paul
Thanks for the affectionate little note and the disconcerting (disconcerting)* photo (how ruthlessly old I look!)* that you have sent me.
When will we meet again in that typical confused chaotic at-mosphere in which we have (and always wanted and needed) lives?
I hug you my dear friend, good luck on your work, good luck yours
   (signed)

*Fiammetta's translation

The first time I discussed age with Fellini, I was forty and he had just turned fifty. He complained he was getting old. "But fifty isn't old, Federico." "You don't understand," he told me. "The number five in fifty is open. The five itself has an open space, Paolino. You have to understand how quickly, how brutally, the five becomes a six, and suddenly you are sixty." Although his hair got thinner and he began to stoop just a bit, he never seemed to lose his vigor or his sense of humor. He would often ask me on the telephone how my sex life was. I always lied and complained that I was exhausted from an abundance of women. He had all kinds of nicknames for the penis and always wanted to know what shape mine was in. He never forgot Betsy or my children, and always asked after them. Once, when we returned to Rome on a visit, Betsy and I had dinner with Federico, and she told him that she now liked Rome. This made him very happy.

In the last year and a half or so of his life, it became apparent that the Maestro was slowing down. "What do you do to your hair?" he asked me. "Do you dye it black? Why is it that you get younger and I get older?" I told him about all my aches and pains, my bad knee, my inability to lose twenty pounds, my smoking habit. He scoffed. "You are like a young boy, and I am an old man." The twinkle was still in his eyes, the wonderful smile that curled his lips up. He still loved to laugh. But he was getting tired—not just physically but tired, too, of the struggles to get his projects made.

The last time I saw him was in Los Angeles in 1993. He had come for the Academy Awards, a special honor "in recognition of his cinematic accomplishments that have thrilled and entertained worldwide audiences." He complained to me on the phone that he was too tired to come but that he probably would because Giulietta wanted him to. As the days came closer to Oscar time, rumors spread that Fellini would not show. He promised to call me from the Beverly Hilton Hotel as soon as he arrived—that is, "If I come. I don't know." Two days later I went to Plummer Park to play my usual Saturday morning tennis. I forgot about Fellini, but when I came home, I checked my phone for messages. "Paolino, I am here in your city in a room, a suite at the Beverly Hilton Hotel. Can you tell me what I am doing here? I know I have made a serious mistake. I should be in Roma, not here. Giulietta is standing next to me and sends her love. Call me. I don't know the number." I ran into the bedroom to tell Betsy. I played her the message.

I called Federico. He told me that he was too exhausted to

see anyone at this moment but that he would make an appearance at the Directors Guild the following morning. "Are you too tired to go to a couple of places with me, Federico?" "Yes, *carino*. I am exhausted." "I want to take you to the Farmer's Market and to the beach at Venice to see some crazies so you'll know there are actually people living in Los Angeles." "I will take your word for it," he said. I knew it was selfish of me, but I wanted to show him a bit of my world. He never understood it. He always asked me why I didn't move back to New York.

The next morning there was a large crowd waiting at the Director's Guild of America. Many prominent directors were there. Some knew Fellini personally, and others just wanted to be there to see and hear him. There was a sudden hush in the lobby, and I saw Mario Longardi come in with Federico. Mario looked great, his sideburns white now, but still a full head of hair, and a smile on his face. Fellini had aged considerably since the year before. Even walking was an effort for him. He wore a dark suit and a maroon sweater vest with a maroon tie. He slumped down in a chair in the lobby, and the mob descended on him. I wanted to rush over and embrace him, but I stayed back for a few minutes. Then I walked over to him. He looked up at me as if to say, *Can you believe it?* "Paolino," he said. And we embraced. I knew he was sick, and I could tell that he recognized my reaction. It was impossible to really talk. We arranged for me to visit him at the hotel the morning after the Oscars.

The Oscars were the usual mixture of the sublime and ridiculous until the award for Federico was announced. The audience rose and gave him a standing ovation. I was home watching with Betsy and a few friends and my daughters. We all began to weep. What else could you do? I knew this was Fellini's last appearance. He made a joke or two, thanked Hollywood for the award, and then thanked Giulietta. He pointed to her in the audience and told her to please stop crying. The camera found her, and, of course, she wept. The waif from *La Strada*, the clown of clowns, acknowledged her husband. It gave us collective goose bumps.

When I got to the suite at the Hilton the following morning,

I was happy to see that Mastroianni was there with Giulietta and Mario. Mastroianni was puffing away, making jokes about Sophia Loren. Giulietta remembered me with affection. Her voice was darker now, but she still had the amazing smile. Fellini talked about the awards. "They told me to say everything I wanted— about this and about that and even to mention Giulietta. Say all of this, but please do it in thirty seconds! What? They are pazzo?" I told Federico that, yes, they were crazy, but that he had performed one last miracle.

Ciao, Federico.

7

Show Me the Magic!

The first time I met John Cassavetes was in 1953. I was working as a juicer at the Salad Bowl, one of the first health food restaurants in New York. The Bowl was located on Seventh Avenue and Fifty-fourth Street, right across from the Stage Delicatessen. George Haines, the owner of the Bowl, would stand near the front of the shop and call out to customers entering the Stage; "Go! Kill yourself with fat!" Remember, this was before all the health crazes of today. My main job was to make vegetable and fruit juices in the large blender in the front window area where everyone could see me. I wasn't exactly ashamed of the job, but I wasn't proud of it, either. (I had already been in Kubrick's *Fear and Desire*, which didn't get me the Oscar I dreamed it would. But I *had* starred in a movie. I also was now married to Betsy and studying acting with Paul Mann.) I was an ace with the blender: carrot juice, beet juice, carrot and apple with a touch of celery.

Perry Como was a Salad Bowl regular. He'd come in once or twice a week and ask me to make him his usual: cabbage and horseradish. This was a foul-tasting blend that apparently opened Mr. Como's nasal passages, thereby enabling him to sing better. He always gave me a twenty-five-cent tip, which was very good for those days. Most of the other customers were ballet dancers who were already hip to health foods, sickly older people who had heard of the "cures," and a few Eastern devotees who studied yoga.

I ate most of my lunches across the street at the Stage, which infuriated George Haines. The other two countermen were George Maharis, who later hit it big on television with *Route 66*, and another actor named Harry Mastrogeorge. Harry was of Greek heritage, and so was Cassavetes. One day John came in and asked Harry if he was going up for this "new movie they're casting over at M.G.M." Cassavetes was a hot young actor in live TV. People definitely knew who he was. "It's a bunch of juvenile delinquent types," said John. "You're perfect." Harry could see the look of envy on my face, so he kindly introduced me to Cassavetes. "You're perfect, too!" said John. "I'll take you both over to M.G.M. I know the casting guy." "What about you?" asked Harry. "Naw. It's not for me. But you guys are perfect." Cassavetes had an exuberance that was rare among the actors I knew. They, like me, were always worried. Will I make it? Will I ever work? Am I good enough? The despair of it all. But Cassavetes was already a Zorba.

The movie Cassavetes took us up for was *Blackboard Jungle*. The casting director, an ex-hoofer named Al, took one look at me and told me I was a great juvenile delinquent type. He asked me what experience I had. Naturally, I lied and told him I'd already been in a couple of Broadway shows and, moreover, I was from Brownsville, Brooklyn. "So you're a tough guy?" Al asked me. "Yeah, I grew up in the Murder, Incorporated section of Brooklyn." Al asked me to do an audition on film the following Friday. I thanked Cassavetes, and he wished me luck.

Two weeks later I was squeezing a carrot, celery, and apple juice for a customer when George Haines came over. "You're wanted on the phone, Mr. Big Shot. What the hell is this, some kind of telephone service?" George was a pain in the ass. I hurried to the phone. "I'll finish your juice, Mr. Telephone Call!" shouted George.

It was Al from M.G.M. on the phone. "Congratulations, Paul. Richard Brooks wants you in *Blackboard Jungle*. You leave for the coast in two weeks." I ripped off my carrot-stained apron and began to whoop and holler. "I'm going to Hollywood! I'm going to Hollywood, George!" All of George's anger vanished. He was very impressed. In fact, he was touched. He called his wife over to tell her my good news, and then in a tone of great respect he asked me for an eight-by-ten glossy of myself that "I can hang on the wall, Mr. Big Shot Hollywood Star."

I never called John Cassavetes to thank him. I didn't even have his phone number. But I knew that if not for his generosity I would never have acted in *Blackboard Jungle*. I wouldn't have met Richard Brooks or Sidney Poitier or Raphael Campos. Campos later married Dinah Washington whom I had seen at the Apollo when I was a kid. Sidney and I are still friends. His demeanor is truly noble. There is a warmth and a beauty to this man, but in those days Sidney and I tossed around the idea of being the first black and white comedy act. I thought of calling us "The Egg Creams." Richard Brooks became a good friend and would often come over to our home and finish off a bottle of ice-cold Slivovitz. Brooks came across like a tough guy in the Humphrey Bogart mold, but underneath he was a marshmallow. When I needed help, he was always there, but with no fanfare. He got me my first agent. After my first screening of *Next Stop, Greenwich Village* at the Directors Guild Theater in L.A., Richard put his arms around me and told me in a choked-up voice, "You did it, kiddo. It's beautiful." We remained close friends until his death. I went to see him a day or two before the end. He was lying in bed watching TV. He was weak, but he was tougher than ever. The imminent probability of death only served to piss off Richard Brooks.

Over the years I ran into John several times. He had by then become a well-known director as well as a movie star. I had great admiration for his work. He was stubborn and tough, and his films had a sense of real life that you didn't often find in American cinema. They were dangerous, loopy. A scene might go on a bit too long, but suddenly Cassavetes would grab you by the throat with a unique and powerful moment of truth. Whenever I'd bump into him, somewhere in Hollywood where I was now living, I'd always remind John that he was responsible for the start of my acting career. He smiled sardonically and quickly changed the subject. He just wouldn't let me really thank him.

By 1980 I had become an established director. I'd had real success with *Bob & Carol* . . . , *Blume in Love, Harry and Tonto,* and *An Unmarried Woman.* I'd had mixed reactions to *Next Stop, Greenwich Village* and *Willie and Phil,* and I'd had a downright flop with *Alex in Wonderland.* Frank Price (one of my favorite studio executives; he later did *Moscow on the Hudson, The Pickle,* and *Faithful*) read *Tempest* and quickly decided he wanted to do it at Columbia Pictures. I was elated. *Tempest* was a complicated and adventurous script based on Shakespeare's *The Tempest.* I'd had the idea of doing this film for years and had tried several forms. Every time I'd finish a film I would think about doing *The Tempest.* But another idea would come along, and I'd table Shakespeare. Once I took it as far as meeting with Mick Jagger. The idea was for him to play an androgynous Ariel in a sort of Marx brothers musical. Jagger was seriously interested. He impressed me with his knowledge of the play. We met in the Palm Court at the Plaza Hotel in New York. At one point I spotted an exotic woman wearing a rather wild hat. She had a great figure, and I could just see her over Jagger's shoulder. "Take a look at that bird, Mick," I said with a bit too much familiarity. Jagger looked over his shoulder. "That bird is me wife, Bianca." The musical version never happened.

Then I toyed with doing the actual play, but I had heard that the great Peter Brook was hoping to film the play. One day in Beverly Hills I was crossing the street when I recognized Peter Brook. I seized the moment and introduced myself. Brook was very approachable. I told him about my *Tempest* fantasies. He suggested a cup of coffee right then and there. It became clear to me that if anyone was to film Shakespeare's *The Tempest*, it should be Peter Brook. (But he never made his film.) Several months later, Leon Capetanos and I wrote a modern film version of the play. It was a very loose adaptation. Prospero became Phillip, an American architect whose marriage falls apart. He ends up fleeing to an island with his daughter, Miranda, and his new paramour, Aretha (Ariel). On the island lives Kalibanos, an eccentric sex-starved goat herder (Caliban). Finally, Phillip/Prospero has either a nervous breakdown or he is indeed a magician. He "makes" a storm. "Show me the magic," says Phillip, holding up his reading glasses to the rays of the sun. "Show me the magic." And sure enough a violent storm ensues.

I loved the project, but I was dubious about studio support. Frank Price changed all that. "Who do you see as Phillip?" Frank asked me. I went down a short list of names. When I got to Paul Newman, Frank stopped me. "Let's get it to him." A few days later I had lunch with Newman at the 20th Century-Fox commissary. He was much smaller than I expected, but he was beautiful. His blue eyes went right through you. There was no pretense to the man. I told him the story of *Tempest* and gave him the script. He promised an answer within a few days. I felt that he was perfect. Not only that, his presence would make the film more commercial. Several days later Newman called me at home from his house in Connecticut. "Pablo [for some reason he called me "Pablo"] I just don't get it." He told me how much he admired my films, but this was not the one for him. "I just don't get it, Pablo." I made no effort to dissuade him.

At my next meeting with Frank Price, I brought up the name of Cassavetes. Frank is a very wise fellow who operates on a combination of brains and instinct, and is definitely not afraid of his feelings (qualities almost extinct in today's Hollywood). "I like John," said Frank. "And we owe him a picture. You know, he did *Gloria* for us." I told Frank my *Blackboard Jungle* connection. We both became more and more enamored with the idea. "I'll make him Greek-American," I said. "And we can shoot it somewhere in Greece. And what about Gena Rowlands as his wife? She'd be wonderful." Frank agreed.

"Get him first," he said. "Then we can worry about Rowlands." I agreed. "Meet him," said Frank. "Who knows what he'll say? He's a strange fellow, but I like him." "So do I," I said.

Cassavetes read the script and responded favorably. We agreed to meet at my apartment in New York. As soon as I saw him walk in, I knew I had found my "Phillip." Talking to John is a tricky thing. You are not always sure what he means. His language makes curious jumps, and he skips from one subject to something that seems almost irrelevant. "I like this script," John said. "He's nuts, which I like, and he loves his daughter, which I like. But what about baseball? I think you need some baseball. You know DiMag hit in fifty-six straight games. Fifty-six! The record! Still stands! Today!" I was a New York Yankee fan and knew all about Joe DiMaggio, but what the hell did that have to do with *Tempest?*

I decided to go with the flow. "Okay, we can put some baseball into this thing," I said. "The script is still open. But I don't improvise that much." I wanted John to be clear about that. He laughed. "Who the hell likes to improvise?" I didn't know if he was putting me on or what. His films seemed rooted in improvisation. "Don't you do a lot of improvising in your movies, John?" "Nah," he said. "That's what they all think. I write, Pauley. I write a script!" I said, "But, John, I do like the idea of Phillip being a baseball nut." "Yeah," said Cassavetes. "And when he's stuck on that bloody island, he can't even get the scores. Ha, ha, ha, ha!" It was already fun talking to John. I knew I was off on a great adventure. Not only was I confident that he'd be fine in the role, but I knew that he'd bring his own visionary qualities to the entire project. It all felt very right.

"What about Gena for 'Antonia'? I asked.

"Oh, you'll have to ask her yourself. But I don't think she'll do it. I think she just wants to take it easy."

We were both smoking furiously. "But won't she want to go on location with you anyway? I'm sure it'll be a long shoot."

Cassavetes chuckled. "You never can tell with her. Maybe she wants to stay home and baby-sit."

I knew Gena Rowlands would make a perfect Antonia. I had

seen her in at least three Cassavetes films. She was beautiful, she was classy, and, moreover, she was a devastatingly honest actress. I started to beg. "John, would you at least ask her to read the script?"

"Oh, I think she already read it. She likes it. But she likes it for me."

"Should I call her and ask her?"

"Sure," said John. "But I wouldn't hold my breath."

To this day I don't know if John was playing a game with me or not. Did he know that his wife, Gena, would play his wife, Antonia? Was he already setting up an adversary relationship with her like the one in the script? I later found out what a genius Cassavetes was in making situations in the script real for himself by carrying the situations over to "real life." In the movie, Phillip sacrifices a goat in front of Antonia after she arrives on the island after being shipwrecked. One day in Rome, where we shot the last month of *Tempest*, Gena came to me and told me she would not appear in the goat sacrifice scene. I was shocked. She was the ultimate pro. How could she do this to me, to the film? She explained that John had told her he was going to sacrifice a real, live goat. "He's disgusting," she said.

"Gena, you must be kidding. We use a live goat only when he holds it up for you to see. Then we cut away to you, and when we cut back, we use a goat skin with fake blood on it. Are you kidding? I'd never let them kill a goat!"

But nothing seemed to assuage Gena's fears. I confronted John in front of Gena. He looked at me and smiled his most devilish smile. "Oh, no. I'm going to slice that goat's neck." And he showed us how he'd do it.

Gena flipped. "You see what I mean? He's going to kill the goat. Count me out!"

For two weeks this charade went on. Finally, I began to believe that John might actually think he would kill the goat. I asked John and Gena to join me for dinner the night before the scheduled goat sacrifice scene. I told them that I was not getting any sleep, that I was worried sick about tomorrow's work.

"Please, John. Tell Gena you're kidding."

He laughed. "I'm not kidding. I'm going to kill that little squiggly, eensie weensie, baaing goat."

Gena excused herself and went to the ladies room. I told John that I knew exactly what he was doing. "You're scaring Gena just the way you'd scare Antonia, and it's working. Come on, John. Stop the games."

Cassavetes looked around. "She's been in the toilet a long time, hasn't she, Pauley?" I realized she'd been gone about fifteen minutes. John got up and went to the ladies room of this fashionable Roman restaurant. He knocked at the door. "Gena, Gena. Come out, come out wherever you are."

All eyes turned to the American movie star pounding on the door of the toilet. John then went inside. People were staring now. A few seconds later John came back to the table and asked for a phone. "She's not taking a piss." He called the Excelsior Hotel where they were staying and asked for his room. "She probably sneaked out the back door," he said, grinning. Then he spoke into the phone. "Hi, honey. You didn't stay for dessert. . . . What? . . . Oh, yeah. I'm going to kill that nasty goat."

I could hear the click on the line. I was positive that tomorrow's work was in the toilet.

The next morning I got to the set at Cinecittà early and tried to decide what to do. How could I explain Antonia's absence in the scene? I was busy figuring out some weak alternatives when I saw John and Gena, arms around each other's waists, strolling ever so happily on to the set. They smiled at me as if nothing had ever been the matter. Not a word was said about last night's aborted dinner. He had put her on long enough to scare her (and me), but now it was time for these two professionals to go to work.

Not only did Cassavetes never admit to his game, but neither did Gena. It was as if it had never happened. Gena was perfect in the scene. So was John. He had shown me something about digging for the truth in acting, about not settling for some comfortable semblance. I don't think John was just playing a game. I think he wanted to carry out the brutality of what he was about to do as

"Phillip"; I think he wanted to go past that comfortable zone that actors can get into. Gena knew what John was doing, but she, too, wanted to take the situation into a more dangerous place so that the work would be richer, subtler, more real, less expected. And, let's face it, it's not every day that an actor is called upon to sacrifice a goat or to react to a husband's slitting a goat's neck.

Earlier in the schedule, my wife, Betsy, had played my wife in the New York segment of the film. Betsy is not an actress, but she likes to be part of what I'm doing, so I try to find something for her. In *Tempest* I played a Broadway producer named Terry Bloomfield, and Betsy played my wife. There's a scene where Gena is throwing a small party, and Betsy and I get up to dance. Cassavetes/Phillip comes in very drunk and embarrasses Gena/Antonia. When introduced to me, Terry, he asks me to dance with him. It's not the scene that I wrote, but we improvised something very real and funny. Finally, Betsy says her one line. She taps me on the shoulder while I'm dancing with Cassavetes and says, "Let's go home." Betsy's delivery was simple, not the expected way an actress would say it. She really did want me to "take her home." When the day's work was over, John said to Betsy, "You are the greatest actress I have ever seen." Of course, Betsy laughed. So did I. Gena, who was standing right next to Betsy, smiled and agreed that Betsy was perfect in the scene. A month later John threw a magnificent birthday party for Betsy at the Bolognese restaurant in the Piazza del Popolo. He toasted her as "the greatest actress I have ever worked with." It was still funny to us. We both knew that John loved to use untrained family and friends in his films. He kept telling Betsy every chance he had, "You should take your acting career more seriously, Betsy." I wasn't sure whether he was trying to make Gena jealous (if so, he didn't succeed), or whether in his mysterious way he really meant it. Maybe my wife, Betsy Mazursky, a woman totally untrained as an actress, who couldn't care less about movies, *was* the greatest actress of her generation.

After we finished shooting we went back to Los Angeles. Cassavetes called and asked to speak to Betsy. I handed her the phone.

"It's John. He wants to talk to you." Betsy got very nervous. She knew something weird was in the offing. I could hear her responding to Cassavetes: "Uh huh, uh huh . . . Peter Falk? . . . Dustin Hoffman? A reading tomorrow at your house? . . . Uh huh . . . You want me to read the woman's part?" Betsy looked at me and shook her head from side to side. She mouthed the words "What should I do?" I nodded vigorously, "Do it! Do it!" Then Betsy said to John, "Is it a big part or just a line or two? . . . Oh, it's the lead? . . . I couldn't do that, John. I'd be too scared. Besides, I can't drive to the valley." John offered to come and get her and drive her both ways. Still he couldn't persuade her. I was very disappointed. I'd never find out if Betsy really was the greatest actress John Cassavetes had ever worked with—unless I asked her to play the lead in my next film.

Tempest was physically tough to make. Shooting began in Atlantic City, New Jersey, moved to New York City for a month, and then on to Athens, Greece, for a week, seven weeks in Alypa, and finally a month in Rome.

Alypa is where we shot the so-called island. It's a unique paradise in the Peloponnesus, an area of Greece called the "Mani." (I used to sing "We're in the Mani" every morning on location.) We all stayed in a rather primitive hotel in a town called Gythion, south of Sparta, right on the water. The rooms were decidedly simple, hot water was an event, and the food was very basic: watermelon, feta cheese, tomatoes, an occasional piece of meat, and more feta. Of course, there was fish, but for some reason the catch that summer was not good.

Most of the shooting was an hour away by car, and an hour back after sunset for the return home. Long hours. Cassavetes never complained about the hours, only about the "fucking rocks I have to climb! I'm not some fucking goat!" Everyone else wept when they saw the cove in Alypa for the first time, it was that beautiful. But John thought I had delivered him to hell. Was this Phillip's reaction or John's? He was right about the rocks. They were difficult to maneuver. Just to walk across the beach over the large white rocks was an adventure. You'd find yourself slipping, tripping, losing your balance.

What I didn't know was that John was in the beginning throes of cirrhosis of the liver, and it was exhausting him. I knew he liked to drink, but he never seemed smashed. He and Gena had the room next to ours, and I could hear the ice cubes tinkling in the glasses all night long. But John was never drunk, just mellow, almost always a delight. He was having a good time. Gena was there; his kids, Nick, Zoe, and Zan, showed up; and so did his fabulous Greek cousin Phaethon. All night long I'd hear laughter, ice cubes, and backgammon.

Betsy and I would step out onto our small terrace to admire the sunset, and the Cassavetes clan would often join us. We were in paradise. My daughters were also there, so it became one large family outing deep in the mysterious Mani where Phillip/John loses his mind, creates a magic storm and eventually goes back to the island of Manhattan, purified by his year's journey. Was this about me? My family? I wasn't sure. I knew that Cassavetes was basing his character more on me than on the guy in the script. He started dressing like me, cutting his hair shorter, striking poses like me—or was it I who was imitating John? As the shooting progressed, the lines of separation became more and more blurred. I knew that John had told someone, "Why doesn't Paul say what he really means? This is about all of us and trying to make things work; it's really about Paul, so why doesn't he come clean? Why is he making this guy an architect? He's a director."

John wore an old blue-and-white Japanese kimono of mine as Phillip. Albert Wolsky, the costume designer I'd worked with since *Harry and Tonto*, loved the idea of the kimono. Albert is a man of impeccable taste and even more impeccable manners. Gossip is not in his vocabulary. (Sometimes someone just slips and tells you something juicy without really intending pain. I remember asking Moss Mabry, the costume designer on *Bob & Carol* . . . about the size of Natalie Wood's breasts. I wondered how she'd look in a bikini. "Mine are bigger," said Moss, "but we'll use a push-up bra and she'll be just fine. She has a darling little ass.") So when Wolsky said the kimono would help hide John's stomach, I realized that John had more of a potbelly than I had noticed. Just like mine. I didn't know if he was feeling rotten or just preparing for the part. When you're directing a film, it's very easy to sweep the possibility of bad health under the rug of art. Only the movie is truly important. You hear people tell you their woes, but all you're really thinking about is the next shot. The passion is all-consuming. Fuck the world! Don't they know I'm making a masterpiece? Nothing is as important as the work!

I was having trouble casting the role of Cassavetes' father. It was a small part but very important. I needed a very strong actor who wouldn't be awed by Cassavetes. I remembered my meetings with Elia Kazan. I mentioned the idea to Juliet Taylor, the casting director, and she loved it.

I had first met Kazan when I was preparing to make *I Love You, Alice B. Toklas* at Warner Brothers. Charley Maguire, the producer of *Toklas* and Kazan's longtime line producer, told me he'd heard I was a pretty good tennis player. "I'm okay," I told him. "I play a lot." "How'd you like to play with Gadge?" Charley asked me. "Gadge as in Kazan?" "Yeah," said Charley. "He's looking for someone to hit with. He's pretty good."

I was thrilled. Kazan was one of my heroes: *Death of a Salesman, Streetcar, Zapata*. Sure, I'd love to play tennis with him. In those days I played at Poinsettia Park in Hollywood. Maguire said Poinsettia would be fine. We set a time for the following afternoon. "He's a good player, and he hates to lose," said Charley. "But don't dog it."

I got to the park early and did some stretching. I kept my eyes out for Kazan. I knew what he looked like, but when he showed up, I was surprised at how short he was. He was very wiry and looked like he could play.

"Paul?" "Yes. Hello, Mr. Kazan." He shook my hand. Powerful grip. "Gadge," he said, smiling. "This is awfully nice of you." "Please. I love tennis." "Let's hit a few," he said. He was testing me to see how good I was. My game was built on speed, smart moves, and bad form. But I was very dogged. Kazan hit pretty well, but I soon felt I could beat him. "Why don't we play a set, Paul." "Sure, Gadge." We got to something like 3–3. He was at least twenty years older than I was, but he was very determined. I forgot any thoughts I might have had about easing up and letting him win. The more we played, the more I wanted to win. I won the first set 6–4. We got some water, and Kazan asked if I was up for another set. He made none of the usual tennis player excuses after a loss. I was just a bit too steady for him. I won the second set. Not a word was ever said that day about theater, cinema, or art.

We began to meet twice a week, and eventually we discussed the "work." But nothing profound ever really passed between us.

Several years later I was invited to one of Arthur Krim's New Year's Eve parties in New York. Kazan was there. He came over and shook my hand. "I really liked your movie *Bob & Carol*. . . . Good work, Paul." Naturally, I was thrilled. I didn't see Kazan again for almost a decade. I knew he'd become a writer. I knew that Barbara Loden, his second wife, had just died of cancer. I had a hunch that maybe, just maybe, he'd be interested in playing Cassavetes' father. I called him. He remembered me. I told him about *Tempest*. "Send me the script," he said. A week later Kazan called me. "I like the script, Paul. It's dangerous. But the truth of the matter is I'm writing now. I don't really want to break my work pattern." I told him I could do the whole thing in just two days, "right here in Queens." Finally, Kazan asked me to come see him the next day. "No promises, but come on over."

I was very excited when I rang the bell to his town house. When he opened the door, I realized how much he had aged. He was glad to see me, but he seemed depressed. The hallway was dark, and as we walked upstairs, I tried to imagine him as John's father. Absolutely perfect! He took me into a dark kitchen and offered me some chili he had made. He admitted that he was feeling blue since the death of his wife. He carried the pot of chili into the darkish living room, and spooned some chili onto a dish for me. It was good, and I told him so. "Yeah, I make good chili. So. *Tempest*. Tell me some more, Paul." I told him about Greece, Raul Julia, Vittorio Gassman, Susan Sarandon, this new fourteen-year-old kid I'd found named Molly Ringwald, Gena and John, the beauty of Alypa, how much he might enjoy a break from his writing. He ate his chili from the pot nodding politely now and then. "It all sounds nice, but I'm really into my book. I just don't want to break my concentration." He looked even older in the dark room, but it was a look of startling beauty: the big Armenian nose, the craggy lines in his face, the depth in the intense eyes. He was so ugly, he was handsome. In a way he reminded me of my own father, Dave. Somehow I felt sorry for Elia Kazan. Why should I be so selfish and take him away from his writing? There was a long silence. "Well," I said, "thank you so much for taking the time to see me, Gadge." Suddenly Kazan grabbed me by the collar, almost choking me. He was livid with rage. "You don't really want me!" he snarled. "If you really wanted me, you'd really go after me! You understand?" His grip on my throat was like a vise. "If you want something bad enough, nothing can stop you. Nothing!" Then, as quickly as he had lost his temper, he let go. "You don't really want me in a desperate way, Paul. If you did, I might have done it." I looked at Gadge, still shaken. "I really want you, Gadge. But I've never really begged anyone to play a part." Kazan stood up. "Good luck with your picture." We shook hands. He smiled at me. "Thanks for the chili, Gadge," I said. As I walked down the stairs, I thought to myself that Kazan reminded me of, well, Cassavetes. A few days later I hired the great Paul Stewart to play John's father. He was perfect.

At the end of shooting *Tempest* I decided to have the entire cast take a theatrical-style curtain call on the rocks of the cove in Alypa. Everyone wore one of their outfits from the film. One by one the cast stepped out of a blue door and took a bow—Molly, Sam Robards, Vittorio, Susan, Raul, Gena looking striking in a black evening gown against the sun-bleached Grecian rocks. We waited for John to make his entrance wearing his kimono. Now that the film was over I was experiencing my first real bit of trouble with John. For some reason that I never quite fathomed, he didn't want to smile and bow. "I don't feel like smiling," he said. As usual I didn't know if he was putting me on or if it was serious. Maybe he felt smiling would break the "magic" spell of the movie. I don't know, but he was getting me riled. I had two cameras on the shot—one wide, encompassing the entire cast, and the other camera using a long lens and getting a medium shot of each bowing actor. Finally, John came out of the blue door. His head was down, no smile, no bow. If anything, a sardonic look that seemed to say, "What the hell is this all about?" When the entire cast took each other's hands to bow in unison, John just stood there with his arms folded, stubborn to the very end. It annoyed me, but I loved him for it.

A few months later, back in L.A., I showed John and Gena my cut of the film. When it was over, John hugged me. "You're nuts," he said. But I could tell that they were both moved. At the New York opening of the picture the audience gave us a fifteen-minute ovation. John, Gena, Raul, Susan, and Molly were all there. It was thrilling.

The next morning many of the reviews were vicious. Who did Paul Mazursky think he was to take on William Shakespeare? I was devastated.

I saw John many times over the next seven years. I'd sometimes go to his house up on Woodrow Wilson Drive. There'd be a reading of one of his plays or films with the usual suspects: Peter Falk, Ben Gazzara, Gena, Elaine May, Dustin Hoffman, Seymour Cassell. John's kids were always somewhere around the house. It was warm and friendly, like one big Greek festival. Lots of booze and grape leaves and cigarettes. But it was impossible not to notice that John's stomach was bulging out more and more. I knew he had cirrhosis. I also knew that he wouldn't go under the knife. As John's body got more and more distorted, he took to wearing a large bathrobe, the only thing he could tolerate. Near the end he had the body of Orson Welles but the still beautiful head of John Cassavetes. He never gave you ten seconds' worth of time to pity him. He was still full of projects—movies, plays, readings. The last time I saw him was in 1989. I was having dinner with Betsy in Hamburger Hamlet on Sunset Boulevard. The Hamlet is a Beverly Hills burger joint that makes a good martini and attracts an amusing clientele. When I looked up from my cheeseburger and saw John and Gena making their way to a table, I gasped. Gena looked beautiful as always, but John was wearing the bathrobe. He had come down from his house on the hill to have a drink and a bite, and he couldn't care less if you saw him with his bloated body. Betsy and I went over to say hello. Gena was under a terrific strain, but she kept it all to herself. John was bone tired, but he still managed some joy. He kissed Betsy. "How's the greatest actress I have ever worked with?" I knew this might be the last time I saw John, and I knew that he knew it, too. I remembered Phillip and Antonia, the goat sacrifice, "show me the magic," the beautiful cove in the deep Mani where we shot *Tempest*. I wished we could all magically go back to the clear green waters and the white rocks right then and there.

8

"Thanks, I Needed That!"

NIGHT CLUB DAYS 1955–1961

Blackboard Jungle typecast me as a juvenile delinquent. Although I was grateful for any part, I was getting frustrated. I was never sent up for the kind of roles that John Cassavetes got—the tough, romantic leading man or the young guy with the problems of the world on his existential shoulders. No. I was always the second or third punk, the rat who licked an ice-cream cone while he scared the hell out of some poor sucker. Where were the great roles? I had dreamed of being another John Garfield, but it was beginning to look as if I'd become another Elisha Cook, Jr. (the great punk "Wilmer" in John Huston's *The Maltese Falcon*).

It was about this time that I ran into Herb Hartig, a friend from my Brooklyn College Varsity days. Varsity was the actor's society, and those of us who were in it were unbearably serious about our careers in the theater. Herb was no exception. Not only was he prepared to play the great leading roles, being endowed with a wonderful dark baritone voice and a handsome profile, but he was also a serious "writer" already at work on his great novel. Herb made sure you knew he was writing something important by carrying it in a bruised brown leather briefcase, crammed with books and papers. Inevitably, someone would ask Herb what was in the briefcase. "Oh, my novel and some research," he would respond oh so casually. But Herb had another side. He was truly funny, and he was already putting it to good use by writing sketches and comedy routines—and getting paid for it. We decided that we were both very funny fellows and that we should do a comedy act together.

There is nothing more serious in this world than writing a comedy act. To start with, there is the business of two massive egos that are positive they know what is or isn't funny. Second, in the early stages there is no one to turn to for another opinion. You can't try out your material in the Stage Delicatessen. The comics wouldn't laugh anyway, and they might steal the jokes. And, finally, Herb had already written some of the material, and I was trying to add my voice to it.

Our meetings took place in coffeeshops and cafeterias in midtown Manhattan. Herb still lived with his parents in Brooklyn, and I lived on Greenwich Street in the west Village with Betsy, by then my wife of a year. We had for some insane reason decided to move from her apartment on Sullivan Street, a warm and cozy nest, to a cold-water flat on Greenwich Street so that we could save $35 a month on rent. The place was so cold that I wore a very heavy brown leather secondhand Arctic navy coat all winter. The coat was so heavy I could barely take two steps in it without feeling exhausted. I would put it on first thing in the morning and never take it off until I went to sleep. At night we'd use an electric blanket that cost us about $20 a month. The apartment was not the best place to work, but when Herb and I finally reached a point where we had to rehearse, the cold-water flat became our nightclub.

We were ready to audition for someone, but we didn't have a name for the act. I would have settled for Mazursky and Hartig, or

Hartig and Mazursky, but Herb would have none of that. It seemed that using the name Hartig could destroy his writing career. "Can you imagine if James Joyce had been a nightclub comic," said Herb drolly one day. "Why, *Ulysses* might never have been published." We fooled around with all sorts of combos: "Herb and Paul," "Two Guys from Brooklyn," "The Funnymen"—each name worse than the one before. Finally, in desperation, we struck upon the idea of "Igor" because Mazursky was so Russian and somewhere in the act, in a spot called "Great Moments in Motion Picture History," I was "Igor," the hunchbacked assistant to Dr. Frankenstein. And since the letter "h" could stand by some miracle for Herb Hartig, we became "Igor and h."

Our first audition was for Max Gordon at the Village Vanguard. Gordon was already a legend who had discovered a lot of new talent. The Vanguard was one of the hippest rooms in town, famous for both its jazz and its comedy. The audition took place in the daytime when nightclubs most resemble graveyards. Most of the chairs are turned up, and there is usually someone loudly mopping the floors while you do your so-called act. Max Gordon was a little man with a friendly smile.

"What's 'Igor and h'?" he asked us as we stepped up on the small stage next to a piano. "The name of our act," said Herb. "Our comedy act," I added. "Okay," said Gordon, "so make me laugh."

We were very nervous, but we managed to get through about ten minutes. The closest thing to a laugh I heard was the wet mop slapping a pail. Gordon thanked us and told us he didn't think we were yet ready to play his room. And that was that.

We climbed up the long set of stairs. The bright daylight made us wince. We were depressed. We blamed the mop, we blamed Max Gordon. "What the hell does he know anyway?" I shouted. "He wouldn't have laughed at Charlie fucking Chaplin!" We had a cup of coffee somewhere and decided to audition for Julius Monk. Herb had written a piece for Phil Leeds, a very funny comedian who looked like a Jewish basset hound. (I later cast Phil as Mr. Pecheles, a nosy comic figure in *Enemies, A Love Story*). Phil knew the great Julius Monk. Monk ran the elegant Reuban Bleu, one of the hippest clubs in New York. Monk was a Noel Cowardish figure who wore stylish British-cut suits with cuffs on the sleeves. He had great wit and a brilliant eye for talent. When I saw him for the first time, he reminded me of Clifton Webb. He seemed to be influenced by no one but himself, a rare combination in show business.

About a week later, after we had honed and polished our act, we took the subway uptown to the Reuban Bleu. This was Fred Astaire and Ginger Rogers time. Black tie and tails! Crème de la crème. The hot comedy act in those days was "Mike and Elaine" (Mike Nichols and Elaine May). They were considered the hippest of the hip. Herb and I thought they were funny, but no funnier than us. Of course, no one had yet seen us except Max Gordon, but what the hell did he know?

Although we hadn't quite formulated it, Herb was the straight man, and I was the zany, manic funny guy. In our Great Moments in Motion Picture history routine, I was the frightened actor about to go onstage on opening night. "I can't! I can't go out there!" I shouted hysterically. "They're all out there. The critics! Atkinson, Kerr, George Jean Nathan! I can't go out there!" At which point Herb would slap me in the face. "Thanks, I needed that!" I responded, suddenly calmed by the brutal slap. (Years later, other comics and even some commercials stole our slap and "Thanks, I needed that" routine.)

There were several other performers waiting to audition. There was a female singer, and she was very good. There was even some light applause from Mr. Monk. Then it was our turn. My throat was as dry as dust. "Name please," said Monk. "Igor and h," we announced and went right into our routine.

Now and then we heard a chuckle from the direction of Julius Monk. We did about fifteen minutes. "Thank you," said Monk. "If you boys have a moment, please wait until I finish my other auditions. I'd like a brief chat with you." "Yes, sir!" "Of course, Mr. Monk."

Herb and I were elated. "We must be in," we whispered to

each other. The rest of the auditions seemed to take a lifetime, but finally we were alone with Monk. Up close, Julius Monk really looked like Clifton Webb. "I think you boys have talent. That's the good news. And I love your name. 'Igor and h' is wonderfully silly and sophisticated. By all means, keep it. Your material needs a bit of sorting out. It's smart and it's funny. It certainly isn't dreary. But you're not ready for the Reuban yet. Maybe you can be a bit more physical. Go home and polish. Cut and recut. Trim, trim, trim."

We practically knelt before the divine Monk. He spent about twenty minutes getting specific about our material, what he liked, what he liked less. He was clear about what to do without ever telling us how. (I never met another like him.) The same Julius Monk who had found Irwin Corey and Jonathan Winters was putting the stamp of his approval on "Igor and h." (The rumor was that Monk had a coffin in his apartment both as decor and as an object that might come in handy someday.) We practically danced out of the Reuban Bleu. "Thanks, I needed that!" I said to no one in particular. We were on our way!

Our next step was to find an agent. Through the comedy grapevine we'd heard about Irvin Arthur. He had a reputation for being open to new talent. (In other words, he'd take almost anybody.) We set up an appointment to audition for him in his office. There is nothing in the annals of show business that can possibly compare with the humiliation of doing a two-man comedy act for an agent in an office the size of a kitchenette. But somehow, between receiving phone calls and watching "Igor and h" perform with manic gusto, Irvin Arthur decided to take us on.

He was a very different type of fellow from Julius Monk and even from Max Gordon. Irvin was brutally practical and to the point. He immediately booked us into the Catskills. We'd play two hotels in one night and get $37.50 a hotel. In other words, we'd earn $37.50 each for one Saturday night's work. Transportation up to the Catskills was a special limousine that would cost us $5 roundtrip, so that meant we'd earn only $32.50 each. Then there was 10 percent of $37.50 to Irvin Arthur for his commission. We'd end up with $29.00 each. "But you can have dinner at the second hotel. They serve a very nice brisket there," Irvin assured us.

We drove up to Monticello with a couple of musicians, an elderly magician, and a fat lady singer who looked like Charles Laughton. Seven of us in one car. We were nauseous by the time we got there. The first performance went well. The youngish crowd laughed at us. It was worth the twenty-nine bucks. We were quickly driven to the second place which was more of a bungalow colony than a hotel. (A bungalow colony is a cheaper place where folks can cook their own meals.) The men in the audience all wore yarmulkes, and the women had kerchiefs on their heads. We did not get one laugh. This confused us. Was there something weird about our act that we could be a hit in one place and totally bomb in another? We were starving, so we decided to have our free dinner. We had to sit with the very audience who had not laughed at us. As we lapped up our borscht, it suddenly became clear to us why we had bombed. "*Zeya gutte de borscht*, hah? *Fashtet?* Hah, boychicks?" said a man sitting next to us. The crowd spoke only Yiddish. That fucking Irvin Arthur! Later, Irvin apologized. "How was I to know? I sold them 'Igor and h.' What did they think you guys were, rabbis?"

A few weeks later Irvin got us an audition for Jorie Remus, the featured hostess at The Purple Onion, a downstairs room at Fifty-first Street and Sixth Avenue. Upstairs from the Onion was another club called Upstairs at the Downstairs. Both clubs were owned by a man named Irving Haber. The Onion had been a successful room in San Francisco, and now Jorie Remus wanted to score in New York. Jorie sang and chatted. She had style and earthiness. She was funky, glamorous, funny, and oddly sexy. She was Tallulah Bankhead, Mae West, and my sweet aunt Ruth all mixed into one. Her laughter at our audition was like a blood transfusion. Her own material was that of the cynical worldly femme who has been around: "I woke up this morning on the wrong side of my life" and "My husband ran away with my best friend. I really miss her."

She loved "Igor and h" and booked us into the Onion. On

opening night all of our doubts disappeared. We were funny. A buzz about us soon began. Ultrasophisticated New Yorkers came by to laugh. We were the new hip comedy flavor. After each show we joined chic couples at their tables to drink in their praise.

Herb and I were getting closer to each other. Maybe he was the brother I never had. (We were both only children.) We were competitive, but we loved each other. But Herb had certain habits that drove me crazy. For example, he was always about thirty minutes late (a form of passive aggression that I still find most irritating in anyone). As much success as we were having, he still considered our comedy act a mere stopover on the way to his "big" novel. But worst of all, Herb gargled his nose every night before we went onstage. This just about put me in the funny farm. We'd both go into the men's room for a last-minute wash and hair comb. Then Herb would pour some water into his palms and shove it up his nose as he tilted his head back and gargled the water in his nose. He never got a drop of water on his shirt front. At first I said nothing, but after many nights I asked Herb why he did this. "To clean out my sinuses," he intoned as if I were a simpleton. I never got over this idiosyncrasy of Herb's, but something about it must have intrigued me because I always went into the men's room at the same moment that Herb did. Why didn't I go in earlier or later? Is it because I wanted to see the dreaded nose gargle? Not just wanted, but had to witness the bizarre ritual.

We were on the bill with Cynthia Gooding, a six-foot two-inch folksinger who played the guitar. She was very good. Then she was replaced by another folksinger, Will Holt (who went on to write *The Me Nobody Knows* and many other Broadway shows). Will was the first blond, blue-eyed Ivy League prepster I'd ever met. He had studied guitar with Richard Dyer Bennett. His great passion was Kurt Weill and Bertolt Brecht. I loved their music, too—songs like "Mack the Knife" and "Bilbao" moved me and made me dream of faraway places. Later, Will married Dolly Jonah, a raspy-voiced, hilarious comic chanteuse who replaced Holt on the bill. Dolly was a one-of-a-kind gal who made me laugh till I cried. (Years later I cast her as Art Carney's tough daughter-in-law in *Harry and Tonto*.) Dolly lived on Jane Street in Greenwich Village. We'd take the subway downtown together every night, laughing ourselves silly at the club's shenanigans, and at the weird New York types on the 4 A.M. train to Sheridan Square. At Fourteenth Street you'd sometimes hear the conductor shout out, "Next Stop, Greenwich Village."

The piano player at The Purple Onion was a songwriter named Murray Grand. He wrote "Guess Who I Saw Today, My Dear?" and "April in Fairbanks," both pungent and witty. He affected a world-weary, eyes-upturned angst that kept me in stitches. Some of his songs were used in *New Faces* and other revues. (In 1980 I cast Murray as the piano-playing friend of Gena Rowlands in *Tempest*. He played "You Must Remember This." Betsy and I danced in the movie, and when the singing ended, Murray ad-libbed a great line: "Does anyone have any pâté?")

Murray also played auditions for me as an actor. I spent several months learning to sing "Mack the Knife." I had a decent voice but no confidence. I feared I'd go flat. I wrangled an audition for Jerome Robbins for this new show, *West Side Story*. They were looking for tough guys for the gang—actors who could sing and dance. Since I could do neither, I told them about *Blackboard Jungle* and then I lied and made up a fake resume of my singing credits. I got through a few bars of the great song and then went flatter than a pancake. Murray turned pale, and as his eyes reached for the sky, I heard Jerome Robbins say, "You're a very good actor, but I'd stay away from songs. Thank you." It was good advice. (In 1957 I appeared in a revue called *Shoestring '57*. I lied again and found myself almost shaking on opening night. I had to sing and dance a tango with Dodie Goodman. In rehearsals I was always off-key, but the number was supposed to be funny, and every time I hit a clinker, Dodie made a funny face. The harder I tried, the more she laughed. The critics liked it. The audience loved it.)

One night Jorie told us that Max Gordon was coming in to catch the act. Herb and I were very skeptical. Gordon had already turned us down once. As soon as we finished our set, Max came backstage and introduced himself. "Hello. I'm Max Gordon. I run the Vanguard." Didn't he remember that we had already auditioned for him? Was this some kind of joke? "I like your act. I want you to play the Vanguard and then maybe move you up to the Blue Angel." We were thrilled. So was Jorie Remus. She loved to see her discoveries succeed.

Irvin Arthur negotiated for us; he called to tell us the numbers. "A hundred and fifty dollars a week," said Irvin, as if that was a fortune. "Each?" asked Herb. "Please, fellas," Irvin said. "This is the Vanguard, not the Copa." Of course, we accepted. One hundred and fifty a week was twice what we were getting at the Onion. "Think of it," I said to Herb. "Seventy-five bucks a week each. Now we can buy that penthouse we always dreamed of."

The truth of the matter is that $75 a week was big money for me. Betsy and I began to talk about moving out of the dreaded cold-water flat, which now had rats. We opened at the Vanguard and were instant hits, especially with the musicians. Not only did they play good, they laughed good. I discovered that you could always count on the band to laugh. They were funny and generous people.

One night Max Gordon pulled us over to the side. "I'm trying out a new singer from San Francisco. Tell me what you think. I might put him in the room." We listened as this handsome young black man crooned a couple of love songs. He had a very distinctive style, but I must confess I had trouble with it. "I don't know, Max. He's awfully mannered," I said. "I don't want to do the kid out of a job, but he's not my cup of tea." Max disagreed, and Johnny Mathis went on to fame and fortune.

Finally "Igor and h" were starting to make a small name for themselves. Popsie Whittaker, who wrote amusing blurbs for *The New Yorker*, came in one night and found us to his liking. He wrote something witty and *très* complimentary. Famous people came into the club and told us how much they liked the act. Still, we didn't know where our next job was coming from.

Then we did an audition uptown at the Blue Angel. Our Great Moments skit played to big laughs: "Say, gang, I've got a great idea! Why don't we put on a Broadway musical?" "Swell.

And my dad's a good egg. He'll let us use his old Hippodrome!"
We thought it went well, but Herbert Jacoby, Max's suave partner,
didn't think we were ready for the big room. Jacoby was a French
Jew with a curious eye for trendy clubs. Herb and I detested him
for not recognizing our talents. (There's nothing like a little ha-
tred to make you feel better after you've been rejected.)

Fortunately, Irvin Arthur booked us into the Bon Soir, a
small club on Eighth Street in Greenwich Village. The club was
run by Phil Pagano. This was long before the days of *The Godfa-
ther*, but one had the feeling that Pagano was close to the boys. He
even had a small shrine to the Virgin in his office. He managed to
be very friendly and slightly menacing at the same time. When he
came over to tell me one night how much he liked our act, he
pinched my cheek hard enough to make me wince with pain.
"You're a good boy, Igor. Funny. And I like funny. Funny makes
me laugh. Nothin' better than a good laugh, eh, Igor?" I loved it
when he called me Igor.

We were on the same bill with two great acts: Tiger Haines,
who sang, played piano, and *tummeled* in his off-the-cuff style, and
"Tony and Eddie," a gay duo who mimed to records using outrageous costumes, sharp lighting, and brilliant comic staging. They
parodied opera, Broadway shows, and movies. They were hilarious and sometimes thrilling. Tough stuff to follow, but "Igor and
h" held their own. We played the Bon Soir for a month. Then one
night Phil Pagano patted me on the cheek and told us we'd be
through on Sunday night. "But weren't we booked for another two
weeks, Phil?" I asked weakly. Pagano gave my cheek the death
pinch. "You boys are funny, and I like funny, but I got commit-
ments which I got to honor. Relax, Igor. You boys will be back."

We never played the Bon Soir again, but we were lucky
enough to get booked into One Fifth Avenue, also in Greenwich
Village. One Fifth was a large, awkwardly arranged room on the
main floor of the apartment building. It featured twin pianos, with
the pianists sitting back to back. That was charming, but there
were mirrored posts that made for tricky visibility. (Years later I
bought an apartment in One Fifth, and at one point shot a scene in

the One Fifth restaurant that had replaced the nightclub. It made me shiver when Jill Clayburgh went through the swinging doors to meet her girlfriends for a post-separation drink in *An Unmarried Woman*.)

Herb and I did well at One Fifth. It was more touristy than the Vanguard and somehow blander than the Bon Soir, but still the audiences were sophisticated enough to get our act. One of our more successful bits involved lines that men used to get a woman into bed. Then the guy needed a line to get out of the relationship. "You don't want to get involved with me, babe. I'm a musician. I'm on the road forty weeks a year." Another routine was the bell. One of us would say what the fellow said. Then I'd ring a little bell and say what the guy really meant. "In the Kierkegaardian limbo of my existential despair, I am often reminded of something Proust said when he bit into the madeleine cookie on that bleak winter day." Bell! "So, what about it, babe?"

It was becoming clear to Herb and me that something had to happen—such as getting into *New Faces*, or getting booked into bigger and better-paying clubs.

I still hadn't given up on my acting career. In fact, I was now studying with the exalted Lee Strasberg. I'd already spent two years with Paul Mann, an actor who became a full-time teacher after he was harpooned during the McCarthy era. I'd gone from Mann to Curt Conway, husband of Kim Stanley. Curt was a very good actor and a fine teacher. (Years later, Curt and Kim Stanley came to see me do my act at the Interlude in Los Angeles. Curt had a loud cigarette smoker's laugh and raspy cough. He loved the act, but he laughed so loudly, he almost blew my punch lines.

I'd met Kim Stanley once before, when she acted in *The Goddess*. The script was by Paddy Chayefsky, and the subject was a thinly disguised Marilyn Monroe. I had been hired as the dialogue director, which meant that I was there to help the actors learn their lines. Costarring with Kim was Lloyd Bridges and Steve Hill. When Bridges couldn't make the first day's reading of the script, I was told to fill in. John Cromwell, the director, told me, "Please don't act. Just read the words. Under no circumstances are you to act." Steve Hill was one of the legends of the Actors Studio. I couldn't wait to watch him work. "Don't act! Don't act!" I reminded myself. The reading began. I had trouble understanding Steve Hill. He spoke very quietly, almost a whisper. Great method actor that he was, he was not yet ready to give a performance. But Miss Stanley threw all caution to the wind. She was inspired. In spite of all the warnings I had been given, I started to act. What could I do? Kim made you laugh, and then she twisted you inside out and made you cry. In other words, this great method actress gave a full-blown performance at the first reading. There just aren't any rules to the magic art of acting. Steve Hill eventually did a brilliant job, even though he approached his role in his own deliberate way. When he needed the goods, he had it. Lloyd Bridges was excellent as the baseball player. But somewhere in my secret soul, I felt that Paul Mazursky would have been better. *(Fantasy Island)*

I had twice failed to get into the Actors Studio, so I did the next best thing and got into one of Mr. Strasberg's classes. He was a smallish man with a peculiar habit of constantly snorting. He was an inspirational teacher. His students treated him like a god and I, too, worshiped at the throne. After several months of exercises, I was actually going to get up and do a scene. I've never parachute-jumped, but I imagine it's something like doing a scene for Strasberg. You almost have to be pushed to perform. I'd rehearsed a scene from a Hemingway short story that took place in a tent in the jungle. The young actress and I were slavish to every detail, but we were both nervous.

We got through the scene, and it felt pretty good. Of course, I expected a critique, but I prayed he wouldn't skin me alive. Strasberg snorted. He looked up at us and said, "No heat." He snorted again and turned to the class. "No heat. I felt no heat!" Immediately, the class began to call out, "No heat." "It was ice-cold." "I never felt a drop of heat!" I tried to defend myself. "You mean no heat as an actor? No emotion?" "No, young man. I mean no heat in the jungle! You might as well have been in Alaska. You're in a tent in the tropical jungle of Africa. Where is the heat?" He snorted several times, and the class nodded and hurled "no heats" at us.

A month later we got up once again to do our scene. If Strasberg wanted heat, I'd give him heat! I poured a glass of water on my head. I soaked my shirt under the arms. My partner sponged herself. We did the scene. I found several places to use my large white handkerchief to wipe my "sweaty" brow. When the scene ended, I expected applause. The room was silent for a long moment, all eyes on Lee Strasberg. Then he snorted and spoke. "Too much heat! And the heat that's there is not specific. There is heat and there is heat. That was too much heat!" Naturally, the class agreed with Lee. And they were probably right.

I decided then and there, however, that I had done enough studying. A few weeks later I started my own class. I'd be the teacher, and my students would come from nightclubs—singers, dancers, comedians. The class would be free, only a dollar a person to pay the rent for rehearsal space. Since they weren't being charged and since I was not a famous teacher, it would either work or fail on its own merit. Dolly Jonah and Will Holt joined Barbara McNair, a beautiful and talented singer who came aboard. Then there was Hank Garrett, a young comic who had been a professional wrestler. Skippy Adelman had been the still photographer on *Fear and Desire*—he wanted to learn to act to help his new goal of writing for the movies. Another student was David Gold, a dancer who had gone to Antioch College with Betsy. He was a talented man but very cheap. Some weeks he'd beg off paying the dollar.

The great thing about the class was the success stories. Barbara McNair learned to sing without broad hackneyed gestures. We did an exercise and tied her hands behind her back. She couldn't make a gesture. The emotion of the song was forced inside, and it came out with purity and power. Of course, I had learned this exercise from Lee Strasberg.

After a scene, everyone would participate in a discussion of the work. It was a refreshing experience that lasted about a year. And in a way I think it was the beginning of my career as a director.

In December, Herb and I flew to St. Louis, Missouri, to play a month's gig at the Crystal Palace, a new club owned by Fred and Jay Landesman. I had known Jay for a couple of years. He published the super-hip magazine *Neurotica*. I had been introduced to his cocktail parties in Manhattan by my then girlfriend, Naomi, a Semitic beauty I'd met at Brooklyn College. She seemed to know everyone at these parties. (She'd already had an affair with Ad Rheinhart, the abstract expressionist. Rumor was that she also had slept with a black man! And now, Mazursky! What a catch!)

Fifty hipsters standing up drinking martinis and talking, talking, talking. Many of them were destined to greatness, but it hadn't yet happened. Among the throng were Norman Mailer, Buckminster Fuller, Jack Kerouac, Gershon Legman, Allen Ginsberg, and John Clellon Holmes. (It was Holmes, I think, who first coined the phrase "The Beat Generation.") Also present was Jay's wife, Fran, who wrote the wonderful song "Spring Can Really Hang You Up the Most." There were Chandler Brossard and Carl Solomon, who was the inspiration for Ginsberg's poem "Howl." Carl may well have been one of the best minds of his generation. He had recently gotten out of the mental ward of Rockland State Hospital. He had written a groundbreaking piece for *Neurotica* about getting shock therapy, using the pseudonym Carl Goy.

One day a couple of months after Betsy and I moved into our cold-water flat, we decided to paint the place. Betsy's father, Bill Purdy, was coming up from Miami to visit us. The apartment was a real dump. We had to clean it—and fast. I hired Carl Solomon to help me paint the living room white. Carl was tall, quite thin, and looked something like an owl with the wingspan of an eagle. Although I could have a fairly normal conversation with him, sometimes the look in his eyes made me nervous. "I'll give you five bucks for each wall, Carl." He answered in a monotone, "Sure. Okay. Five bucks." I gave him a can of white paint and a brush. He sat down in front of the wall and dipped the brush into the can of paint. I hurried out of the apartment to get some bread and cheese. Half an hour later I returned to see Carl dipping the brush toward the can but just missing it. He had not painted one foot of the wall. He seemed catatonic. "Carl," I said, "you don't quite have the hang of it." Betsy's father arrived the next day and found the place charming. "Could do with a coat of paint," he said.)

At the Landesman parties I held my own by doing my imitation of Marlon Brando torturing Albert Basserman. Brando was the king of Broadway, and Basserman was a cult favorite who had a prominent role in the film *The Red Shoes*. No one laughed more at me than Jay Landesman.

Herb and I arrived at the Crystal Palace just in time to see a fine production of *Waiting for Godot*, directed by Ted Flicker and starring Flicker, Severn Darden, and Tom Aldredge. This was more like it! A cabaret theater where great plays were done, where the new comedy got on its feet. Mike and Elaine had played there. Barbra Streisand had sung at the Palace. "Igor and h" was a big hit, but within two weeks, Herb and I found ourselves missing the Apple. We were tired of the same small group of midwestern hipsters who came in night after night. As a result, in spite of the hospitality of the Landesmans, I felt like I was at a party I wanted to leave. A short time later Irvin Arthur booked us into the Pirate's Den, a club for honeymooners on the island of Bermuda. Paradise! The pink coral beaches made for a pleasant stay for Betsy and my daughter Meg. We were in love. Life was good. The all-black staff of the Pirates Den threw a party for Meg, whose first birthday was on August 27, 1958. She had just started to walk. Herb worked on his novel and I got into bodysurfing. Betsy and I had two close black friends in New York, and one of them had a brother living in Bermuda. He was the principal of a high school. Of course, I invited him to our opening night. He smiled at me. "Oh, Paul, don't you know, we are not permitted to sit in a white establishment." I flipped. Herb was sympathetic. We went to the night manager of the club and told him we wouldn't perform if our friend couldn't see our show. The manager was a friendly chap who actually wore Bermuda shorts. Like Solomon, he came up with a solution. My friend and his family could watch the act from the kitchen. They could stand just away from the swinging double doors. As beautiful as Bermuda was, I never forgot how ugly life there was for the blacks.

When we got back to New York, Herb and I decided to split up. We had just been offered a tour to play some big rooms in hotels across America. The money was good, and the exposure would have been big time, but Herb felt that this would be the end of his career as a writer. "I don't want to pull my pants down in public," he told me. I couldn't believe what I was hearing. "We've been pulling our pants down for two years now, Herb! What's so different about the hotel circuit?" Herb did not agree. It was decided that I could use our material and try to make it as a single. Herb was very generous. I'll never forget that. I experimented with ways to do the act alone. In "Great Moments in Motion Picture History," I played all the parts. I even slapped myself in the face right before I said, "Thanks, I needed that!" I tried out the new act at One Fifth Avenue—a onetime performance to show my single wares. I asked Albert Grossman to catch my act. Grossman was an important and sophisticated manager. He handled "Peter, Paul and Mary," among others. It would be a coup if he agreed to manage me. (About a year later Albert asked me to listen to a tape of a new young folksinger. I thought the twangy sound was oddly moving, but I couldn't understand the nasal lyrics. "He needs speech lessons, Albert," I said. But Bob Dylan needed nothing more. I was fast becoming a barometer for singers. If I didn't like them, they were sure to become stars.) I was introduced as that up-and-coming new comic, Paul Mazursky. I didn't want to be Igor anymore. The show at One Fifth went well. There were a few bumpy moments, but I felt that I could make it on my own. I was elated. Grossman, a dour man who looked more and more like Benjamin Franklin as his hair got longer and longer over the years, was very kind. He didn't know how far we'd get, but he'd start the ball rolling and try to get me some bookings.

Grossman had superb taste and a great instinct for deals. (See *Don't Look Back*, the documentary about Bob Dylan. Albert figures large and is devastating at deal making.) Within a few weeks I was kissing Betsy and Meg good-bye and heading for Boston to play my first date at Storeyville, a supposedly hip room. I was on the bill with Roberta Sherwood, a pleasant middle-aged lady who wore a sweater over her shoulders and shook hands with the audience during her opening song. Just what I needed. I should have known I was in trouble when they introduced me to the pianist who'd play my cues. He was a very good musician, but he was blind. This meant that he could only guess when to play certain cues. Amazingly, he was always on the money.

Storeyville was owned by George Wein and managed by Charley Bourgeoisie. George had started the Newport Jazz Festival. Charley, originally from New Orleans, had immaculate taste in clothing and in music.

The night before I opened, I saw the final performance of the star, the inimitable Myron Cohen. Mr. Cohen was a master of longish and very funny stories, told with a slight Yiddish accent. He was about sixty, and he was bald and dapper and very self-assured. The audience loved him. It scared me silly. Here I was about to follow the great Myron Cohen. Was I nuts? If they loved Myron Cohen's stories, how could they possibly like my satirical routines? Satire! What I needed was a couple of good, short jokes: like "Schwartz meets Ginzburg in the garment district. 'I heard about the fire,' he says. 'Ssssh! Tomorrow!' says Ginzberg." I spoke to Myron Cohen after his show and confessed my anxiety. "Well, young man, you have every right to be nervous. Comedy is a very dangerous profession."

He was right. The Roberta Sherwood crowd didn't really get my humor. They came to see Roberta and merely tolerated me. Only the band laughed, but I learned a few things about doing the act solo.

I had heard about the high level of sophistication at my next booking, The Gate of Horn in Chicago. I was to be on the same bill as Frank Skildt, a Dutch folksinger, and the great Odetta. The Chicago winds were howling. I had to hold on to chains to cross the street. I wondered if this was a metaphor for what I was in for. But no, the atmosphere was more like a good college course in nightclubbery. The audiences were smart and responsive. I got a great review from Irv Kupcinet, even though I'd seen him dozing in the front-row seat.

In the afternoons I started doing improvisations with a group of actors who were about to start their own club: Severn Darden, Barbara Harris, Mina Kolb, Eugene Troobnick, Alan Arkin, and Howard Auk. They were going to call it "Second City." (A few months later, after we'd moved to Los Angeles, Auk called to offer me a spot in "Second City." But I felt that I couldn't afford yet another upheaval. Besides, even though I really liked working with these improvisers, what the hell was "Second City" going to add up to?) Albert Grossman called with good news. He had set up three bookings in a row at $500 a week each. A month in San Francisco to play the hungry i, a month in Los Angeles to headline at the Interlude, and finally a month at the Statler-Hilton in Dallas. Twelve weeks' work. $6,000!

Since most of the television work had moved to Hollywood, I started thinking about our moving to California. San Francisco was the most beautiful city I'd ever seen—full of charm and energy, and a thrilling harbor.

At the hungry i, I caught the final performance of Jonathan Winters. I had last seen the extraordinary Winters at the Reuban Bleu in New York. He was a comic genius, totally unpredictable and wonderfully dark. He began his show that night by telling the audience that he missed his wife and kids. "On the road a lot," he said. It wasn't funny, but the audience figured it to be the prelude of a new bit. They chuckled. Winters seemed more and more depressed as the minutes ticked by. Then he took out his wallet and showed the audience photos of his family. There were real tears in his eyes. Not a sound from the audience. We all knew that Jonathan Winters was having a nervous breakdown. The bartender walked onstage, took Jonathan's arm, and led him off. "My God," I thought. "Is this what nightclubs can do to you?" (Twenty-one years later I cast Jonathan in *Moon Over Parador.* He loved to remind me of "the good old nervous breakdown days." "Boy, that funny farm was really funny!" he told me, going into a ten-minute riff on psychiatric wards. *Parador* was shot in Brazil. We all spent a month in a small town called Ouro Preto. Most of the people there spoke only Portuguese, but Winters would often stand on a street corner with Sammy Davis, Jr., and try to make Brazilians laugh at some wild improvisation in English. He didn't have much luck, but he was perfect in the role of an American businessman who turns out to be a CIA agent.)

Larry Adler, the harmonica virtuoso, was the headliner at the hungry i. He was as comfortable with Bach as he was with Gershwin.

Enrico Banducci ran the club with an iron fist. No drunks, no wisecracking hecklers. It was as much a theater as a club. My act was successful. I was really on the way.

I called Betsy, and she agreed to move west. She'd try San Francisco with me for two weeks, and then we'd try L.A. My heart was pounding when I saw Betsy and little Meg get off the plane. I was twenty-nine years old and was finally moving away from my mother, Jean. Two weeks later, we were confused. San Francisco was a splendid place, but somehow it seemed more like a social club we didn't belong to. On to Dreamland!

The week before we left, I called my old friend Andre Philippe. "Betsy and I are coming to L.A. Any ideas on where we could stay? Cheap? And room for the baby?" André, whose real name was Everett Cooper, had no hesitation. "You'll stay with me. I have a beautiful house and a swimming pool. Stay with me for a month." What a generous offer. I'd known André at Brooklyn College. He went to Paris on the G.I. bill to study cooking at Le Cordon Bleu. While in Paris, he got a gig singing at a small club called Le Cave. That's when he changed his name from Everett Cooper to André Philippe. By the time I was working as a juicer at the Salad Bowl, André was singing at the Copacabana. I was very impressed, but I refused his offer of a fifty-cent tip.

André met us at Union Station in Los Angeles. He was dark, handsome, and really looked French. He drove a smallish Austin-Healy convertible. The three of us barely fit in, but somehow we managed—baby, luggage, and all.

In 1959, L.A. was more like a hick town than a powerful metropolis. Our drive down Sunset Boulevard took us past giant plastic hotdogs and funny dog-shaped huts that sold chili burgers and tacos. Tacos! It was all stucco and gas stations, and looked more like a movie set than a real city. Betsy was already dubious. "Where are the people?" she asked me. Even the baby was crying. I was very nervous. But as we pulled up to André's house on Sherbourne Street just north of Sunset Strip, I felt more hopeful. "Here we are, folks," said André. It was a charming stucco and wood house. A bit more Mediterranean than most of the crap we had passed. "Where's the swimming pool, André? In the back?" "Oh, let me show you the pool first. You might want to take a dip." Without losing a beat, André led us to a wooden fence separating his house from a tall apartment building next door. There was a loose slat in the fence, and we could see next door. Sure enough, there was a large swimming pool. "But this belongs to the building," said Betsy. "I don't want to sneak in." André smiled. "I'm dating this yoga teacher who lives in the building. You just say you're visiting Virginia Denison."

I was beginning to wonder if there actually was a house. There was, but it had almost no furniture. André smoothly explained why that was. He'd been seeing Nina Foch, the actress. She'd caught him in bed with another woman and immediately had all her furniture removed. "Yesterday," said Andre. "What could I do? I didn't want to scare you guys off." Since the only furniture André possessed was a wooden kitchen table and two chairs, the house seemed empty. "Where do we sleep?" asked Betsy. André led us to a sunny room that had a large blanket and two pillows on the floor. "It's only temporary," he said. "I'll find you a bed by tomorrow." "And where does Meg sleep? In some room in the building next door?" I was pissed. Like a magician, André pulled out a small blanket and laid it down on the floor. "She can sleep on this until we get her a crib. My cousin Diane has an old crib. All we need now is a mattress," he said.

Somehow we got through the next few weeks, and we found our own apartment. But my stint at the Interlude was rough going. As usual, I went to the club for the closing night of the comic. This time it was Lenny Bruce. He was brilliant. His act was a mixture of showbiz humor, great imitations, and strong social comment. He talked about jerking off. I didn't know if I was square or yesterday's news, but it shocked me. Jerking off! Lenny held the audience, and they were a tough group. Many of them had come to pick up women, not to hear Lenny Bruce. Lenny, with his dark good looks, reminded me of a Jewish Turhan Bey, Rudolph Valentino crossed with a Catskill comic. (Years later I used Lenny's mother, Sally Marr, as the "Cat Lady" in *Harry and Tonto*. Sally was a former comedienne. She always wisecracked funny and made it clear that she was the force behind her son. I met her on the street in Westwood one day. "I just saw Dustin Hoffman in this movie about Lenny," she said. I asked her how it was. "Oh, Lenny was a much bigger junkie than that!" she said, waving her hand at some invisible fool.)

My opening night at the Interlude was brutal. To start with, a waitress stepped onto the tiny stage right in front of me and took her drink orders while I did my act. I couldn't believe it! As soon as the set was over I found Gene Norman, the owner. "It's humiliating, Gene! The waitress is taking orders for Scotch on the rocks while I try to be funny!" Gene's advice sent a chill up my spine. "Just wait until she finishes taking the order and then go on with the act." Things never got much better than that for me. I was very tense even though I'd occasionally have a good night. But I was beginning to worry about my next booking in Dallas. Maybe they roped steer there while the comic did his stuff.

By now we had found a two-bedroom apartment in West Hollywood for $85 a month. The neighborhood was filled with young marrieds just like us. You could walk to the grocery, the park, and even to the library. Betsy got a job as a part-time children's librarian. I bought a sharp-looking used Studebaker. Then it was time to go to Dallas.

I was the only performer on the bill. Music was by Sandy Sanderson and his band. The lobby of the Statler-Hilton featured a large photo of me. I wore a checkered cloth hat and posed like Frank Sinatra, but the joke was lost on everybody. I think the audience expected a singer, not a little Jewish guy from Greenwich Village. Since you weren't allowed to buy liquor at the tables, the cowboys and cowgirls arrived with bottles of Scotch and gin wrapped in brown paper bags.

I got no laughs in forty minutes, probably a record. But the audience gave me enthusiastic applause at the end of my act. They thought I was a monologist! I had another set to do. Desperate to tell them they could laugh, I came out in my tuxedo, laid some newspaper on the stage floor, and had the band give me a drum-roll. Then I knelt down, put my arms in front of my head, slowly kicked my legs up, and stood on my head. I had learned to do this from André's girlfriend, Virginia Denison, the yoga teacher.

"Good evening, ladies and gentleman," I said, upside down. I told the "Schwartz meets Cohen" joke. Nothing. I bent my up-turned legs into a difficult position. Slight applause. I was getting ready to faint. I knew I couldn't stay upside-down much longer, but I also knew that they thought I was a contortionist, definitely not a comic. I suppose these experiences broaden a performer's palette, but truthfully I was miserable.

The next morning the Dallas newspaper critic called me "filthy," a cross between Lenny Bruce and Don Rickles. I should only have been that good. The manager of the Statler-Hilton in-formed me that they would pay me for the full four weeks, but I was just too dirty for this "family-oriented" room. I was relieved. Then he asked if I would play one more night, since the new comic couldn't make it until Tuesday. I agreed. When I got to the club that evening, I was surprised to see that they had opened the double doors of the room to handle the huge crowd. It seemed that all the hipsters in Dallas had read the review and come to see Paul Mazursky. They laughed the same way the folks at the hun-gry i had laughed. They got everything. After the second and final show, the manager told me he was "real sorry. . . . I never did think you were that dirty."

When I got back to L.A., I told Albert Grossman I didn't want to play these tough commercial clubs anymore. I went out hustling for acting work, and took a job as a messenger boy for Red Arrow. I had to drive my smoking Studebaker all over L.A. to deliver scripts, gifts, postage stamps. To make matters worse, I had to wear a jacket with a lightning bolt and a Red Arrow on the sleeve. Somewhere along the way I met Ben Shapiro.

Ben had opened a Greenwich Village–type coffeehouse on Sunset Boulevard. He was tasty and amusing, and had fought for Israel with the Irgun. I liked him, and he liked my comedy act. At that time Ben handled Miles Davis, and that really impressed me. He offered to book me at his club, The Renaissance, for $35 a weekend—Friday, Saturday, and Sunday—two performances a night, plus, at my request, all the cappuccinos I could drink.

I was on the bill with Jimmy Witherspoon and Lord Buckley. They were incredible, and the audience loved them. I went over big, too. It was like being back at The Gate of Horn in Chicago. But I was more confused than ever. Was I a comedian, an actor, a sketch comic, or a messenger boy?

A couple of months later I moved my act to another sophisticated coffeehouse, Cosmo Alley. This was a small brick-walled room run by a man named Herb Cohen. One night my old *Blackboard Jungle* friend, Vic Morrow, came in with his wife, Barbara Turner, to catch my act. Vic, Barbara, and I had studied acting in New York with Paul Mann. We had done scenes in class together. Vic wanted to direct Jean Genet's powerful play *Deathwatch*. He asked me if I would coproduce the play with him. "All we need is a couple of hundred bucks," said Vic. "And I want you to play "Maurice." Maurice was a young homosexual in love with "Green Eyes," his powerful cellmate. But the third man in the cell, Lefranc, will have none of it. He, too, loves Green Eyes. "Who'll play Lefranc?" I asked Vic. "There's a guy named Leonard Nimoy," he said.

I agreed to everything. I was now a coproducer and an actor once again. A tall, handsome actor named Mike Forest played the murderer Green Eyes. Maurice was a unique and dangerous role, especially since playing homosexuals was daring for 1961. I rehearsed wearing a woman's housecoat and slippers. I shuffled around the prison cell as if I were a woman. Nimoy and Forest were very strong. I guess I made a very convincing Maurice because during many performances, as I lay on my prison cot, I'd feel a strange hand groping my leg. The audience sat very close to the set. The play was a success. We ran for about four months, which is an eternity for L.A. I was through with being a nightclub comic. I was back to my childhood fantasies of playing *Hamlet*, when I used to lay in the bathtub in Brownsville reciting "To be or not to be . . ."

9

Citizen Welles

In 1965, Larry Tucker and I got an interesting call from Bert Schneider and Bob Rafelson. We were the hot oddball comedy writers working for Danny Kaye. Bert and Bob had an idea. They wanted to do a television pilot about a new American rock 'n' roll group. They screened the Beatles' films *A Hard Day's Night* and *Help!* They wanted to create something madcap, irreverent, and different from the cliché-ridden sitcoms. Tucker and Mazursky came up with a lively half-hour. We wanted to call the show "The Turtles," but since turtles are slow creatures, we decided on monkeys, since they are wild and unpredictable, just like our rock group. Bert and Bob included us in on casting the four young men who were to make up the quartet, and I was set to direct seven out of the first thirteen episodes if the show was picked up.

As soon as the show went on the air, we knew it was a hit. The Writers Guild of America called Larry and me. It seems there was something called merchandising rights, and we stood to make a bundle since we created the show. Out of the blue Rafelson and Schneider claimed that they created "The Monkees." They went as far as to say that the title "Monkees" was their idea. It was getting silly—and ugly.

The Writers Guild took our case, and we went before an arbitrator and won. We never really understood why Bert and Bob, who were making a lot of money, wanted to screw us—especially since we were all on the same wavelength. Several years later, I ran into Bob coming out of a bookstore in Beverly Hills. We smiled and shrugged and agreed to forget our past troubles.

In 1973, years after our Monkee business, I was surprised to get a call from Bert Schneider. We were no longer enemies (in fact, I had great respect for Bert), but we never called each other. "Orson Welles wants you to be in his new movie," Bert said. I didn't think that was funny. "Come on, Bert," I said. "Don't play games with me. Why would Orson Welles want me?" Bert said, "I don't know why. He just asked for you." I was in the midst of post-production on *Alex in Wonderland*. "I'm really busy, Bert. When would this thing work?" I asked. "Tonight," Bert answered very dryly. "Tonight?" I was positive that it was some kind of stunt. "Yeah," said Bert, "tonight at eight o'clock. At his house. I'll give you the address." "Bert, this is not amusing—" Bert cut in and gave me an address on Benedict Canyon.

Five hours later I found myself driving up to Orson Welles' house. Half of me was thrilled, but the other half believed this to be a Bert Schneider trick. "All I know is what Orson told me," Bert had said. "He's doing a picture called *The Other Side of the Wind*, and he wants Paul Mazursky for a party sequence." It all sounded fake, but I couldn't take a chance and not go. At a quarter to eight I slowed down and saw the house. I drove past it and decided not to get there too early. After waiting five minutes, I rang the bell. In a moment the door opened wide. There was Orson Welles! He was huge, almost the size of Larry Tucker, dressed all in black. A sort of black smock hung over black trousers. He wore a beard and had a jumbo Churchill cigar in his hand. He took one look at me and started to guffaw. In his inimitable voice he went "Ha, ha, ha, ha, ha! Ha, ha, ha, ha, ha!" Almost like Santa Claus.

"I can't tell you how happy I am that you've come to my party," said Orson. He congratulated me on *Bob & Carol*. . . . I was in seventh heaven! "What is it you want me to do, Mr. Welles?"

I looked around and saw a large living room with two 16-millimeter cameras set up. Sitting at a small table was Henry Jaglom. Henry had auditioned for the leading role in *Alex in Wonderland*, and when we decided not to use him, he accused us of bowing to studio pressure. This wasn't true, of course, but we could never convince Henry. We weren't exactly enemies, but we certainly weren't friends. I knew that something fishy was in the works. Jaglom was known to be close to Welles, and he probably wanted something from me that would help Welles.

"Hello, Henry." "Hello, Paul."

Orson laughed and laughed. He was overjoyed. "Paul, I want you to sit here, right across from Henry. You know each other, but you have opposite opinions about Jake Hannaford." This time he laughed so loudly I thought he was nuts. Welles, the genius who had made *Citizen Kane, The Magnificent Ambersons, Chimes at Midnight*, and *Touch of Evil* was actually directing Paul Mazursky.

I looked over at Henry to see what his face might tell, but he just sat back and smiled. Then it came to me. Henry knew I was good at improvisation. Welles wanted an improvised argument between us. "Johnny Huston is going to play Jake Hannaford, but since John is not available tonight, I'll be off camera so you have someone to refer to." "And what sort of man are you, Mr. Welles?" I corrected myself. "I mean, Jake Hannaford."

Welles found this very amusing. He smiled and poured me a large brandy in a snifter. I was getting loaded. Welles went on: "Jake Hannaford has been living in Europe for some time. A director, filmmaker, someone who's been blackballed by Hollywood. A great man!" He laughed so loudly, I thought the neighbors might complain. "And he's come back to Hollywood after all these years. Peter Bogdanovich makes a documentary about Jake. I've already shot that. And someone throws a party for Jake, a great, big, juicy Hollywood party. That's where you boys are," said Welles. "I've already shot some of the people at the party: Lili Palmer, Edmond O'Brien, Paul Stewart, and this new kid Dennis Hopper. Welles pointed at a darkly beautiful, exotic-looking woman who was holding a lantern. "This is my friend Oja Kodar," said Welles. "She makes the transitions between scenes at the party. The lantern crosses the frame, and there you are." (Oja was Welles' companion for many years and can be seen in *F Is for Fake*.)

I smiled. "Jake sounds a lot like you, Mr. Welles."

"Ha, ha, ha, ha, ha! He is not Orson Welles! You can be sure of that! Even though he's back in Hollywood trying to raise money!" He roared with laughter at this bit of irony. "Now, Paul, you take Jake's side. You love his films! Henry will go the other way. But, please, for heaven's sake, never say Orson! It's not about me!" With that he broke his own record for laughing.

Then I heard Orson Welles, the greatest director of all time, say, "Action." Jaglom looked at me and quickly said that he despised *Bob & Carol & Ted & Alice*. He characterized it as a cheap exploitation picture. I accused Henry of being a spoiled rich boy. We went at it for about ten minutes. I was getting drunk by now. I spotted Welles coming toward us, and I told Jaglom how much I admired Jake Hannaford's work. "He's a bigger fake than you are," said Jaglom. Our improvisation kept crossing back and forth between our real feelings and this story that Welles had devised. I no longer felt that I was improvising.

"Cut! Cut!" shouted Welles. "Don't say a word! We're reloading! It's brilliant! Absolutely brilliant! No talking, please! Save it for the camera!" Welles was using *Second City* techniques, I thought to myself. In less than two minutes Welles called out "Action" again, and Henry and I went back to our "scene." We were the young Turks of Hollywood circa 1972. We shot for three hours. My brandy snifter was constantly refilled by an excited Welles. At one point he handed me one of his Churchills. I hated cigars, but I was not about to turn down this one. Welles took great pleasure in lighting it for me. I knew that I looked foolish, sipping brandy and puffing a huge cigar, but I was too drunk to give a damn. Besides, I was trained to always listen to the director. And if the director was Orson Welles . . .

Finally, near midnight, Welles called a final "Cut." He thanked me profusely. Of course, I knew that he was the "director" in *The Other Side of the Wind*, that Orson Welles had suffered mightily at the hands of Hollywood. Unable to get financing for his projects, he was forced to act in some clinkers to pay for his films (not *The Third Man* by Carol Reed, written by Graham Greene. Welles' "Harry Lime" is a sublime piece of acting in a great film). Maybe this new film was his way of telling the world Orson was back in town.

As I drove down Benedict Canyon, I felt my mood of elation disappearing. If they treated Welles like that, what could I expect? I was very nervous about how *Alex in Wonderland* would be received. (Unfortunately, I was right to be nervous.) I realized that this was neurotic self-pity—after all, who the hell was I to compare my problems with those of the great Orson Welles?

The next morning I was at my desk at M.G.M. when my secretary buzzed me and said that Orson Welles was on line one. I breathed deeply and cleared my throat, then I picked up the phone. "Hello." Welles laughed. "Now I know I have a film! "You were absolutely brilliant. Both you and Jaglom. Brilliant. I was getting worried about my party scene. I shot the Hopper kid last week. He can't improvise!" Welles did an imitation of Dennis Hopper. "Boring! But you boys will liven up that party. Thank you! Thank you!" I thanked Welles for the compliments. "I hope I can see you sometime and just talk," I said. Welles responded, "Of course, Paul, but don't call me. I'll call you as soon as I'm done with this thing." He hung up. I leaned back to savor the moment.

I never heard from Orson Welles again. Now and then a bit of gossip about *The Other Side of the Wind* would float by in *Daily Variety:* Welles needed more money. Welles needed more time. Welles no longer owned the film.

I ran into Henry Jaglom. We shook hands and felt genuine warmth for each other. Henry told me that Welles had cut our scene down to about ten minutes and that it was sensational. He mentioned a couple of people who had also seen it and loved it. "Will I ever see this movie?" I asked Henry. "I hope so," he said. "But I think it's going to take a little time."

Welles died in 1985, about thirteen years after *Wind*. He never finished the film, although a cut sequence was shown the night he was honored by the American Film Institute. Orson made an inspirational speech that night, once again reminding us of his greatness, his wit, and his huge appetite for life.

As the years rolled by I'd occasionally meet Henry Jaglom, and we always talked about *Wind*. I learned that an Iranian group was involved. It seems that a relative of the Shah had invested in the movie and gained control over it after Welles' death. It all sounded too complicated. I'd never get a chance to see the film, let alone my performance. "Were we that hateful?" I asked Henry. "I think we did exactly what Orson hoped we would do," he told me.

It is now 1998. A few weeks ago I found myself sitting next to Henry Jaglom at an Academy meeting of directors. Henry smiled when he saw me, his odd crushable hat down to his forehead as usual. "I think you're going to see our movie. Oja Kodar has worked out the financial problems, and Bogdanovich is finishing the cutting according to Orson's notes." Thirteen years after his death, Welles' film seemed destined to finally come out. "I hope we're still in it," said I, ever the hopeful actor, to Henry. "Oh, I think so, Paul. Our scene is too good to be cut," he said confidently. Then Henry shrugged. "But you never know . . ."

One of the other directors at the meeting, Norman Jewison, brought up some business about what standards we should use to accept new directors into the Motion Picture Academy. There was a heated discussion, and soon I forgot about Orson Welles and *The Other Side of the Wind*.

Several weeks after writing this piece, a stranger came up to me in the Farmer's Market where I have my morning coffee and asked me if I'd ever seen myself in the Orson Welles film. I asked him who he was, and he told me he had twenty hours of tapes including my "great" scene with Henry Jaglom. There was talk about cutting it together, but not with Peter Bogdanovich. He said that Bogdanovich wasn't cutting this film, and there were no notes from Orson Welles! But "If you want, you can see my tapes of your scene." I readily agreed. "This Thursday I'll get you the tapes." I never heard from him again.

P.S. Six months later I finally saw an hour of cut film. My scene with Henry was down to about fifteen seconds. But at least I had been directed by Orson Welles.

10

Bob & Natalie & Elliott & Dyan

Mike Frankovich, the powerful producer of my first shot at directing, *Bob & Carol & Ted & Alice*, suggested I fly to London to meet with Natalie Wood. She had read the screenplay and was interested in playing "Carol." Natalie had been a big star for many years, but she hadn't been in a real hit since *Gypsy* and *West Side Story*. I thought she was beautiful and could act, but I was worried about her ability to handle satire. I knew that if she was in the movie, we'd get some instant recognition, but I had large doubts and was determined to meet her on my own terms. Freddie Fields, the great agent who handled Natalie (and me), said he would join us for lunch at Claridges in London for the first meeting to help break the ice.

The year was 1968, and I'd never been to London. I checked into a hotel near the Marble Arch and ran out into the streets. London was very vital and, appropriately enough, looked like a

Beatles movie, with all sorts of exotic types parading down Kings Road wearing flowered shirts and long hair. And, of course, there were the bobbies, the Bentleys, and Buckingham Palace. It seemed to me that London was what New York should have been. It was cleaner, safer, and had better theater. Why the hell wasn't I British? I wondered.

At a quarter to one in the afternoon I went into the Claridge's lobby. Freddie was already there, and he quickly told me that Natalie was a "great gal" and perfect casting. She just needed some reassurance that I knew what I was doing. "You gotta remember, pal, this is your first picture. How the hell would she know you can direct?" "I'll do the best I can, Freddie. But I have to tell you, I'm not sold on her yet. I mean, this is satire." Freddie winced. "Yeah, but satire can be funny. And Natalie Wood can be funny. Plus she's a huge star."

I agreed with everything Freddie said, but I still had my reservations. We went into the restaurant. Exactly on time came Natalie Wood. No entourage. Dressed simply. The great smile. By the time she said, "How nice it was of you to fly all the way to London to meet me," all my reservations disappeared. I was desperate for Natalie to play "Carol."

The headwaiter came over and told Freddie there was a phone call for him. For the first time I was alone with Natalie. I described some of my ideas for the film. I told her I had taught acting and had directed in the theater, that I was confident about working with actors, that I was assembling a fine team of technicians including Charley Lang—a genius at lighting women. I was sure Natalie knew of him. He had won two Oscars for cinematography. She seemed very enthusiastic.

Freddie came back to the table, white as a ghost. "You okay, Freddie?" I asked him. He seemed depressed. "Yeah. That was Sellers. I can't go to my kid's graduation tomorrow. I have to fly to Cannes to see Sellers." Natalie and I urged him to forget Peter Sellers and fly to Los Angeles for his daughter's high school graduation. What could be so important in Cannes? Freddie smiled ironically. "His lordship has a new record player on his yacht. It has some kind of gyroscope so it'll keep playing even if the yacht sinks. Which would be okay with me. He says I have to see it." I knew how nutty Peter could be, but this ranked high on the list.

After lunch, Natalie and I took a walk through Hyde Park. By now I was speaking with a slight British accent. I learned that after her marriage to Robert Wagner and then her divorce from him, she still considered him her best friend. (I figured she was telling me all this personal stuff to establish a real relationship with her director.)

She was now living in London with a Brit named Richard Gregson. They were very much in love and were planning to get married. Gregson had been an agent and was now a producer. I met him the next day and liked him a lot. He was intelligent, witty, handsome, and had a wonderful haircut. (British barbers cut men's hair longish, almost arty. You don't know if you're meeting an actor, a barrister, or a cab driver.)

By the time I returned to L.A., I knew that Natalie Wood was going to be "Carol." While I still had a glimmer of anxiety about the business of satire, I was about eighty-twenty sure she could handle it. Her radiant beauty could only enhance the film.

"Can you imagine," I said to Larry, "how hot the audience will get when this gorgeous thing tells her husband who has just confessed to adultery that she's glad he told her?" "Not only glad," Larry added. "She loves him even more for his honesty!" We laughed. This was going to be a very funny movie. Now on to casting the other three leads.

Robert Culp was costarring in the television series *I Spy* with Bill Cosby. He was a good-looking leading man who had not yet scored in pictures. He, too, was Mike Frankovich's idea. Larry and I met with Culp. He loved the script and seemed to really get it. We thought he'd make the perfect mate to Natalie—the result being a delicious, pseudo-hip, trendy L.A. couple. Even in his real life Bob wore outfits with zippers down to the ankle and up to the neck. Playing a documentary filmmaker going up to the "Institute" for research on a movie idea fit him like a glove. (The "Institute" was based on Esalen where Betsy and I had gone for our own weekend marathon. Later, the people from Esalen read the script and would not let us use their facility for the movie. I don't think humor is part of their curative vision.)

Once Culp was cast as Bob, we began the search for Ted and Alice. Ted's a lawyer; he's not a nerd but definitely not the swinger Bob is. Alice is confused about her life; she has a beautiful child and a good husband. She plays tennis, shops, and sees a psychiatrist once a week. But Alice doesn't have much enthusiasm for Carol's confession to them one night that "Bob had an affair. He told me all about it. I'm so happy!" Later, in the car going home, Alice asks Ted to pull over to a Jack in the Box so that she can throw up.

For Ted we met just about every thirtyish actor in Hollywood, from Richard Benjamin to James Caan to Alan Alda. They were all good, but none seemed quite right. Perfect casting usually comes at unexpected moments, but when it comes, it leaps out at you. You are immediately positive you've found your actor. But we were confused. Frankovich gave good advice, as usual: "What's the big hurry? Just keep looking, boys."

We were also meeting women for the role of Alice. At one time we were hot on Paula Prentiss and Richard Benjamin. (I think they would have been very good.) But somehow we didn't feel sanguine. Then Dyan Cannon, who had been married to Cary Grant, walked into the office. Frankovich knew her and thought she might make a good Alice. She had once guested on the Danny Kaye show as a singer, and I remembered how adorable she was. She had long blondish hair, full lips, the face of a baby lioness, the smile of a sphinx, and a spectacular figure. Wow! Natalie Wood and Dyan Cannon!

Dyan read for us and did very well. She seemed perfect. Larry and I agreed that she could do the part, but we couldn't make a final decision until we found our Ted. So we put Dyan on hold for a few weeks. I probed a bit and asked her what life with Cary Grant had been like. Dyan smiled. "A great education," she said. "Of course I had LSD with Cary, and I don't know how great that was." She seemed perfect for the sexually repressed, thoroughly square Alice. I couldn't wait for the scene near the end of the movie when the foursome goes to Las Vegas and decides to finally have an orgy. Alice leads the way as she takes her blouse off. Bob unzips his pants and jacket and gets down to his undershorts. Ted sees them and starts stripping. Finally Carol, too, goes along with the orgy idea.

Frankovich had another casting notion. "You boys know Elliott Gould? Streisand's husband. He's funny. He just finished *The Night They Raided Minsky's* with Britt Ekland. Why don't you meet the boy?" Frankovich had already been responsible for three great casting ideas, so it was with interest that we met with Elliott. We had had so much trouble with the role of Ted that we were beginning to think it was a script problem. We were rapidly losing confidence in the character. When Elliott Gould came into our office at Columbia, all he said was "Hello," and Larry and I looked at each other as if to say, "This is the guy!" He was Ted in every way. He was tall and handsome in a Jewish kind of way. He seemed a bit vulnerable, and that was exactly what we were looking for. Elliott read for us and halfway through the scene I said, "You've got the part!" Elliott Gould completely validated our writing.

We decided to put Dyan through a screen test. She would be one of three actresses to test with Elliott. They'd all do the same scene, one in which Ted is horny and wants sex with Alice. Alice, however, is too disgusted by Carol's behavior to even think of sex. Ted quickly develops a terrible headache. Alice gives him a massage which only gets him hotter. Finally, in a moment of complete despair, Alice asks Ted, "Would you want me to do it just like that, with no feeling on my part? Would you, Ted? Would you, darling?" To which Ted instantly replies, "Yeah." No one has ever done anything funnier in one of my films. (At the preview in Denver when Elliott said "Yeah," the audience exploded. You couldn't hear the dialogue for the next five minutes.)

All three tests were good, but it was no contest—Dyan Cannon became our Alice. I, too, was coming up roses because I'd directed the tests with such professionalism. We knew the picture was going to be a hit. Elliott and Dyan made a perfect couple. The scene was funny and sexy. Mike was elated. "Why that scene is so good I'm thinking of showing it to the distributors at the national convention." (He later did, which helped start the buzz about the film.) Frankovich sipped his martini. "This'll give those boys a hard-on for our movie." We toasted each other.

I hired Pato Guzman to be the art director and Stuart Pappé to edit. They had both worked on *The President's Analyst* for Ted Flicker. Ted was the only director I knew, so I just followed his trip. Pato did almost all my films for the next twenty-two years. Stuart has cut eight of my films so far. With the help of both these men I set out to learn how to shoot a movie—how to design a sequence, how things would cut together. I developed a technique I've used ever since: prepare and prepare, then prepare again; find the locations and dream up shots long before the cameraman arrives on the job (usually two weeks before you start).

For two weeks I rehearsed with the cast. They jelled quickly. There was a moment or two when I felt that Natalie lacked irony, but I came to see it as a stroke of luck. Her adorable sincerity about the business of being "open" was perfect for Carol. At the end of the two weeks I showed the fully rehearsed scenes to Charley Lang, Pato, Stuart, and a few others. They loved it. "I've never had the privilege of seeing one of my movies this way," said Charley. "Paul, I can really visualize this film." I felt ready to start shooting.

But I had a restless weekend. Monday I got up very early and went over my notes for the first day. I knew the shots, and I knew the staging. I strode onto the soundstage full of bravura. This kid was going to wow them! About twelve actors and actresses, including Natalie and Bob, were assembled for the first scene. There were also at least fifty crew members, and they all called me "Boss." Their expectant smiles seemed larger than life. Charley Lang asked where I'd like to begin. The actors smiled expectantly, and the technicians got ready to move. All they needed was a word from their boss.

Then my stomach turned sour. Everything I had prepared seemed silly, clichéd. I was a first-time director with absolutely no idea of what to do. Why did I give up my job as a messenger boy? I thought.

Charlie recognized my panic. "Why don't we go up on the crane?" he suggested. "There may be a nice shot from above."

I'd never been up on a crane before, so it took an extra minute or two to strap me in next to Charley. Up and up, higher and higher we went. I don't like heights, so the elevation only added to my anxiety. At the top, Charley spoke in a quiet voice, almost a whisper. "The good thing about being up here, Paul, is we can figure out what to do down there and nobody can hear us. Now, why don't we begin with a master shot of the entire group? But first rehearse the scene, and I'll watch it with you." I was relieved. "Okay. Thanks, Charley," I said. "Take her down!" Charley called to the one of the grips.

The rehearsal went well. The actors were comfortable. Charley and I figured out the first two or three shots. Much of what I had planned was working. Soon not only was I feeling better but I was getting cocky. By God, I was finally doing what I was born to do!

At least once a day after that I would go from extreme arrogance to abject fear, but still the shooting zipped along. We all had bonded—Natalie and Robert and Elliott and Dyan. They seemed to be real couples confused about their sexuality. They totally accepted me as a director. I felt I could do no wrong.

Then came the day of the scene where the foursome decide to have an orgy; that's when I ran into my first big problem. They are in a hotel suite in Las Vegas. Elliott and Natalie are in the foreground, sitting at a small bar. Dyan and Robert are in the background. Elliott and Natalie are against an orgy, but Dyan angrily insists they go all the way. Still in the background, she begins to strip.

Natalie suddenly turned to me and said, "I won't do this shot. I'm not going to sit here talking to Elliott while Dyan and Bob are undressing in the background." I explained to her that the humor of the scene counted on the juxtaposition of these two things happening at the same time. "That's what's funny!" I insisted. But Na-

My bar mitzvah photo.

Next stop, on
my Greenwich
Village rooftop.

The day I fell
in love with Betsy.

4

Acting in Genet's *Deathwatch*. *Left to right:* Leonard Nimoy, Mike Forest, yours truly.

The entire cast and crew of Stanley Kubrick's first film, *Fear and Desire*.

"Igor and h," the new comedy team, 1955. (With Herb Hartig).

Second from left, me, the punk teenager, in *Blackboard Jungle*.

Zeda and Bubbe (holding Meg), Dave and Jean.

9

I loved Natalie Wood.
Can you blame me?

T*oklas.* Peter Sellers and Leigh
Taylor-Young. He fell in love
with her.

10

11

P eter, Paul, and Larry on the set of *Toklas.* That's Larry on the left.

12

Elliott Gould,
a complicated
comic genius.

13

Bob & *Carol* & *Ted*
& *Alice*. From the New
York Film Festival,
1969.

With Jeanne
Moreau on Hollywood
Boulevard for a dream
scene in *Alex in
Wonderland*.

14

15

Me, in hippie hat, directing Donald Sutherland and Ellen Burstyn. Larry Tucker looks on.

16

Lunch in Rome at the Nuevo Fico. *Standing:* Mario Longardi, Fellini's right hand man. *Seated:* Me, Fellini, and Robin Williams.

With the fabulous Shelley Winters in Cannes for *Next Stop, Greenwich Village.*

17

18

Two of my favorites, Alan Bates and Jill Clayburgh. *An Unmarried Woman.*

19

Robin Williams, Maria Conchita Alonzo, and me at opening party for *Moscow on the Hudson.*

Leon Capetanos and me in Moscow doing research.

21

22

Perhaps the purest
actor I ever worked
with—Art Carney in
Harry and Tonto.

My darling Meg,
1979, at a party for
Willie and Phil.

They all came
for my *Willie and
Phil* party. Margot
Kidder, Jill Clayburgh,
Dyan Cannon, and
Natalie Wood.

23

With Sven
Nykvist on a barge
in Benares, India,
(from *Willie and
Phil*, 1979).

Strolling in
Cinecittà with
Fellini, 1981. He's
asking me about
my sex life.

John Cassavetes: "Will you dance with me?" Me: "Well, okay."
Gena just smiles.

Raul Julia, me, Sonia Braga, Richard Dreyfuss in Brazil
during *Moon Over Parador*. Three brilliant actors.

Lining up a shot for *Moon Over Parador* in Brazil.

Betsy Mazursky and her husband in *Parador*.

Jean, my Gypsy mother, sitting with my friend Norman Cohen.

30

31

32

Albert Wolsky (costumes), Pato Guzman (production design), me, Stuart Pappe (editor). We've worked together for twenty-five years.

In the "Amazon" with Michael.

33

Four women I love—Betsy, Meg, Jill, and Betsy's late mother, Margaret.

With Bette.

34

Richard Dreyfuss, Nick Nolte, Bette Midler.

35

36

As Leon Tortshiner in *Enemies, A Love Story.*

37

Pato Guzman, me as Tortshiner, and Roger Simon in Coney Island. *Enemies, A Love Story.*

Enemies, A Love Story. The supreme ensemble cast—Ron Silver, Margaret Stein, Angelica Huston, and Lena Olin.

38

Bette and Woody.
Their marriage is over
in *Scenes from a Mall*.

39

40

41

Acting with
the great Jack
Nicholson in
Man Trouble.

Betsy in one of her
greatest roles,
opposite Danny
Aiello in *The Pickle*.

Back to
Brownsville after
forty years.

September, 1998.
My daughter Jill
holding my
granddaughter Molly.

I'm a lucky guy.
Steve, Meg, Betsy,
Kate, Jill, Paul, and
Carly, Monza and
Snowball.

talie was adamant. I told her I'd cover her with her own close-up, but she must have realized that I'd end up using the four shot.

With a grim determination I hadn't seen before, she marched into her trailer. I told the assistant director (Tony Ray, son of Nicholas Ray) to take a ten-minute break, and I followed Natalie into her trailer. I pleaded my case again, but to no avail. Now I was getting angry. "Well, Natalie, if you won't do the four shot, I won't shoot the scene at all. Someone else will have to direct the rest of the picture." I couldn't believe the words coming out of my mouth. We looked at each other, and it was clear neither one would bend.

I left the trailer and called Larry Tucker and Mike Frankovich. They hurried down to the set. Larry tried his best with Natalie. Even Mike couldn't budge her, but he didn't try to force me to give in to her. He knew I was right and that somehow this would all end happily. I called lunch and went back to Natalie's trailer. I asked her to "at least take a walk with me" outside the soundstage. She agreed.

She was more attractive than ever, wearing Carol's miniskirt, her wonderful dark eyes full of passion. We strolled slowly in the hot sun. I told Natalie about my childhood, my mother, my dreams of greatness. It was, I guess, a soliloquy about my stubborn need to follow my instincts. I tried to convince her that if the scene didn't work, I would use more conventional two shots and close-ups. I told Natalie that nothing would change my mind. I hoped she would at least agree to try it once. Then she stopped walking and said, "Okay, Paul." I embraced her. We were both close to tears. The former child star who had been brought up on a diet of conventional movie rights and wrongs showed real class.

That afternoon we did the scene, and it was hilarious. I remember Elliott's exit line (written by Larry Tucker) as the troupe walks into the bedroom: "First we'll have an orgy, and then we'll see Tony Bennett."

Next came the orgy scene. The cast had been asking me for weeks what exactly was going to happen since the script was a bit vague on this point. I kept telling them I'd discuss it when we got closer to the actual filming. I wanted the actors to "really" get anxious about what would happen when the four of them got into bed together. The truth is that I wasn't sure myself. Larry and I had talked it over many times. Have the orgy. Don't have the orgy. On the one hand, it was daring; on the other hand, I didn't believe they would actually go through with it. But I pretended to the cast that I was the Cheshire cat with my smug grin.

There was an air of great expectancy on the set as the foursome arrived. I had ordered a closed set, no visitors, thereby raising the expectation of something very wild and sexual. The actors were mostly giggling nervously. I arranged Natalie, Bob, and Dyan in the king-sized bed, sitting up under the covers. They were waiting for Elliott (Ted) to join them. He was in the bathroom doing a last-minute breath spray and underarm cleanup. He was very funny.

When Elliott entered the bedroom, he climbed in next to Natalie. I told him I wanted him to take his jockey shorts off under the blanket and then toss them out so we could see them. Elliott did it perfectly. Only later did I learn that he wore two pairs of jockey shorts so that he wouldn't be totally naked under the blanket. Just like Ted! All of this went very well. It was funny and kind of poignant.

Then the cast looked to me for the wisdom I had promised them. "What do we do now, Paul?" they asked. "Just do what you want," I said. "Whatever feels right." I'm sure they expected something more profound, but no one complained. By now their trust in me and the film was total. I was curious to see what would happen. The cameras rolled. There was an initial nervous giggling. Then Bob reached under the blanket and caressed Dyan. She turned red and began to laugh. Natalie was the aggressor with the shy Elliott, but you could tell he was warming to her. Elliott and Bob had a brief chat about the stock market, followed by a long, funny, awkward silence. Then Natalie kissed Elliott with great tenderness. It was beautiful. Bob and Dyan kissed passionately. Remember, this was 1969 when the sight of two married couples just getting into the same bed was daring! But, finally, they couldn't go through with the "orgy." They exited the hotel arm in arm and outside joined a Felliniesque circle of dozens of couples, all searching for the "answer."

I still wonder what might have happened if I had told the cast to really get it on, really have an orgy. I think Bob Culp could have handled it, but no one else. I think.

11

What Are
Friends For?

Michael Greene is my best friend. We are almost complete opposites except that we are both extremely judgmental, egotistical, and control freaks. Mike—or "Big Mike," as he is called because he's six feet six—is an actor, which tends to make him very up and downish. If he has a role, any role, in anything, even a commercial (he does a lot of them), he's a happy camper. But if he's out of work, as he often is, he gets moody and self-pitying.

"I think I'm going to quit the business," he'll tell me mournfully. "What are you going to do?" I ask him, my tongue way up in my cheek. "Become a shaman or move to Maui and catch waves or maybe just meditate in a cave for a year?" "Hmmmm," Mike answers, "become a shaman . . ."

Mike and I ride our bicycles every Sunday morning on the bike path in Venice. We go all the way to Temescal Canyon and back, and during the ninety-minute ride we play games. If we see a beautiful girl (and we often do; bikini-clad young things on roller-blades are heart-stopping), we use the word "purple." As the maiden approaches, one of us will say, "Did you bring your purple jacket?" thereby alerting the other to a gorgeous nymph. If the other guy doesn't think the girl is that great, he'll say something like, "Oh, I didn't bring my purple jacket." But if both of us agree on purple, we then move on to ranking in the usual manner, with ten being best. Some Sundays we actually see three or four purple tens, and we are overcome with fantasies of what we'd do: "How much would you pay for that?" Mike asks me. Quickly I answer, "Five thousand for a three-day weekend." Mike: "I'd pay ten in a flash." "No way. Maybe ten for a full week." "If I had the bucks, I'd pay ten for a weekend," says Mike.

Another game we play is switching. For thirty minutes or so as we ride our bikes we switch roles. Mike is me, and I'm Mike. You have to really know the other person well to do this, but it can be quite beneficial. If the other is good, you get a sample of what your own bullshit sounds like.

At one point, mostly in the sixties and seventies, Mike experimented with drugs—with a vengeance: speed, grass, psychedelics. Every day! Today, amazingly, despite his earlier excess, he is in excellent shape. He has a healthy diet; he hikes every day; he begins every morning with an hour and a half of meditation. I ask him if the meditating does him any good. "Oh, sure," he says. "Can you imagine what kind of prick I'd be without it?"

Even though I've tested the waters of many of the New Age trips and the psychedelics and the gurus, and participated in marathon weekends with Sufis, I still basically distrust it all. I'm fascinated and maybe even hopeful for a miracle, but I don't believe in gurus, especially when they charge. Mike thinks I'm closed to some "great experience." "You're so conventional," he'll tell me.

We've taken several trips together. We trekked in Nepal for three weeks. We've been to Avignon, Positano, Naples, and Dallas. But our wildest journey was to the Amazon.

I don't like ordinary vacations, so when I heard about the

Wild Mushroom Trip on the Amazon, I was immediately hooked. It is run by a couple in Connecticut who own an Amazonian arti- fact shop. The man, Gerry, has been going down the Amazon for twenty-eight of his fifty-odd years. He has lived in the jungle for long periods of time with the Indians—in particular with shamans who conduct Ayahuasca ceremonies. Ayahuasca is a potent psy- chedelic drug made from vines that grow in the jungle. Gerry told us that taking the drug induces hallucinations. I figured it was like the peyote rituals of the American Indians. Gerry and his wife, Chris, seemed very legitimate. I told them I'd love to take the trip. Betsy, however, was worried about bugs, piranha, and malaria, so this was one vacation she would not be taking. "Why don't you go with Mike?" she suggested.

In late March 1995, Mike and I flew to Miami to catch the plane to Iquitos, Peru. Even the name "Iquitos" was thrilling. We spent a night in Miami in an air-conditioned hotel in South Beach, the Art Deco section where the beautiful roller-bladers meet the elderly in walkers on the bike path.

We tried to imagine the trip. We had seen pictures of the *Delfin*, the boat that would take us down the Amazon. It was fifty- seven feet long and looked like the old junk heap Bogart cap- tained in *The African Queen*. We'd been warned that the boat was not fancy. We'd be taking the trip with a dozen other people whom we were to meet the following morning at the Miami air- port.

The next day Mike and I waited by the Peruvian airline ticket counter. One by one the group arrived. There was Marita, the lovely wife of Fred Murphy, the cameraman who had shot *Ene- mies, A Love Story* for me. Marita loves to travel, and when she heard about this trip, she asked if she could join us. (Fred was busy shooting a film.) Marita turned out to be a great traveler. She had also invited two good friends of hers: Gigi, who was married to Herbie Hancock, the musician, and Beverly, another old friend. Both of them rarely left the *Delfin* during the trip. There was an intelligent Belgian woman named Miriam; Peter, who had spent a lot of time in Central America; (I thought he was CIA); a couple into "seeds"—he had been on the trip several years before and was back for more seed research, this time with his newest bride, a tense woman who kept a diary going all day long. He assured us the trip was safe and interesting. Then there were the artist and his wife, both about sixty. He barely spoke. She was a vivacious New Yorker with a lot of money who talked for both of them. Three men completed the cast of characters: Two were from Minnesota, good friends, one quite heavy and the other quite fit. The fit guy was a dentist, and the other one was into computers. Both men complained constantly about the miserable quarters (they *were* miserable) and how much they missed their usual food. (One day we were served river rat, and the chef proudly held up the huge dead rat for all to see. It tasted a bit like chicken, but you had to hypnotize yourself to get past the fact that you were chewing on a rat leg.) The last man on the trip was a waiter from Connecticut who had seen the trip advertised on a bulletin board and spent his hard-earned money to join up. He was plainspoken, blue-collar, and drank beer like a fish. Everything he wore told you he was about to go on an exotic adventure deep in some jungle: weird knives, jungle jackets, exotic hats, vests with sixteen pockets—the whole bit.

After fifteen minutes or so of introductions, we all began to ask the same question: "Are you going to take Ayahuasca?" Of course, Mike and I were definitely going to take it. That was our main reason for the trip. Where else could you find a vacation complete with three shamans? Maybe, at long last, we would find the magic formula for peace, happiness, and spiritual well-being via a natural psychedelic experience in the jungles of Peru.

The twelve of us arrived in Iquitos, which is a jungle port, at 11 o'clock at night. The small airport, more like an airstrip in a war movie, was makeshift and kind of dark. I looked around for Gerry and Chris, but there was no sign of them. Then, through a set of glass doors, I saw Gerry waving frantically at us. "There's Gerry!" I called to the group. Then I saw that both his arms were bandaged from his fingers up to his armpits.

We nervously made our way to Gerry, who said, "I'll explain

this after we get on the bus. We're going to go right to the boat." By then it was near midnight. We were apprehensive, driving in an old bus through a jungle town with the sounds of parrots, screeching monkeys, and howling cats assaulting us.

On the bus Gerry told us that three weeks before, he and Chris had been sleeping in their jungle compound, which is about two and a half hours from any town, when thieves burst in. Fortunately, Gerry heard the thieves a split second before they got to him, and he reached for the gun he always kept under the bed. Shots were exchanged in the dark. Gerry killed one of the intruders, but he was badly wounded as well. The other thief, also wounded, fled into the jungle. With great courage, Chris raced through the darkness, a lantern strapped to her head, and found some natives in a small village. Two hours later they got Gerry onto a boat and took him to the hospital in Iquitos.

Naturally, this story made our group nervous. We weren't even at the boat, and we were already flipping. Could we get a refund? Should we go back to Miami? Are Chris and Gerry in some kind of cult? But we all boarded the *Delfin*. Gerry told us that he wouldn't be with us the first week because he had to stay in the hospital, but Chris would look after us. She seemed very hyper and intensely in denial, but we accepted the situation. After a week, if the doctor said it was okay, Gerry would rejoin us.

Before we knew it, we were clomping down dozens of wooden steps in the moonlight to board the *Delfin*. We were shown our tiny staterooms and the four toilets that doubled as showers. We were exhausted and nervous, and I immediately started drinking beer. By the time I finished my beer (Peruvian beer is very good), my throat was killing me. I decided it was probably a strep that I had caught in the air-conditioned hotel in Miami, so I asked Chris, who was wild-eyed with anxiety, whether I should take an antibiotic. Chris suggested I see a shaman and introduced me to Leo. He was about seventy, sweet as sugar, very thin and quite lame. Like the other two shamans traveling with us, he wore old Reebok sneakers, a shirt, and a baseball cap. What, no feathers? I wondered. I later learned he had once been attacked by an anteater in the jungle during an Ayahuasca ceremony. The other two shamans looked down on Leo because of that experience, which they interpreted as bad karma. They believed he had been paid back for some wrong act.

In Spanish (I don't speak Quechua, the Amazonian tongue) I told Leo about my throat. We were on the upper deck of the boat, which by now was gliding down the river. He sat me down in a chair and had me point to where on the throat it hurt. Then he lit a cigarette that was about five inches long and very wide—pure tobacco, not grass—and he began to chant. He was doing this rhythmic chanting in Quechua and blowing smoke at my head and my throat. After several minutes Leo got down on his knees in front of me and began to kiss my throat. It tickled, but I was too scared to laugh. He began to suck on my throat at the spot I'd indicated. He was trying to suck the strep out. Finally, he went to the side of the boat and spat out the bad "stuff."

The others watched intently, laughing nervously every time Leo sucked my throat. He repeated this ceremony the next morning and the following night. Twenty-four hours later my strep was all gone. I'm not like Mike, who is definitely a believer in native healing, but Leo either cured me or it was an amazing coincidence. Or maybe I cured myself. Who knows?

Pretty soon the other passengers on the *Delfin* started telling Leo their problems, and he was chanting and sucking people's throats, stomachs, arms, anything. Everybody wanted to be cured of something. Then the other two shamans got into the act. It wasn't long before all three shamans were smoking, chanting, and sucking various parts of the human anatomy.

For the next week we cruised the Amazon, and it was wondrous. Big Mike took the upper berth in our tiny room, and I slept two inches from the musty floor. It was hot and buggy and barely tolerable, but we loved it. The natural beauty of the river was overwhelming, though we didn't see many animals apart from some birds, monkeys, and one alligator. We swam in the brownish waters of the Amazon only after our crew of six jumped in to show us it was safe. We stopped at villages and met the natives. The

Bora tribe painted our faces and had us chewing cocoa leaves. I swallowed some and almost fainted.

This was all good and well, we thought, but when would we take Ayahuasca?

Back in Iquitos for a pit stop, Gerry joined us on the boat, bringing with him a Peruvian doctor to change the dressing on his wounds every day. Gerry knew his stuff. Soon he was chatting with the shamans in Quechua. He told us we would have our first Ayahuasca ceremony that night. The session was held in a room in an open hut in a clearing in the jungle. The shamans go during the day and find a spot they think is copacetic. The ceremony always takes place after dark.

Leaving behind three of our group (Gigi, Beverly, and one other) who chose not to partake, we were taken from the *Delfin* by canoes to the jungle house. There we sat on chairs arranged in a circle, the only illumination coming from an occasional flashlight. The Ayahuasca was in an old wine bottle, prepared days before. Every shaman has his own technique. Gerry and Chris had warned us that the drug had a foul taste and that you were more than likely to throw up. You'd feel wobbly, we were told, sort of like being seasick. But don't worry, they said. Throwing up was good. It purified the body, like a spiritual high-colonic.

Everyone was nervous. The shamans began to chant, passing the Ayahuasca around in shot glasses. I quickly tossed down two shots. I was going to be a warrior! At first I felt nothing except the sour taste of the drink. Then the shamans, who had already drunk their portions, began to vomit, making violent sounds. I could hear some of our group getting nauseous. I started to feel queasy myself. Then I began to trip out. I had a vision of a giant spider creeping into the room. It was about ten feet high with furry tentacles and huge black eyes. Somehow, though, I was not scared. Then I saw a large black jaguar, moving in soft footsteps, looking right at me. (The next day the shamans were very impressed when I told them about the jaguar.). Then I saw myself as a five-year-old child. I saw my grandparents, my *bubbe* and *zeda*, my parents, Dave and Jean, and then Betsy and Meg and Jill. I began to cry. I could hear the others throwing up; some of them were writhing on the ground, attended to by Chris or a shaman. Mike told me that nothing much had happened to him, but since he was an old pro at psychedelics, maybe that was only natural. The whole thing lasted three or four hours. Whatever it was, I was glad I'd done it. We got back on the *Delfin* feeling very tired but strangely elated.

Two days later Gerry told us that the second Ayahuasca ceremony would be that night. This time, though, it would be led by the other two shamans, and it would be more powerful. The shamans were grouchy, expressing their feeling that the first trip had been too soft. Our group of Ayahuascans shrank from ten to four: Marita, the CIA guy, Peter, Mike, and me. The canoes took us to a jungle clearing where there were no structures, just half a dozen folding chairs on the grass. Jungle noises were all around us in stereo, bugs were swooping down, and there was clawing humidity.

I swallowed three shots of the brew. Already the intimacy of there being only four was better. The chanting began. It started to drizzle, and I put on my rain poncho. In about fifteen minutes I began to feel acute nausea. I also began to sweat profusely.

Mike began to moan: "I think I'm dying. I'm out of my body. I'm dying!" This scared me. I knew that Mike suffered from fibrillation. "I'm flying in space! I'm an astral traveler!" he groaned.

By now we were all throwing up, much more intensely than during the first trip. The chanting continued. I began to see visions of a sort of wide-screen David Lean movie with Inca warriors, and beautiful Inca women with red painted lips lying on divans, saying, "Come into the room with me." The more I threw up, the sexier it got. Then there were beautiful Inca children and tall warriors carrying a leader on a divan—stuff I'd never seen in a museum. The vomiting and the visions didn't seem to interfere with each other.

During all this I remained worried about Mike. Had his pulse gone up to two hundred? I knew he never should have taken Ayahuasca. Chris came over to Mike and soothed him, rubbing his back. In the darkness I could see his body stooped over as he threw up, howling "I'm dead! I'm flying!" Marita seemed to be more in control; Peter was lying down on the grass, throwing up. One of the shamans began to blow smoke at Mike's heart.

I tried to stand up, but I was so dizzy that I fell down. "I have to get back to the boat," I told Chris. They carried me to the canoe. The rain came down harder. They got us back to the *Delfin* and brought us pails so that we would not throw up on the deck. Then they helped us into our rooms. I began to calm down. My heartbeat slowed, and I prayed that Big Mike was enjoying a similar fate. Then I felt the overpowering need to throw up again. I made my way to the rail. For about thirty minutes I heaved black bile into the murky waters. I finally managed to get to sleep around five in the morning. Mike lay in the upper bunk, snoring. I was exhausted.

When we woke the next morning, the visions had almost disappeared. We ate some bread, our first food in fifteen hours. (During that time I had lost about ten pounds. Was this the Ayahuasca diet? I wondered.) Then the oddest feeling of well-being took over, almost as if I had been purified. The well-being feeling lasted for about two months. Then the usual showbiz silliness took hold, and I was back to my normal angst.

The next day the shamans told me that the songs they had chanted in Quechua were about Stone Warriors. Many of the things they described I had seen in my visions. How was I able to see visions sung in a foreign language? I was baffled. Was it synchronicity? Weird coincidence? I don't know. The shamans told me that I was a very good subject but that if I really wanted to take Ayahuasca again, I would have to totally purify my body and my mind by abstaining for three months from salt, sugar, and sex.

Two days later we got ready for the third and final trip. We were almost at the end of our Amazon journey and would be heading for Machu Picchu in a few days. Although I was tempted to try the drug a third time, I didn't want to get nauseous again. Mike agreed. Marita and Peter were also not willing to do it again. The shamans suggested that we go with them into the jungle for the third ceremony, and they would take the Ayahuasca to complete the circle of three journeys. That night we took a tape recorder to record the chanting. (I still play it on my car radio as I drive through Beverly Hills.) The shamans were very pleased that we had come. If there is such a thing as an Ayahuasca contact high, I had it that night.

Later, back in L.A., when riding our bikes along the beach path, Mike and I would recall our trip with awe:

MIKE: It's the greatest thing I've ever done.
PAUL: I'll never forget it. Do you still listen to the tape?
MIKE: Every day. I love it. Did you bring your purple jacket?
PAUL: Luckily, I did.
MIKE: Did you see that? Deep purple. A twelve!
PAUL: A nine and a half. But she's only fourteen.
MIKE: I'd pay ten thousand for one night.
PAUL: Five thousand . . .
MIKE: I'd like to take her to the Amazon . . .

12

The Betty Ford Clinic

We were living on Alpine Drive in the flats of Beverly Hills. One day I went into the lush alley behind our house to throw some garbage into one of the large green Dumpsters that the city of Bev Hills gives you, when I saw a homeless man pushing a supermarket wagon filled with old clothes, tin cans, and a small brownish dog. The man stopped at a Dumpster halfway down the alley and found some food in it for his pooch.

Lightning struck! I saw scenes from an old French film run through my mind: *Boudu Saved from Drowning* by one of the masters, Jean Renoir. In that humorous and touching film, Boudu is a *clochard*—a bum—in France of 1930. He's sick of life and tries to commit suicide by jumping into the Seine, but a bourgeois shopkeeper sees him jump and saves him. The shopkeeper takes Boudu into his home, and Boudu proceeds to turn everybody's life upside down.

I hadn't seen the film since my New York days where it had screened at the Museum of Modern Art, so I arranged to see it again. I called Leon Capetanos, my writing partner, and shared my flash with him: We'd make a modern-day *Boudu*, only this time the homeless guy tries to drown himself in a Beverly Hills pool. Leon loved the idea. We saw *Boudu* the next day.

As great as *Boudu* was we still imposed our own ideas on it, satirizing the nouveau riche of Bev Hills and coming up with a new ending. (In the original, Boudu gets married, but at the last minute he fakes a suicide and ends up floating down the river on his back, happy to be free again. We didn't think a homeless man today would be happy to be free, not in the violent world we now live.)

We pitched the idea to Guy MacElwaine, one of my former agents and now head of Columbia Pictures. Guy loved it and gave us the green light for the script. But three weeks later there was still no deal memo. Finally, Guy explained to my agent Jeff Berg that he was having trouble remembering the plot. This was a very strange canard, but who wanted to work with an executive who had memory loss? We immediately went to Frank Price at Universal. Frank had backed two of my toughest films, *Tempest* and *Moscow on the Hudson*. He agreed to finance the script, and Leon and I went to work.

About four months later we had a very good script. But I sensed something wasn't right. Price said he liked the script but wanted a new ending: He wanted Jerry (The Bum) to go off down the alley with the Whiteman daughter.

After a day of thinking about it, I told Frank that Leon and I disagreed. I wanted to shoot my ending, and if mine didn't work, then I'd shoot the alternative. A few days later Jeff Berg and Sam Cohn informed me that we were officially in turnaround, meaning that Universal wasn't going to go ahead with it. Turnaround usually means pure hell; a script that someone has passed on can get stuck in the studio swamps forever. But we knew this was a good script, and sure enough, within two days the agents told us that everyone wanted *Down and Out*. They recommended that we go with the new team at Disney, Michael Eisner and Jeff Katzenberg, and we did. My early meetings with Eisner and Katzenberg were splendid. They had very few notes; it was all a matter of casting.

During the period Frank Price had the project, I met with Jack Nicholson to discuss his playing Jerry (Boudu). The meeting took place on New Year's Day at Jack's house on Mulholland Drive. Various bowl games were blasting away on several TVs. A fellow I knew from New York was cooking veal and pasta. He welcomed me by offering a forkful of delicious hot veal. He was a crony of Jack's who owned a restaurant on Tenth Street in Greenwich Village, and he had flown in just to cook for his pal. There were others wandering around the house, but I was too intent on my upcoming meeting to pay any attention. I had gotten word from Jack's agent, Sandy Bressler, that Jack liked the script. Otherwise why the meeting? And on New Year's Day to boot. What a coup! Nicholson as Boudu (Jerry)! The quintessential rebel with the piercing smile picking garbage out of a Dumpster for his dog, Kerouac.

The smell of marijuana wafted through the air. Merely sniffing the stuff got me a little high, and I became a bit concerned—I didn't want to meet a stoned Nicholson. Rumor had it that Jack was almost always high, but that he functioned well and was totally professional. After a few minutes Jack asked me to join him in the living room to watch the games and "chat."

"How are ya?" he asked, smiling at me. Although we'd known each other since the early days at Columbia, I confess that I was excited to be sitting there with the great Nicholson. "Try this Maui Wowie. It's great shit," said Jack, offering me a toke.

I sucked in a deep puff and found myself suddenly unaware of where I was. "What did you put in this shit—Gorilla?" I asked. Gorilla was a pacifier used for large apes and had somehow become a popular drug.

"No, sir. It's pure Maui Wowie," Jack assured me.

We chuckled at nothing in particular. I found myself eating a piece of prosciutto. It was divine. I saw a quarterback throw a pass that seemed to hang in the air for minutes. Everything was very pleasant.

Then Jack leaned forward and lit another huge joint. "Try some of this Sensamilla. We're talking Russian River up north. Killer shit." I took a couple of drags on the new shit. "To tell you the truth, I'm too stoned to know the difference." I said. Jack smiled. My God he was perfect for Jerry. "What the hell. You don't have to know the difference to tell the difference, and if you knew the difference, it wouldn't make a difference. Let's go upstairs to my den for a chat."

I followed Nicholson up a set of winding stairs, passing paintings by several great masters. Jack sat down in an overstuffed chair, and I sat opposite him. There was no TV on, and the silence was welcome. Jack allowed as he'd like to play Jerry, but he'd do it only if I would play Dave Whiteman, the man who saves Jerry. I didn't know whether or not I was hallucinating. Me play Dave? Was Jack putting me on? He assured me he wasn't. I explained how tough it would be for me to both act and direct. "I'll need all my energy for you, Jack." But he would have none of it. I agreed to do it, already flashing my Oscar speech through my drugged mind: "I want to thank Mr. Jack Nicholson for believing in me . . ."

Then Jack threw a bombshell—I'd have to wait for him to finish another movie. "Are you shooting it now?" I asked. "Nah! It's a thing I promised Bobby Evans I gotta do. *The Two Jakes.*" "When would you do it?" I asked. Jack chuckled. "That's the problem, amigo. Could be a year from now. Just no telling. And I don't want to hold you up." My high dropped very low. I couldn't wait a full year, not even for Jack Nicholson.

A few days later I met with Richard Dreyfuss to discuss the role of Dave Whiteman. I'd known Richard since the early seventies when I tried to get him to play Larry Lapinsky in *Next Stop, Greenwich Village*. We'd also had a brief fling about Richard's playing the lead in *Moscow on the Hudson*. Both times it didn't work out. Years later Richard turned his car upside down in an accident. He walked out alive, but it was clear he'd been high on cocaine at the time of the accident. Now nobody was hiring this brilliant actor. I'd seen him in a play at the Mark Taper and checked with Gordon

Davidson, the director, who assured me that Richard was in fine shape.

When Dreyfuss came to my office, I asked him, "Who do you want to play, Dave or Jerry?" Richard smiled. "I'd be happy to play the dog, Kerouac." (There is a great dog role in the film.)

We agreed on Dreyfuss as Dave Whiteman. On to the search for Jerry. I thought about my old friend Warren Beatty. I imagined the handsome Beatty as the filthy bum who later gets cleaned up and yuppified. It would be very funny. Beatty expressed interest, but I knew that didn't really mean anything. In the past I'd met with him about doing roles in several of my films, but he'd done none of them. Years before, I had breakfast with Warren at the Beverly Wilshire Hotel to discuss *Alex in Wonderland*.

Blume in Love was a three month wait. Warren wanted to play Stephen Blume (George Segal eventually did it). But Warren made it clear that he'd do it only if his girlfriend, Julie Christie, would play his wife. Since I admired Miss Christie, this was a most delicious problem but four months later the whole thing fell apart.

Now, years afterward, I found myself waiting for a phone call, a message, anything from Warren indicating his decision. I'd wait three days and say, "Tomorrow I'm moving on to Nick Nolte," but then I'd give Beatty another three days, which took us into the weekend which gave him almost another week. Everyone I spoke to about Warren told me that waiting a long time for his decision was par for the course.

Beatty had told me he was going to Las Vegas to see his parents and his sister (Shirley MacLaine) and that he'd call me from there. That was four days ago, and I'd heard zip. Then my home phone rang. My teenaged daughters and a couple of their friends were in the downstairs bedroom, and Betsy was upstairs taking a bath, so I answered. It was Warren, speaking in a very intimate voice. "What are you doing?" I realized who it was. "Warren?" "Yeah. What's your address?" I was excited and pissed at the same time. "I gave him my address." "I'm in my car. I'll be right over." Before I could say another word, he hung up.

I ran into the next room and told my daughters that Warren

Beatty was coming over. They shrieked wildly. Two of the girls visiting them were quite beautiful. I also knew that girls of fourteen made Warren tremble. My God, I thought. Here I am using my own children and their friends to land a star for a movie!

"Betsy," I shouted up to Betsy's bathroom, "Warren Beatty is coming!" She called back, "I'm taking a bath." "I know. But come down and meet him. It's Warren Beatty." "I just got in the tub,"said Betsy.

The bell rang. I opened the large Spanish door, and there stood Beatty. He was very handsome even though he squinted at me. "Hi," he almost whispered, looking around. "What a nice house." I heard the girls shriek. Beatty turned. "Who's that?" "My daughters and some of their friends. Teenagers. You know." Beatty went right to the girls' bedroom. I introduced him. I must admit Warren handled it with great aplomb—just a nice, friendly fellow.

Then he joined me in my den. The den's walls are covered with family portraits and photos of many of the people I've worked with. Warren spotted a beautiful young blonde in a tub, her breasts covered with bubbles. "Who's that?" he asked me. "Betsy," I said, "my wife." "Wow," said Beatty. I commented, "That's an old picture. I mean, she's still beautiful. As a matter of fact, she's taking a bath right now." I shouted up to the second floor, "Betsy! Warren Beatty is here! Come say hello!" Apparently, she didn't hear me, since she never came down to meet Warren. He talked about the photo of me and Fellini, then said, "You want Jack. I know you do." "Jack can't do it," I responded. "He has to do *The Two Jakes* first." Beatty smiled. "Yeah, but you want Jack." I tried to convince Warren that he would be perfect for the part. I reminded him of how close we'd come to working together in the past. I wanted him even more than Jack now that I'd seen him again. Warren was perfect for that pure Americana white-bread guy who ends up down and out and loses all hope.

Warren said he'd let me know. He said good-bye to the girls and even called up a wan good-bye to the invisible Betsy.

I waited about a week to hear from him, but no call came.

I sent the script to Nick Nolte who, like Dreyfuss, was not

exactly having a thrilling career at the moment. The rumor was that he was drinking but I loved his work, and I thought he was right for Jerry. Nick read the script and asked to meet me.

I drove out to his place in Malibu. Nick was very warm but also very nervous. He seemed like a wounded bear, rough and grizzly and right on for Jerry. We poked around the script; finally I suggested that we read through the entire piece. He'd read Jerry, I'd play all the other parts.

Sometimes Nick read in a voice so low I couldn't make out what he was saying. But after a while he started to feel comfortable, and I knew he would make a brilliant Jerry. (Nick is one of our great actors, but he's never obvious about it; he just does the work without telling you how he does it.) Embarrassing as it was, I asked him about his health. Clearly I was talking about booze. Nick said he was just fine and added, "Why don't we drink to that?" I laughed, and we drank a grapefruit juice and vodka concoction while I offered him the role of Jerry.

All that remained to be cast of the three principals was Dave's wife, Barbara Whiteman. I'd always been a Bette Midler fan, so I arranged a meeting in my office on Beverly Drive. Miss Midler was announced. I opened my door and in walked a woman with reddish purple hair and a wide coat collar wrapped around her face, making it impossible to tell what she looked like.

"Hi," said Bette very shyly. She was even shorter than I'd expected. "I've seen just about all of your shows, Bette. I never went to the baths, but I've seen the others. You're great!" "Oh, that's so sweet of you," she said demurely. "But," she added, "I decked my last director. We got into a nasty spat, and I punched him in the face." "Was that Don Siegel?" I asked. I'd heard that she and Siegel had gotten into an argument, that Siegel had swung at Bette, and that she had decked him with a clean right cross. "Yeah. I knocked the little bastard on his ass." I laughed. "Then you're perfect for me."

Even with the collar covering her face I could tell she liked what I'd said. Bette slowly lowered the collar, and I could see her face: no makeup; looking tired. She had presented herself in this bizarre getup almost challenging me not to use her. Wild hair, sloppy outfit. It only served to turn me on. "You'll be great in this film, Bette." "Come on, Paul. Look at me!" "You'll get a makeover at a Beverly Hills salon, and you'll be Barbara," I told her. "Do you really think I can play this part?" she asked me. "Bette, you were brilliant in *The Rose*. And you'll be brilliant in *Down and Out*. Just don't hit me." She smiled, almost purring.

A couple of days later I met with Eisner and Katzenberg. "-I've got my cast," I told them. "Richard Dreyfuss as Dave." Eisner shrugged, "He's good. Fine." "Nick Nolte as Jerry." "Can he be funny?" asked Eisner. "I mean, I discovered Nolte when I was at ABC. Does he have any humor?" I explained that he didn't have to act funny. The situation was funny. He only had to be believable." Katzenberg nodded in agreement. Eisner said, "Okay, I'll go with Nolte. But who plays Barbara?" I paused. I knew my choice would either be met with joy or outrage. "Bette Midler," I said.

Eisner suddenly stood up and jumped, touching his hands to the ceiling. "I love it!" he shouted. Katzenberg grinned. "Bette is perfect! It's a stroke of genius!" said Michael Eisner. "See you in April."

He was in effect telling me to go make the movie. I was very happy. Later, in a meeting with Jeff Katzenberg, who is a great executive, I discussed the history of my three stars. I could tell that Jeff was a little worried. I had no anxiety about Bette but Nick and Richard might be trouble. "You mean why did I cast this film at the Betty Ford Clinic?" I asked him.

The trio of stars was on their best behavior for the entire shoot. I had zero problems. Often, rumor is more believable than truth in Tinseltown.

〰

Some of my fondest memories of *Down and Out* have to do with Mike the dog and Little Richard. When you cast an animal for a large role, you meet the trainer and the animal. Clint Rowe, the trainer, brought Mike to my office. Mike was a black-and-white Australian sheepdog. I asked the dog to sit down on my couch.

Clint said something, and Mike jumped up on the couch and sat there facing me. He looked as if he knew he'd get the part. There was no question in my mind that the dog understood what was going on and wasn't the least bit nervous about it. Most actors are nervous at auditions, but Mike the dog sat there confidently, his tongue partway out of his mouth.

Clint asked me questions that are usually asked by actors: "How old do you see Mike in your show?" "Does he like Dave more than Barbara?" "Does he believe Jerry's stories?" Sometimes Clint would say to me, "I don't think Mike would do that." I was astounded. "You're telling me the dog wouldn't put his chin on Nick Nolte's leg? Why? Why not?" Clint looked at me as if I was naive. "Because he'd know Nick is lying in this situation." "You're telling me a dog knows when someone is lying?" Clint frowned. "Absolutely." By God, I was working with a Method dog. I fell in love with Mike. He probably got more laughs than my three stars, and they never let me forget it. "That fucking dog is stealing the picture!" howled Bette in her best Mae West imitation.

Little Richard was my choice for the Whiteman's next-door neighbor, Orvis Goodnight. He'd never really acted before, but he was a hilarious personality, and I knew we could use a song or two of his. When I met him, I asked if I should call him Little Richard or Little or just Richard. "Oh, my," he said, "Richard is just fine, Mr. Mazursky." He pronounced my name perfectly. Everything he said and did made me smile.

I read him for the role and knew he could do it. I had only one fear: Could he learn the lines? The first scene with Richard was a night shoot on the back lot with a police helicopter overhead. The dog has accidentally set off the Whitemans' burglar alarm. Little Richard races out and complains to the police that they come right away for a white man (Dave Whiteman) but not at all for a black man. Then Mike the dog nips his trouser leg, and he flees into the night.

It was potentially a great scene, but Richard could not get through one take without blowing the dialogue. I begged him to just go on talking even if he missed a line. I had large cue cards with his lines printed up, but that didn't work because you could tell he was reading. The hours were passing. I was desperate. I took Richard aside and told him that if he didn't get it right on the next take, I was going to replace him with Sidney Poitier. "Oh, my!" he said, looking very worried. "I just love Sidney Poitier. Oh, my. Oh, my. Oh, my!"

The next take was magnificent, hilarious. We shot for a couple of hours more, until the sun was threatening to come up. I called a halt and told everyone we'd be back the following night to finish.

"Oh, but good Lord, tomorrow's Friday," said Richard. "I can't shoot on Friday night. That would take me into Shabbus." I did a double take. Little Richard was Jewish? I figured it was a scam to avoid working another night. I spoke to Richard's manager who was on the set and told him that Richard had to work. The manager responded with a straight face, "He really is Jewish, and he has to be at a synagogue on Saturday."

I went to the white stretch limo that Little Richard was sitting in. The darkness of the night was turning into that lovely early morning light. "I didn't know you were Jewish," I said. "Good golly! I certainly am, Paul. I'm a good Jew. I have to be in Sacramento on Saturday for the service." I couldn't believe what I was hearing. "You're a rabbi?" Richard frowned. "No, sir. I just help lead the Shabbus service. There is no way I can work Friday night. The good Lord would be angry with me. No way!" "Let me ask one question, Richard. Were you bar mitzvahed?" "No, sir. I became a Jew too late for the bar mitzvah." I saw an opening. "Well, I was bar mitzvahed, and I'm going to work tomorrow night." "I didn't know for sure you were Jewish," said Richard. I said, "Richard, if you don't work tomorrow night, it'll cost you about one hundred thousand dollars. Why don't you ask the good Lord to let you work this one Friday night?"

Richard thought about it for a moment, then said, "I think the good Lord would let me work, but only till two A.M. Then I can still make Sacramento."

"That's great!" I told him. What I didn't tell him was that a really devout Jew wouldn't travel on Shabbus. In any case, it all worked out, and Little Richard gave a brilliant performance that Friday night. That Saturday he led the service in a Sacramento synagogue. I wish I had been there.

13

To the
Finland Station

After completing the screenplay of *Moscow on the Hudson*, which was based mostly on interviews with Russians in New York and Los Angeles, Leon Capetanos and I felt we needed a trip to Russia to find out how accurate our screenplay was. There was no way to shoot in the U.S.S.R., not in 1983. I knew we could get in, but only as tourists, with enough freedom just to smell around. I wanted Pato Guzman, my production designer, to go with us so he could see the way Russians really lived: the apartments, the wallpaper, the furniture, the appliances, the cafeterias—in effect, the life. But Pato held a Chilean passport, and after the overthrow of Allende by the Pinochetists, he had, in fact, become the mayor of a small town in Chile called Pirque. These anticommunists were not welcome in the Soviet Union. So how to get Pato into Russia was a real problem.

I went to the Venice Film Festival before the planned trip to

Russia, and arranged for Pato to join me. Our strategy was to fly to Moscow via Vienna. I met Jack Valenti at the festival and confided in him. Jack, the suave head of the Motion Picture Association and former press secretary to Lyndon Baines Johnson, knew his way around. "I don't want the Russians to know I'm researching a movie about them. But how do I get Pato in?" I asked Jack. He told us that the head of the Russian film delegation was there in Venice. "Those boys want to show the world that you can do business with them," intoned Jack.

I don't remember the Russian's name, but we met at one of the great outdoor cafes in Venice. He wore a dapper brown corduroy jacket draped over his shoulders and used a cigarette holder to smoke his exotic cigarettes. The effect was a bit like Claude Rains. I told him I was going to Russia to visit Kiev, the city of my grandfather, that Pato was my best friend who wanted to go with me. Jack Valenti allowed as how pleased he would personally be if the Russian could help.

"No problem," the Russian told us. "I will take care. Please go to Vienna and apply for visa at Russian embassy there," he told Pato. It was a done deal.

We thanked the Russian and Jack Valenti, and flew to Vienna. Pato went to the Russian embassy, where they had him fill out a standard visa form and told him to bring in a new photo of himself later that day. We were very enthusiastic. Obviously, the Russian had pulled some strings.

Pato went back to the embassy two days later to pick up the visa, but he was notified that the request had been denied. They gave Pato the form with the photograph, and he left the building. Outside, he glanced at the form before tossing it into a wastebasket. He was shocked! The photograph they had given him was not the one he had taken two days before but was clearly a photo taken twenty years earlier. Amazingly, the Russians had an old photo of Pato in their Byzantine files, and they wanted him—maybe me, too—to know this.

It was with a certain misgiving that I took off from Vienna alone. Would I be met at the airport by the KGB? Had they secretly gotten hold of the script of *Moscow on the Hudson* from a spy at Columbia Pictures? Would Leon Capetanos arrive as scheduled two days later, or had the Russkies found a way to veto his visa as well?

✻

The airport in Moscow was dark and smelly. Everything seemed to move at a very slow pace. Every now and then somebody lugging a large refrigerator or a television set on his back would pass by. Large families of peasants wept as they said good-byes to relatives. The pungent aroma of pickles, salami, garlic, sweat, tobacco, and vodka hung in the air.

As I got closer to customs, I looked out at the sea of faces to see if anyone was there to meet me. All I had asked of Columbia Pictures (they paid for the trip) was to have a driver pick me up, but I could see no one holding up a sign with my name on it.

The silver-toothed customs man was very curt. There was obviously no concern about how tourists were treated. To put it simply, he was rude. "Purpose of visit?" (Visit was pronounced "wisit.") "I'm a tourist. Tourism is the purpose of my visit. My grandfather was born in Kiev." I smiled sheepishly at the customs man, the way one does when you feel guilty even though you've done nothing.

After about fifteen minutes I was out with the crowd. I must have been more nervous than I knew because by then I was sweating profusely; the incident with Pato had filled me with justifiable paranoia. I spotted a desk where other tourists were congregating and I gave my name to the woman behind the desk. "I'm supposed to go to the Intourist Hotel," I said. She looked down at a sheet of paper, then spoke to me in English: "Mr. Mazursky. Yes. You please will take taxi outside. Show this to driver." She wrote something on a piece of paper and handed it to me.

Ilya Baskin, my Russian actor friend whom I'd cast as the "Clown," an important role in the film, had told me that when in doubt tip and/or bribe with Marlboros. Also, don't be afraid to be rude. The Russians respect rudeness. I handed the piece of paper to the taxi driver with a pack of Marlboro Reds. He smiled with appreciation and started the motor. It coughed weakly and died. After the third try we were on our way.

The city I saw through the taxi window seemed more like the Old West than the capital of the U.S.S.R., but I was excited. Russia! Moscow! Land of my forefathers! Everything looked drab until we got further into the city, when some larger buildings came into view and I saw crowds on the streets. I waved as if to say hello; no one waved back. I wondered if they all knew that I was here to research their lives: ("Look in taxi, comrade. There is Mazursky, capitalist spy.") Suddenly paranoid again, I wondered if I should hire a food taster.

We arrived at the Intourist Hotel where I was met by a doorman wearing an ankle-length blue coat with oversized gold epaulets that must have survived czarist days. I handed him a pack of Marlboros, and he tipped his hat. The large hotel lobby was almost as grim as the airport. The concierge, a woman of about forty, checked for my name. "Yes. Mr. Paul Mazursky. You have fine room, sir. Very best suite. Maeterlinck Suite." I asked her why it was called the Maeterlinck Suite. "Miss Elizabeth Taylor has lived here to make film *Bluebird* by Maeterlinck. Also, Mr. Brezhnev stay in Maeterlinck Suite." Why was she trying to impress me, I wondered. I was positive they knew who I was and that as a result I was going to be spied on. I had asked for no special treatment, so why the hell were they rolling out the red carpet?

I carried my bags up to the room since there was no bellhop in sight, and let myself in with a key the size of a cucumber. It wasn't a room—it was six rooms. There was a grand piano, a dining table for twelve, three bathrooms, two bedrooms, and one small piece of used brown soap. The furniture was early Tijuana. I tried the telephone to call someone Ilya Baskin had suggested I contact, but I couldn't get through. Either the line was busy, or I wasn't really calling out of the hotel. After ten minutes I gave up and took a hot bath in a huge tub. I began to relax but soon found myself staring at the ceiling looking for hidden wires.

I went down to the hotel restaurant for my first Moscow

meal. I asked the waiter if he spoke any English. "Yes, sir. How may I be of service?" I pointed at the menu. "Is the borscht hot or cold?" He leaned in and whispered, "Two hundred rubles for your wristwatch, sir." I laughed. Now I knew that our script was accurate, that Moscow was as fucked-up as we had imagined it to be.

Later that night, after reading for an hour or so, I was hungry again. I went down the long corridor of the hotel to find the floor woman—every floor of every hotel in Russia has one. This was a woman of either sixty, which she looked, or thirty-five and the victim of Russian life. I told her I was hungry. I used sign language since she didn't speak English. I mimed myself eating and patted my stomach as if to say, "I'm starving." She shook her head negatively. "Restaurant closed," she said in English. So I went back to my room. Fifteen minutes later there was a knock at the door. I opened it, fully expecting to see the secret police. It was the floor woman, holding a large can of pineapple from Afghanistan. She smiled and handed me the can. I was astounded. Then she took an old-fashioned can opener out of her pocket and plunged it into the can. As soon as the can was opened, she practically curtsied. I thanked her profusely and she exited. I couldn't find a spoon or a fork, so I ate the pineapple with my fingers. It was gooey and super-sweet, but it hit the spot.

I went into the bedroom, looked up at the ceiling to the invisible bug wires, and said good night to my new Russian friends, whoever they might be.

The next morning I joined a half-day tour of the Kremlin. It was quite beautiful, just like in the postcards. The Intourist guide, a woman of thirty or so, spoke excellent English. I tried a joke or two on her, but she didn't react. At the end of the tour I asked her if the bus could let me off near the Aragvi Restaurant, and she happily agreed. "Good lunch in Aragvi," she said.

I'd been told by Ilya Baskin that the Aragvi was a favorite of sophisticated, well-off Russians, the kind who might speak English. The area in front of the restaurant was busy with people, and at the door I was stopped by another man in a long blue coat with gold epaulettes. He shouted something negative to me in Russian. I responded, "American. Americanski! Hungry! Lunchski!" The man waved at me, telling me to go away.

Then a man of about forty-five with a neat black beard and a handsome gray corduroy jacket said to me in English, "The Aragvi is too crowded, sir. You will not get in." I looked at the guy. "You speak English very well," I told him. "Thank you, sir. My name is Vladimir." "My name is Paul. Pavel in Russian." He responded, "If you are hungry, Pavel, we can eat in Minsk." I was astounded. "But Minsk is far from Moscow," I said. For the first time Vladimir smiled. "Minsk Restaurant. Ten minutes away. I drive you in my car." Was he KGB? I didn't know, but I was hungry. I agreed to go with him.

His car was tiny, sort of like an Italian Fiat. He handled the car with a certain brio, and we made it to the Minsk Restaurant. By now Vladimir had told me he was married, had two children— ages ten and seven—and lived in an apartment on the outskirts of Moscow. I told him I was a writer visiting the land of my forefathers. I said nothing about movies.

Just before we went into the restaurant, Vladimir told me not to speak English too loudly, that we would be seated at a common table with other people. Sure enough we were seated next to an army officer with a chestful of medals and a civilian in a European-cut suit. The Minsk was a very cheerful place. I saw no reason not to speak English, but I kept my conversation down to a whisper. The food was excellent.

Vladimir told me that he was a lawyer specializing in real estate. This surprised me. I didn't think the average Russian owned much real estate. "We are not talking average, Pavel," whispered Vladimir. When the check came, he insisted on paying for me. I was confused. Why all this sudden generosity from a total stranger? Was he gay? He said he was married, but that didn't mean anything. Was he KGB assigned to me?

Back in the car, he asked me if there was anything more he could do for me. "Well, Vladimir, I would love to meet your family and see your apartment." I explained that I was doing research for a book about Russia. "But of course, Pavel. Are you free tomorrow?" I explained that my friend Leon Capetanos was arriving that day. Could he come too? Vladimir assured me that it would be fine. He arranged to pick us both up in front of the hotel at 9:00 A.M. If this fellow was a spy, he was an awfully friendly spy, I decided.

I was happy to see that Leon had already arrived at the hotel. In a manic rush I told him everything that had happened. "Sounds like KGB," said Leon in his southern drawl. He was wearing a black beret and an olive raincoat, and looked like either a CNN reporter or a CIA agent.

The next morning, Vladimir seemed happy to meet Leon. He had driven all the way from the suburbs to pick us up and take us back to his apartment. In about thirty minutes we spotted a huge ring of tall, drab gray apartment buildings. "My home," said Vladimir.

We parked in a forlorn spot with a few bare trees and odd bits of garbage on the grass. The lobby was small and dark, all illumination coming from a single bare bulb. The place stank of piss. We got into the ancient elevator, after first letting out a woman of about sixty wearing a purple shawl on her head. She looked at us with a scowl of distrust. Vladimir smiled and told us that everyone in the building was suspicious of strangers. We met Vladimir's wife and his two adorable children. The apartment was furnished like a movie version of one's idea of a Moscow apartment: There was cheap-looking furniture that seemed to be from the forties, but beautiful glasses with silver handles for the tea we were served.

Vladimir's wife did not seem surprised by our presence. (Was she a spy, too?) I made Donald Duck noises for the kids. (I do a great Donald Duck.) They laughed at me. "Donald Duckski!" I said, like a moron.

On the way back to our hotel, Vladimir asked what we would like to see the next day. I told him he'd already been too kind, but he insisted. I said I would like to see the zoo. He was astonished but agreed.

Then he told us about his mistress. "She has apartment in Moscow. Also, I have two dachas. One for wife and one for mistress." Dachas are summer cottages.

"That sounds like a nice arrangement," said Leon.

I was impressed. "Big dachas?" I asked Vladimir.

"Oh, yes. Right on water."

"I hope they're not next to each other."

"Sounds like a good idea if they were adjoining dachas," said Leon.

Vladimir told us that he would like us to meet his mistress the next evening. "She will make party for you. Herring, black bread, vodka, sturgeon, caviar, Pavel! We have party for you and Leon. You will meet very interesting Russian people."

The next morning, outside the hotel, we waited near the curb for Vladimir. I had asked him to meet us in the lobby, but he refused. "I don't like to go into hotels. They know you are there."

"Who knows you are there?" I asked him.

"Authorities know."

Leon said, "You mean KGB?"

Vladimir shrugged. "Is better to meet me in front of the hotel."

The doorman in the long blue coat seemed to be staring at us. Just then Vlad pulled up in his car. "We go to zoo first," he told us. "You still want to go to zoo?"

"Oh, yes," I said. "You can learn a lot about a country from its zoo."

Vladimir looked forlorn. "Then we are in trouble in Soviet Union. Animals are starving."

The zoo was old, shabby and cold. Like almost everything I'd seen in Moscow, except Red Square and the Kremlin, it desperately needed a paint job. The animals seemed to know what a shithole they were living in. The ennui was apparent everywhere. We stopped in front of the lion cage where two lions dozed—exhausted, I imagined, from dealing with the Russian bureaucracy. A zookeeper in shabby green overalls shoved a large chunk of raw meat into the cage, then said something to the lions and left. Before the lions rose to claim their meal, an elderly man with a cane and a fur hat hustled up to the cage. He deftly poked his cane through the bars and pulled the meat to him. In less than ten seconds he was gone, with the meat hidden in his black valise. Leon and I began to laugh. This was a first! Stealing dinner from a lion. We had to get that into our script.

Vladimir shrugged. "People are hungry in Moscow."

The mistress's apartment was not far from Red Square, in a building that looked much more agreeable than Vladimir's. We noticed that all the shades were down even though it was still light. We asked Vladimir about this. "Oh. We don't want people staring at us."

The mistress, Tanya, was about five feet ten inches tall and quite attractive. She spoke no English and appeared to be sad. She opened a bottle of cold vodka for a toast of welcome. Later we realized that the Russians toasted everything. The table in the tiny apartment was filled with delicacies that Vladimir had purchased: caviar, potatoes, herring, yogurt, olives, meatballs, bread, butter, cookies, and half a dozen bottles of vodka.

There was a knock at the door. Tanya excused herself, then reappeared with two men in their twenties accompanied by a woman in her twenties. She was beautiful and dressed very well. One of the men carried a guitar and the other a tennis racket. The guitar man was introduced as the son of a famous Russian general from Kiev. The tennis man was a biologist, and the new woman was his girlfriend.

"I am Raissa," she said. "I am going soon to be arrested. I have already lost my post at TV station. Because of God. You see, I go to church. I am Christian. Is very dangerous to be Christian in Soviet Union, but I go. I believe in God. I would rather go to prison than give up my belief."

We were amazed that she would pour all this out to American strangers, but by then the toasts were coming fast and furious, and things had begun to blur.

Tanya put some soulful music on a record player that looked like a relic from the fifties. Vladimir urged me to dance with

Tanya. "I don't like to dance," he confessed. I could see Leon suppress a double take as I put my arms around Tanya. My head reached just above her sumptuous breasts. She was quite drunk and held me close. Leon was looped and began to chuckle. The dance ended. I wondered if Vladimir had noticed our erotic waltz. Was this another setup? Was Tanya another Mata Hari or Tokyo Rose?

I sat down at the table and ate a piece of salted herring, and suddenly I was back in Brooklyn, eating with my grandparents. Raissa went on with her despair. She said she knew that it was "only matter of time before they arrest me. I am Christian." "So am I," said Leon. "I am Greek Orthodox." Raissa smiled. "Oh, is so beautiful." Leon asked why she couldn't go to church; in our travels we had seen people entering one. "Old people," said Raissa. She told him that the government didn't want young people to go to church.

The general's son, Ivan, said that his father was a right-winger. "He hates me, sir. No freedom here, sir! No freedom!" (I remembered the Russian dentist I'd interviewed in Los Angeles. She'd told me that in Russia she woke up every morning feeling an invisible string attached to her head. The string jerked her here and there. She was a puppet. She had no freedom. But oddly enough, she confessed to me, now that she was free, she missed the puppeteer.)

The biologist disagreed with the general's son. "We have good life in Moscow. Plenty of freedom for those who take it. Today I played tennis." He told us that there were splendid tennis courts in Moscow, available free of charge to all citizens.

Vladimir laughed. "Available where?" he asked. "In Kremlin?"

Ivan began to play his guitar. I thought I could make out the tune to "We Shall Overcome," but I decided that I was just drunk. Then Ivan began to sing in a thick Russian accent: "Ve shall overcome, ve shall overcome. . . . Dip in my heart I do believe . . ."

It was all very confusing. Surely this amazing evening couldn't be a setup by Vladimir.

Finally, it was time to go. Vlad had to get back to his wife. We said our good-byes, hugging everyone, tears in our eyes. We had one more toast for the road.

The next day we were to leave for Kiev. Vladimir told us he would pick us up in front of the hotel and take us to the circus. Robin Williams was going to play a saxophonist in the circus orchestra, so it was vital that we see the real thing. By morning it had turned cold. The one-ring circus was charming and dynamic. Everybody seemed happier here, even the animals. The audience was filled with parents and children and grandparents. They stamped their feet on the floor to show their approval. My favorite act was the gray house cat who was held aloft on his rear legs by a trainer on a horse. As the horse circled the ring, another horse galloped by with a monkey on the saddle. The first rider tossed the house cat onto the other horse. Now the gray cat rode with the monkey. It was sublime.

Moscow was beautiful, funny, mysterious, dirty, depressing, filled with great energy. It reminded me of New York.

Vladimir was driving us back toward the hotel when suddenly he stopped the car and confessed that he had a brother living in Queens. He was, for the first time, very emotional. He said he wanted us to take his brother two wooden crosses, and he showed us a parcel wrapped in brown paper. It was about eight inches high and five inches across. "For you, Pavel, is easy to take to America. For me, not possible."

I looked at Leon. I told Vladimir that since we were eventually to leave Russia by way of the Finland station, I could not take anything out for him in a train. "Too dangerous," I told him. I was positive that Vladimir had found me in front of the Aragvi and had befriended me to get me to smuggle stuff out.

He understood what I was saying, and he assured me that we were still great friends. Then it was time to say good-bye. With tears in his eyes, Vladimir embraced me, a clumsy exercise in the tiny car. As he leaned over to hug me, he accidentally banged his elbow on the glove compartment. The door to the compartment fell open, and a gun clattered to the floor. It was a Biretta. I lifted it up gingerly. Vladimir smiled, tossed it back into the glove compartment, and closed it. "Is just toy. Toy gun for my son."

I didn't look at Leon, but I knew that we both knew this was not a toy gun. Later Leon and I tried every permutation of the Vladimir story. We finally decided he was KGB assigned to us but that he was also an intelligent and nice guy.

When we got back to L.A., I told Ilya about Vladimir. "Paul. He was most definitely KGB. Intelligent and nice guys can also be KGB." "But what about the crosses?" I asked. Ilya grinned. "KGB can also be Christian. Besides, who knows if they were crosses?"

From Moscow we flew to Kiev. The Aeroflot plane smelled as bad as the zoo. The seatbelts didn't work. The food was cold and bland. Half the people on the plane were Chinese men in dark blue Mao suits. The bulky stewardesses seemed right out of a Mel Brooks movie about Bulgaria. But finally we landed.

My grandfather had told me how green Kiev was, how many parks there were. On the ride into the city, the gloom of Moscow gave way to the possibility of joy. We checked into a cheerful hotel and had a decent lunch. Everyone was polite. There seemed to be less bureaucracy here.

We bought tickets to the Kiev circus and then went for a walk. In less than five minutes a young man came up to me and asked in English if I wanted to sell my Reebok sneakers. "No," I told him, adding, "What would I wear then?" The man assured me that he had plenty of sneakers available, but not Reeboks. He seemed quite open and intelligent. He told us he was an engineer, but by now Leon and I had come to understand that might mean a dishwasher. We asked if we could see his apartment. He was surprised, but agreed. We began to stroll toward his place on a lovely, wide, tree-filled avenue. At one point he saw two soldiers approaching us, and he whispered, "No English, please!" Then he pointed to a tall building across the street. "KGB," he said. Leon asked Pyotr (that was his name) if the KGB was watching us. "You never know," he said bitterly.

He lived in an old building dating back to the time of the czars. The lobby stank as usual. There were about ten names listed by the door. Pyotr explained that this once had been one family's home, but it was now divided into ten apartments, although they all shared one kitchen and one bathroom. When we got to the second floor, we encountered a dark entryway with half a dozen large doors that seemed to be exactly alike. One of the doors suddenly opened, revealing an angry-looking man of about sixty. He wore a striped bathrobe and was coughing and smoking. He scowled at us, and shouted something in Russian. Pyotr shouted something right back at the old guy, who then slammed his door shut. "My father," Pyotr said, dragging us into his apartment. "He hates foreigners."

A pretty woman of about twenty-two was introduced to us as Pyotr's wife. The small room contained a sofa bed with a colorful blanket on it; the walls were covered with dozens of American pins with English printing. Pyotr was very proud of his pin collection. Unfortunately, we had nothing to contribute, but we told him that at our hotel we had Marlboros, American magazines, and cologne that we would give him.

We heard a baby gurgle, and the young couple led us to a crib near the only window. "My baby," Pyotr said with a smile. His wife lifted the round-faced baby up for us to admire. "A boy?" I asked. "*Da,*" said the wife. The baby smiled.

Pyotr reached under the sofa and yanked out a flat cart on wheels. On it were two dozen or so pairs of blue jeans. "I buy from Finn people. Finns love wodka. Russians love blue jeans!" There was a tiny closet in the room. Pyotr opened it to reveal another dozen pairs of jeans. We told him apologetically that we were not in the market for jeans.

I had to pee. Pyotr led me out to the hall past the dark kitchen where a woman was cooking cabbage. She frowned at us. The small toilet had an unbearable stench. Someone had strung up several pairs of thick black socks and a few pairs of underwear to dry. I flushed the toilet. After an ominous sputter, it worked.

I went back to the hallway. Six doors that were exactly alike

stared at me, and I didn't know which was Pyotr's. It was like a
scene out of Kafka. Tentatively I called out "Pyotr," but nothing
happened. I knocked at a door, and it flew open. It was Pyotr's angry, coughing father. Another door opened, and Pyotr yanked me
in. His father, he informed us, was an old-line communist and was
pissed because his son hated the communists.

We thanked the young people for their hospitality and made
an appointment to meet Pyotr the next morning with our care
package.

Later that day we took a taxi to Babi Yar, the shrine com-
memorating the brutal slaying of a hundred thousand Jews by the
Nazis and their Ukrainian fellow anti-Semites. In spite of the huge
communist-style statuary, Babi Yar was profoundly moving, and
seeing it, I better understood Yevtushenko's great poem. We saw
several wedding couples and their families posing for photos. Why
there? Why Babi Yar? It's Russia, we told ourselves.

That evening we went to the Kiev circus. There we saw
happy families, amazing trained poodles dressed like men and
women, monkeys who played Frisbee, and careening horses ridden by wild Gypsies. I could just see Robin Williams playing the
saxophone on the bandstand of this arena.

The next day we returned to the spot where we'd met Pyotr.
We had all his goods in a plastic bag: a copy of *Time* magazine,
some cologne, and six packs of Marlboros. We saw Pyotr approaching, a worried frown on his face. He was obviously scared.
"Please to keep walking," he said. We followed him. Leon held up
the plastic bag—"This is for you, Pyotr. Nothing much. Just some
Marlboros and toilet water and *Time* magazine." Pyotr peeked in
the bag and suddenly started to run. "Too dangerous!" he cried.
"*Time* magazine too dangerous!" he said, tossing the bag into a
wastebasket. We never saw Pyotr again.

That afternoon we hired an Intourist guide. She spoke perfect English, but she wasn't very friendly. I told her that my grandfather, Samuel Gerson, was a Jew from Kiev. "I want to go to a
synagogue," I told her. She assured me that there were many syna-
gogues in Kiev. "Good. Please take me to one," I said. "A very sim-

ple matter, sir," she said. She spoke to the driver in Russian. For
the next hour we rode around the streets of Kiev, but they couldn't
find a synagogue. Then the car stopped. The guide pointed to an
old redbrick building across the street. "There, sir! There is your
synagogue. But you go alone. I don't go to synagogue!"

Leon and I crossed the street. As we approached the building, several women hurried inside. They seemed to be afraid of us.
Then an old man wearing a brown fedora leaned out of a window
three flights up. He shouted something in Russian, and he
sounded angry. "Americanski!" I shouted back. He seemed confused. Then I cried out in my best ragtag Yiddish, *"Ich bist a Yid!"* (I
am a Jew!) The man smiled and said in Yiddish, *"Com stu, boy-
chick!"* (Come up, sonny.)

The synagogue reminded me of the little storefront shul in
Brownsville where I'd been bar mitzvahed. And it was Rosh
Hashanah! New Year's! What synchronicity! I was not a believer,
but it was getting dicey. The man in the brown fedora was the
shammes, the caretaker of the synagogue. He told us he had a sister
in Queens. It seems almost everyone in the Soviet Union has a relative in Queens. I asked him if there was a Gerson in the congre-
gation. He shook his head. I asked him if things were bad for Jews
in Russia. He looked at me with utter resignation. *"Vu den?"*
(What else?) Then he invited us back for the New Year's services. I
still regret that we did not go.

The next morning we flew to Leningrad (now St. Peters-
burg). We were getting to be old Russia hands. We were now used
to the planes, the food, the almost constant stench, but nothing
prepared us for the beauty of Leningrad. It was Paris combined
with Venice! Hordes of energetic people on the wide streets, people who appeared to be right out of a Dostoyevsky novel. Men with
long wild hair, Rasputin style. Women in short stylish skirts and
long colorful dresses. Everyone seemed to be in a great hurry.
There were many female vendors selling ice-cream cones and pickles and hot sweet potatoes. Every now and then we'd see a group of
people scurrying to form a line. "What are they selling?" I asked a
trotting soldier. "Who knows?" he answered as he got into line.

As usual we took a stroll near some restaurants, and sure enough, a young man came up to me. "Three hundred rubles for your coat, sir." I told him no. I said we were writers interested in Russia, wanting to see if this scared him. "What kind of writers?" he asked. "We write for movies," Leon said. As we crossed a large avenue, the young man said, "Do you know Mr. Dustin Hoffman from *Kramer vs. Kramer?*" (Kramer was pronounced like the word "cram.") "Why, yes, as a matter of fact I do know Dustin Hoffman," I told him. He was mightily impressed. We decided to have lunch together. He seemed fearless. He told us what seemed to be the same old story—that life in the U.S.S.R. was brutal.

〰️

There was no circus in Leningrad that week, but the Kirov Ballet was opening that evening. I hurried down to speak to the concierge at the hotel, a stout, corseted woman. "I need two tickets for the Kirov for tonight," I said innocently. The concierge snorted. "My dear sir, there are no tickets for the Kirov tonight! This is the Kirov, sir! The world-famous Kirov! Tonight they dance *Swan Lake.* Opening night, sir! No tickets, sir!"

Things looked grim, but I remembered what Ilya Baskin had told me about being rude and tough on the Russians if I really wanted something. With quiet power I leaned in toward the concierge and said, "And what is your name, please?" She blanched but gave me her name. "Thank you," I said. "My name is Paul Mazursky, and I am the head of the New York City Ballet. If I don't have two tickets for tonight, I will have to report you." "The New York City Ballet?" She was aghast. "But, sir, please return in twenty minutes. I will see what I can arrange." She was all smiles now.

I hurried away, very pleased with my lie. Fifteen minutes later we appeared at the concierge's desk. She smiled coquettishly and handed me a large envelope. "Front row, center," she said.

Leon and I had learned that in Russia you were not likely to get food after 9:00 P.M. The ballet would not be over until 10:00 P.M. so we bought a very large bar of chocolate, one that seemed large enough to feed a family of four. When we arrived at the Kirov, we were secure about food.

The building was magnificent, and the crowd walking up the ornate staircase was wonderfully cosmopolitan: Men wore well-cut suits, capes, sweaters over a shirt and tie, here and there a man in blue jeans and a tweed jacket. Women in gowns, short skirts; peasant women wearing babushkas. True democracy in action, we thought. The Soviet Union may have been long on spying and short on freedom, but ticket prices made it possible for everybody to go to the theater, the circus, and the ballet. It was a powerful reminder of how little the U.S.A. cared about the arts.

We found our seats, which were indeed in the front row. As we looked about us, Leon and I tried to guess what various people did for a living. The two seats to my right were occupied by two attractive young women. I nudged Leon, and he smiled. I asked the girls if they spoke English. They shook their heads. "Americanski," I said. "We are American." They seemed to understand. I made some silly-looking ballet movements and asked them if they liked ballet. They giggled. Leon giggled.

Then I remembered the chocolate. I took it out and offered it to the girls. "Would you like a piece of chocolate?" I asked, affecting a Russian accent. The girls looked at each other, and then the one nearest me took the huge chocolate bar. We were very pleased. Maybe we could find a club later and have a drink with these young women. They proceeded to strip the tinfoil off the chocolate and eat the entire bar. They reminded me of piranha as they sucked the chocolate down. One of them folded the tinfoil into a small, neat square and gave it to me. She thanked me in Russian. Leon and I went to bed hungry that night. But, the *Swan Lake* was breathtaking.

The next morning we took the train to the Finland station. We had a compartment to ourselves, but we soon made friends with people in the other compartments. None of them were Russian, and all of them couldn't wait to get out of Russia. As soon as the train started, two young soldiers came into our compartment to check our passports. They questioned Leon about a large book he was carrying, something about space by James Michener. Leon tried to explain that it was a novel, not a scientific treatise, but they didn't understand what he was talking about. They asked to see our wallets and proceeded to empty them. I was glad we hadn't brought Vladimir's crosses. After about fifteen minutes of this routine, the young soldiers left.

The trip through the Russian countryside was dazzling. Somehow we were sad at leaving. We saw villages made mostly of wood, beautiful old churches, animals grazing, an amazing sunset. Absolute Tolstoy! Finally, after many hours, we passed from Russia into Finland. It was an invisible passing except for a lone sign that read FINLAND. As the Russian soldiers got off to return to Leningrad, everyone on the train began to cheer.

In a few months Robin Williams would play a Russian saxophonist who defects for freedom. Leon and I had begun to believe in our script.

〰️

In 1991, about nine years later, I went back to Moscow for the first Moscow Jewish Film Festival, at which I was to show *Enemies, A Love Story*. I brought my two daughters with me. I wanted them to see the land of my grandfather, but they hated it, which upset me greatly. They insisted on eating mostly Pop-Tarts, which they had bought at the airport in L.A. All they did was complain: The hotel was disgusting (It was, but so what? We stayed at the Rossiya, probably the largest and worst hotel in the world); the food was vile; and the place was dirty. Also, we had trouble finding each other at the Rossiya. The girls stayed in one wing, and I had a miserable roach-filled room in a wing a block away. Everything wrong with Russia was crammed into that hotel.

The festival had been organized by several bright women from San Francisco with very little money but a lot of heart. Anti-Semitism was still going strong in the new Russia, but there were signs of freedom. In fact, the Jewish Film Festival could never have taken place ten years earlier. Things were so open now, rumor had it that the KGB was going on strike for shorter hours and higher wages.

I finally got my daughters out into the streets. We drove to an outdoor market that reminded me of Tijuana, Russian style. They were selling old nails, used pots and pans, cherries, rocking chairs, Marlboros. A four-piece band played "As the Saints Go Marchin' In."

The screening for *Enemies* took place in an old shabby theater. There were no subtitles; the translation was done live on a microphone, by a Russian woman who had seen the film that morning. She played *all* the parts. I dreaded the experience. But the audience of Russian Jews liked the film. When it was over, many of them were weeping. My daughters, too, were in tears, which made me happy.

Afterward, a man in the audience stood up and told me that he had spent six months in prison after being caught watching a black market videotape of *Moscow on the Hudson*. "It was worth to be in jail for your movie," he said. Then he walked up to me and took his watch off. He was giving me a gift, his Russian army wristwatch. I tried to refuse the gift, but he would have none of that. Later that evening I tried the watch on. It looked wonderful, but it didn't work. Russia!

How ironic. In 1991, freedom was in the air—but still nothing worked.

14

Ode to Shelley

In 1975 I made *Next Stop, Greenwich Village*. It was a rite-of-passage movie, mostly about my own experiences in the early fifties. It's about a twenty-one-year-old Brooklyn boy who finally leaves home and gets his own apartment in Greenwich Village. He wants to be an actor. I was remembering my life of twenty-odd years ago. Both my parents, Jean and Dave, were dead, so I could write without fear (although I was positive at the time, and still am today, that Jean was watching).

My "big" romance with my girlfriend Naomi was a centerpiece of the movie. I changed her name, and I changed Howard O. Sackler's name. Sackler had written *Fear and Desire*, the first film I acted in. He also two-timed me and broke up my relationship with Naomi. I cast Ellen Greene and Christopher Walken in those roles.

For my mother, I picked the legendary Shelley Winters.

Many people warned me that Shelley would be a pain in the ass, but I was fearless. My father was played by Mike Kellin, and he was uncanny. He caught every nuance of this hardworking, brow-beaten man.

I auditioned just about every young actor in Hollywood and New York for the role of Larry Lapinsky. Is it possible that no one seemed right or quite good enough because the actor I wanted was really me? At the eleventh hour, Juliet Taylor, the ace casting director, told me about a young theater actor, Lenny Baker. He had a hook nose that Alan Ladd, Jr., thought you could "cut bread with" (spoken at the first day's dailies by Laddie). Lenny Baker was perfect. It was apparent to me during rehearsals that this could be an extraordinary film.

Shelley came up to me one morning and asked me if my mother had been a great typist. "Who told you that? I asked, stunned. "Nobody told me anything," said Shelley. "Answer my question." I told Shelley that my mother could type 120 words a minute. She was a whiz. "She had a lot of part-time typing jobs," I added. "I knew it," said Shelley. "I just knew it. She also loved the movies, didn't she?" "Yeah, but you can tell that from the script." (One of my favorite lines is when Shelley says to her Hollywood-bound son at the end of the film, "If you happen to see Clark Gable, tell him your mother loves him.") "Oh, yeah," Shelley said with a smirk. "Where in the script does it talk about her loving foreign films?" In some uncanny way, Shelley Winters was fast becoming Jean Gerson Mazursky. I didn't realize it, but I was reacting more like Shelley's son than the director of a movie.

For the most part Shelley behaved very well, but then came the scene of the parents' first visit to Larry's Greenwich Village cold-water flat. Shelley takes one look at the place and is disgusted by the rathole her son has moved to. She opens a huge shopping bag full of goods. First she hauls out her son's shirts and underwear, which she has washed and ironed (just as my mother had done). Then item by item out of the brown paper bag comes lox, cream cheese, apples, his rubbers (for the feet), a bag of rye bread, a chicken, and a pot to cook the chicken in.

In the middle of this hilarious sequence, Shelley suddenly stopped acting. She opened the bag of bread, looked at it, and sniffed it as if it were poison. "This is not rye bread!" she shouted. "What do you think, I was born yesterday? I want real fucking rye bread!"

The dreaded moment had come. There was madness in Shelley's eyes. I took the bag from her, and sure enough there was a loaf of commercial rye bread, not the authentic Yiddish rye. "But this *is* rye bread, Shelley!" She flipped. "It stinks! It's practically white bread, it's so bad! It smells like a detergent!"

I looked around and saw the crew staring at us. Was Mazursky going to handle Winters? I had a divine rush of inspiration. "Shelley, do you mean a rye bread like the rye bread from Ratner's?" "You'd better believe it!" said Shelley.

The property master leaped into the fray. "That'll take at least an hour, boss. Probably more with traffic and all." Shelley shouted at him, "Why the hell didn't you go there in the first place?"

I opened the loaf of bread and smelled it deeply. "Ahhhhhh! Now that is a Ratner's rye bread if I ever smelled one." Shelley looked at me as if I was Hitler. "Shelley, you are one of the great actresses of our time. You've gone from playing a sexy ingenue in *A Double Life* to that that poor miserable girl in *A Place in the Sun.*" I could see that my words were having some effect. Shelley peered at me, "I also happen to know, Miss Winters, that you teach at the Actors Studio. I find it difficult to believe that you cannot find a sense memory from your past of the smell of a Ratner's rye bread."

The crew turned their heads from me to Shelley, to me, and back to Shelley. I think they thought the jig was up. "Besides, I am not waiting two hours for a Ratner's rye bread!" I said this with great authority.

With a sudden flirtatious smile, Shelley looked at me and said, "Of course I can make myself believe it's a Ratner's rye." "Thank you, Shelley," I said. Then Shelley smirked. "But don't think I fell for that other crap, kiddo!"

I can truly say I love Shelley Winters. Here's what Pauline Kael had to say about her in *The New Yorker:* "You can't get enough of Shelley Winters' performance. With her twinkly, goo-goo eyes and flirty grin, Shelley Winters is a mother hippo charging—not at her son's enemies but at him. Fat, morose, irrepressible, she's a force that would strike terror to anyone's heart, yet in some abominable way she's likable." This was an uncanny piece of writing. Pauline Kael had just described Jean Mazursky.

The reviews for the film were mixed, but Miss Kael's rave made me feel very good. Business in the States was only fair, but we were chosen to go to the Cannes Film Festival. I was thrilled but nervous. I knew that *Bob & Carol . . .* and *Harry and Tonto* had been successful in Europe, but I also knew that it was impossible to predict a festival audience's reaction. So it was with some trepidation that I walked into the Palais du Cinema with Shelley Winters on my arm.

The movie began, and within minutes the audience began to stamp their feet loudly at the sounds of Dave Brubeck. I whispered to Shelley, "They hate it! Let's go!" "No. They love it!" she said. "In France foot stomping is good." The mostly French audience went mad for the film. When the lights came on at the end, Shelley and I took a ten-minute bow. I was stunned. Later that evening, at a party for *Next Stop*, Alan Ladd, Jr., came over to congratulate me. Laddie is not normally a man who shows much emotion, but it was impossible for him to hide the single large tear that rolled down his cheek.

I wished that Lenny Baker had been there to savor this moment. (Lenny died of cancer a few years later. He was only thirty-six.) The next morning Denise Breton and Marc Bernard, the French publicists for the film, told me that Shelley and I should wait around in Cannes because we had a real chance to win the grand prize. The French press was highly complimentary, and we were now a dark-horse favorite. Denise Breton was the hardest-working publicist I've ever known, and she had already done wonders with *Harry and Tonto* in France. Marc Bernard was a dark-haired man in his late thirties who chain-smoked Gaulois and complained of piercing migraine headaches. I liked both of them.

Shelley and I agreed to stay until the prizes were awarded. The buzz on the winner was getting more and more pro *Next Stop. . . .* I was certain that the worst we could do was best actress for Shelley. On the fateful morning Marc Bernard told me to wait in my suite. The jurors decision would come at high noon, and Marc would rush up to give me the word. Marc chain-smoked three Gaulois just to give me this bit of news. He complained of a killer migraine. I told him to relax. "It's only a movie," I lied.

At five after twelve there was a knock at my door. "Come in," I called. The door opened, and Marc stood there, crestfallen. "*Rien,*" he said with a sigh. "*Rien.* We have nothing." "Not even Shelley?" I asked. "*Rien.* . . . Paul?" I was depressed. "What, Marc?" "Who will tell Shelley?" He lit another cigarette. I felt pity for this poor publicist about to feel the wrath of Shelley Winters. "I'll tell her, Marc." He thanked me and fled.

I had a moment to myself. Why the hell was I so blue? After all, the film had had a great reception. I took the elevator up to Shelley's suite, knocked on the door, and Shelley opened it. I shrugged. "Nothing, Shelley. We got nothing." Without pausing to take a breath, Shelley shouted, "Those anti-Semitic French bastards! Let's get out of this joint!" She picked up her two suitcases, which were already packed. I hurried down to get my bag, and in a matter of fifteen minutes Shelley Winters and Paul Mazursky were on their way to the airport.

"How come your bags were already packed?" I asked Shelley. "Are you kidding? The minute you want to win real bad, you're bound to lose!"

The first time I worked with Shelley was in *Blume in Love* with George Segal and Susan Anspach. That was the first film I made after living in Europe for six months. Segal played a Beverly Hills divorce lawyer whose own marriage falls apart. Shelley Winters played a hysterical woman who wants a divorce. It seems her husband has fallen in love with an airline stewardess. "A cockeyed air-line stewardess!" she wails. I wanted her to be sobbing right at the beginning of the scene. "Then I need *Madame Butterfly*," said Shelley. I didn't know what she was talking about. She explained that the one thing that made her cry was to hear the aria "Un Bel Dia" from the opera *Madama Butterfly*. Naturally, we didn't have a recording handy, but Shelley was adamant. It took about forty-five minutes, but we found a tape. Shelley listened to a few bars and began to weep.

Now came the first take. The tape was in a stereo next to her chair. First she took a large vitamin bottle out of her enormous purse and drank from it. It was wine. Then she turned the stereo on, and the aria began. In seconds, Shelley began to weep hysteri-cally. Then she deftly turned off the recording, continuing to weep, and nodded to me to start shooting. The scene was hilari-ous. Shelley did it at least five times. As soon as each take ended, she quickly stopped crying. She repeated the same process every time—the vitamin bottle, the aria, the weeping, and the nod to me. Amazing!

About twenty years later I again cast Shelley as a version of my mother. This time the film was *The Pickle* with Danny Aiello as Shelley's big-shot movie director son. He's been living in Paris and is down on his luck, but he has finally made another film. Un-fortunately, he hates it. It's teenage drivel about a flying cucum-ber. He goes to see his mother in Coney Island and commiserates with her.

The scene was set on the boardwalk. Shelley immediately told me there was no way she could walk that entire "rotten boardwalk. My back is killing me." I got the bright idea of putting Shelley and Danny in one of those boardwalk carriages. "No way," said Shelley. "They'll think I'm crippled if I ride in some cart. This is a woman without self-pity!" I reminded her that she had just told me her back was killing her. "That's my business," said Miss Winters. "Let's shoot it already. I'll walk even if it kills me." She did the scene beautifully. As soon as the take was over, the cart was rushed to Shelley, and she rode back on it to do the scene again. "You know something," she said, "I kind of like this cart."

15

Love in Bloom

I wrote *Blume in Love* in Los Angeles after I returned from living in Rome and London. First, I tried to raise money for *Harry and Tonto*, but no one wanted to finance a film about an old man and his cat searching for a home. Josh Greenfeld and I had written a poignant and funny script. Many people admired it, but no one would put up the money.

I had lived in Europe with the romantic notion that it was a better place for an artist. Now I was back in Hollywood, and the same old crap was hitting the fan. I didn't know what to do. Out of desperation I agreed to direct a script called *Flasher* about a cop who secretly flashes. It was meant to be a black comedy and would star Burt Reynolds.

The night of the day I agreed to do the film was a long one. I couldn't sleep. I turned the movie over and over in my burning brain. At seven in the morning I called Freddie Fields and told him

I wanted out of *Flasher*. Freddie didn't argue with me, but he insisted that I personally call the Universal studio executive. I did so and was very relieved. For better or worse, I was going to stick with my old game plan and write or cowrite my own films. Even though *Harry and Tonto* was sitting there, it didn't mean it wouldn't eventually get done.

I got a free office in my agency's building. I had a typewriter and paper and pencils. For several days nothing happened. My mind was blank. I began to regret not doing *Flasher* because here I was sitting in a room without an idea in my head. But at the end of the first week in the office, an entire script miraculously appeared in my mind. A man is sitting in a cafe in Venice, Italy, surrounded by lovers of all ages. His voice-over tells us that he is a divorce lawyer from Los Angeles who is also madly in love. The problem is that he's in love with his ex-wife. The script poured out of me— the present, the past, the immediate past, back and forth between Venice, Italy, and Venice, California.

Blume's one indiscretion had been a romance with his secretary. When his wife, Nina, came home early one day and discovered the two of them in bed, she just walked out of the house, never to return. The idea came from a show business couple I knew. One day the newly married wife came home early and discovered her husband in bed with his secretary. Without a beat, she ordered her husband out of the house and it broke his heart, just like Stephen Blume.

I hired George Segal to play Blume and Susan Anspach to play Nina. I completed the principal casting with Kris Kristofferson as the hippie musician Nina starts seeing, and the unknown Marsha Mason as Blume's new girlfriend. The shooting went well except for one thing: There was a bizarre tension between George and Susan. Maybe it was the actors identifying with their roles. Maybe George/Blume was mad at Susan/Nina because she kicked him out of the house. I had no idea why; I only knew that this probably was not good for the film.

By the time we arrived in Venezia, George had become more irritated with Susan. When Susan heard about it, her skin would turn deep red. She's a great actress who cannot hide her sensitivity. But somehow George masked his true feelings on screen. (George Segal, one of our best comedians, has a sense of irony and a feeling for urban man that makes you both like him and care about him. In spite of tension between my two stars, the shooting went well.)

Venice is the most beautiful city in the world, and it worked its usual magic. After three weeks we returned to Hollywood for the last few weeks of shooting. Things continued to be tense (just like the relationship between Blume and Nina. Blume somehow wormed his way back into Nina's life. He is now part of a *folie à trois*—Nina, Blume, and Elmo), but the dailies were consistently excellent. The film was coming to an end without a major incident. Then the dam broke.

I arrived on the set at Warner's Burbank and was immediately greeted by the assistant director, Tony Ray. "George is in his trailer and won't come out," said Tony, chain-smoking. I lit my own cigarette. "What's the matter?" I asked, a sudden feeling of nausea overcoming me. I could see by Tony's eyes that this one was going to be tough. "George says that Susan stole his Eye Bleu." "And what does Susan say?" Tony explained that Susan not only denied the accusation but was weeping hysterically in her trailer. "What the fuck is Eye Bleu?" I asked Tony. "Some French eye-drops that make your eyes shine. A lot of movie stars use them." So banal I couldn't believe it. "Why the hell doesn't he use another bottle?" Tony smiled grimly. "There is no other bottle of Eye Bleu. Not in this country." "You think she swiped it?" I asked Tony. He smiled. "Naw. She's a method actress. She makes her eyes shine from inside." Tony knew a lot about acting. He had starred in John Cassavetes' first film, *Shadows*.

I headed straight to George's trailer and knocked on the door. "Yes?" I heard George say very calmly. "It's Paul. I want to talk to you, George." "Sure. But I won't act until she returns my eyedrops." I opened the trailer door. There was George sitting in a cross-legged yoga position, wearing a short Japanese robe. His expression was blissful. "George, you know she didn't steal your Eye Bleu." "Oh, yes she did." "But why? What good would it do

Susan?" George chuckled. "It's bad for me. That's what's good for her." "But why is it bad for you?" I asked him. "Because I act better with Eye Bleu in my eyes. It's that simple, Paul." I told George that I was going to talk to Susan and straighten this thing out. "You're wasting your time," George said, closing his eyes and going back to his meditation.

I hurried over to Susan's trailer. I could hear her weeping. I knocked at the door, and she sobbed, "Come in." Her tear-stained face was a bright crimson. Even if we went right to work, makeup would have to redo her face.

"Susan, I know you didn't steal George's eyedrops." This made her cry even more. She blew her nose. "I'm a method actress. I don't need eyedrops to act." I tried to reason with her, improvising that George was probably suffering end-of-film blues. "We're coming to the scene where you open the door to take him back. It's very emotional." Susan turned a shade redder. "It's very emotional for me, too, Paul!" I tried my best to calm her down, but to no avail.

I went out and found Leo Lotito, the wily makeup man. "Come on, Leo. Can't you find another bottle of this French shit?" Leo shook his head. "It's all gone, boss. And you know it comes from Paris, France." "Look again, Leo! There must be another bottle of it!"

I hurried back to Susan's trailer and put my ear up against the door. I heard subdued sobbing. I rushed over to George's trailer and heard absolutely nothing. Maybe my paranoid star was sound asleep while I was on the verge of cardiac arrest. Then I saw Leo hurrying toward me. He held up a small, dirty bottle of Eye Bleu.

"I found an old bottle, boss. But there isn't jackshit in it." I grabbed the bottle from Leo's hand. It had a bluish tint. I whispered, "Get some Murine and put a few drops in the fucking bottle, Leo! Then wait a few minutes and tell George you've found some Eye Bleu!" Leo, who'd been around movies for many years, didn't even blink. "Yes, sir, boss!"

A half hour later my two stars came out of their dressing rooms. Susan's coloring was almost normal. George seemed very content. His eyes shone with the joy of triumph. Only Leo and I and Tony Ray knew that we had faked George Segal into thinking Murine was Eye Bleu.

To this day I don't know the truth of the matter, but I strongly suspect that Leo had indeed run out of Eye Bleu. I do know that Segal and Anspach were terrific in *Blume in Love*. When I saw the finished film, which ends with the very pregnant Anspach joining Segal in the Piazza San Marco to the strains of the love theme from Wagner's *Tristan und Isolde*, I felt a deep urge to weep. Art, after all, is magical.

16

How I Became
a Woman

Film ideas come from strange places, sometimes in your dreams, sometimes from the daily paper, sometimes from a word or a phrase. *An Unmarried Woman* came about because a friend of Betsy's and mine—Caroline, a divorced woman of about forty-five—told us that she had just bought her first home. Caroline showed us the deed of purchase, and on it I read that she was identified as "an unmarried woman." The State of California apparently identified women as married or unmarried. That was enough to get me going on the script. *Moscow on the Hudson* was written because a young Russian student at NYU had told me about his miserable life in the U.S.S.R.

Sometimes an idea doesn't work right away, but you keep at it; it can take a month or two to realize you don't have anything. So it was with a great deal of cynicism that I took a phone call in my L.A. office. My secretary informed me that a man on the

phone had the rights to old movies that were flops, "but he thinks
they have great ideas." This was impossible to resist. I told the
gentleman, whose name was Gary, that I was very skeptical. "Just
tell me one of the ideas, okay?" Gary reeled off a brief plot, and I
instantly rejected it. "No wonder it bombed!" I told him. He
pitched another bad movie idea, one even sillier than the first. I
just wanted the conversation to end when Gary told me about a
fifty-year-old film with Akim Tamiroff playing an actor who pre-
tends to be a South American dictator. I loved Akim Tamiroff. (All
the comics used to impersonate him in his role in *For Whom the
Bell Tolls*. His famous line—to Gary Cooper, I think—was "I don't
provoke.") I arranged for Gary to show me the film. He had a
video of it, not a print, which was not a good sign.

But Gary was right: the movie, as bad as it was, had a great
premise. An actor in a second-rate touring troupe is forced to impersonate a Latin-American dictator when the real dictator dies in
an earthquake. In my mind, a story fell into place very quickly. My
film would be as much about the desperate need of actors to "act"
as it would deal with the absurdity of Latin-American politics. I
showed the video to Leon Capetanos, my longtime writing partner, and he liked the notion. I pitched the idea to Frank Price who
was now the head of Universal. We quickly made a deal. A week
later Leon and I went to work. We invented a country called
Parador, which was run by an alcoholic dictator and his insane
minister. Our actor would be shooting a low-budget film in
Parador when the summons to "play" the dictator arrives.

In 1988, Pato Guzman and I settled on Brazil as the best
place to shoot *Moon Over Parador*. Pato, Leon, and I had already
scouted Guatemala, Salvador, Veracruz, Mexico, and various back
lots in Hollywood, but none of those places seemed right. Location scouting can be fun, but it can get confusing. You are looking
for a dream you've had of an unknown but familiar place.

Guatemala was too dangerous. (At the American embassy the
chargé d'affaires told me that filming in Guatemala would be a bit
like walking in Central Park at night.) Also, the extras in
Guatemala would be brown skinned; I wanted black people, a

Caribbean texture, for this comic-opera film I had in mind. Salvador was even more ominous. Almost everywhere we drove we saw buses stopped at the sides of highways while armed soldiers rudely searched the passengers who stood meekly, arms over their heads. It was a page right out of a report from Amnesty International. We were getting good stuff about dictatorships for our film.

We tried Jamaica, but there was no large plaza. At one point we considered Chile where Pato was from, but we didn't think that Pinochet the dictator would approve of a comedy about a man like himself. Pato Guzman was my closest friend and coworker, a brilliant production designer with endless humor. The paradox of this situation was that Pato sympathized with the Pinochet government but could also laugh at its pretense: the outrageous uniforms of Latin American generals, the vulgar machismo, the hilarious pomp (eight thousand extras doing aerobics in the plaza as their dictator leads the way), the curious tango of daily life.

Finally, visiting Brazil, Pato and I saw Ouro Preto. It was my dream come to vivid life. Ouro Preto is a "designated landmark" town, and it looks today just as it did three hundred years ago. It has a plaza of enormous charm built in the Portuguese style, not to mention the availability of thousands of black extras at seven bucks a day from the nearby Samba schools in Minas Gerais, the mining center of Brazil. Everything fell into place. "The dictator can make his speeches from that balcony!" I said. "And we can do the aerobics scene right here in the plaza." Scene after scene leaped into our minds. Gita Engelhart, our vivacious Brazilian production manager, assured us that she would get all the necessary permits. "We need permission from every shop in the plaza plus an okay from the museum. I will get it! I promise you!" We phoned L.A. and told the studio we had found the perfect location.

Back in Rio, as I was preparing for the return flight to L.A., I found a message waiting for me at the hotel. "Please call Adolpho Bloch," it read. I presumed the reference was to an actor looking for a job, since in Brazil it is not uncommon for the actor to call the director himself.

I dialed the number. A secretary answered. "I'd like to speak to Adolpho Bloch please," I said. "Who shall I say is calling?" "Paul Mazursky." I found it strange that an actor had a secretary, but I figured it was a service.

In a few seconds I heard a heavily accented voice say to me in English, "Mazursky?" "Yes," I answered. "I am Adolpho Bloch. I am your *'mishpucheh'*." His accent seemed Russian-Jewish with a taste of Portuguese.

"My *mishpucheh?*" I asked him with some skepticism. *Mishpucheh* was a Yiddish term for relative. As far as I knew, I had no relatives in Brazil, but I also knew that actors were capable of going to bizarre lengths to get jobs, especially Brazilian actors looking to score in a Hollywood film. "I'm afraid this is a bad time, Mr. Bloch. I'm just about to leave for the airport." Bloch just kept talking: "Mazursky, I want to make for you blintzes and chicken soup and matzo-brei. Hot pastrami and pickles. Yiddish food." Did the guy work in a delicatessen? I wondered. I repeated to Bloch that I had to go, but I promised to call this desperate actor when I returned to Rio in a month.

Downstairs, in my car, I asked Gita if she knew of an actor named Adolpho Bloch. Gita looked at me as if I were crazy. "Why do you ask me this, Paul?" I explained about the phone call. She was thrilled. "If Adolpho Bloch says he is your relative, then please, Paul, I urge you to be his relative." She told me that Adolpho Bloch was the owner and founder of the Manchete publishing and television empire. "Is like *Time* magazine," she added. "Very powerful. He is for sure one of the richest men in Brazil. He can help with anything—permits, money. My God, this is wonderful news, that you are related to Mr. Bloch."

"How old is he?" I asked. I was beginning to wonder if I could have a distant relative in Brazil. "Oh, about eighty years. I don't know him personally, but he is very powerful man. Oh, boy, he is rich!"

A month later, back in Rio for preproduction and rehearsals, I remembered Adolpho Bloch and decided to call him. "Mazursky. Come please for lunch. Tomorrow at my office." It was an offer I couldn't refuse. I decided to take Pato with me. At about twelve-thirty the next day we took a taxi to the Manchete building. I was wearing a pair of tennis shorts to fight the heat in Rio. Pato wore his usual good-taste outfit, a pair of chinos and a white shirt. As soon as we got out of the taxi, I knew I was badly underdressed. It was a magnificent structure overlooking Sugar Loaf Bay. The lobby walls held extraordinary modern art. The receptionist looked at me as if I was a nervy delivery boy. When I announced that Senhor Mazursky was here for lunch with Adolpho Bloch, she suspiciously called up. Someone said something to her, and she turned to me and flashed a great Brazilian smile. "Mr. Bloch is expecting you, senhor."

Pato and I got into the elevator. Pato said, "I have the feeling that I am underdressed for this event, Pablo." "You? Look at me! I'm in my underwear!"

The elevator doors opened, and before we could say a word, I heard a man shout, "Mazursky!" I quickly looked around. We were in a massive room with a fifty-foot dining table. At least fifty men and women, many of them in full-dress military uniforms and others in suits and dressy frocks, stood facing us, smiles on their faces. Then the voice reached us in person. He was a Russian-looking man, squat, full of energy, about eighty. He embraced me. "Mazursky! I am Adolpho Bloch. I am your *mishpucheh!*" His arms gripped me tightly. This old guy was strong. "I didn't realize that lunch was going to be formal, Mr. Bloch. Sorry. I'm wearing my rehearsal clothes," I apologized. "Wear what you want, Mazursky. Come, have a caiparinha." He picked up two glasses off a passing tray and gave one to me and one to Pato, whom I had just introduced. Adolpho explained that he had arranged this luncheon for many of the great people of Brazil. "They want to meet my relative who is a famous film director." We drank a toast. The caiparinha is composed of sugarcane, alcohol, ice, limes, and lots of sugar. After one sip you are in near oblivion! All my inhibitions about my tennis shorts vanished. I smiled at Pato who was taking his second sip. He weakly whispered to me, "I can do no more work today, Pablito."

Bloch led me around the table for a series of introductions. Most of the crowd was perfect for *Parador*. Then suddenly, tears in his eyes, Adolpho cried out, "My sister! Here is my sister! She was married to Mazursky!" An attractive, smallish woman of at least seventy, dressed with great style, came up to me. She took a long look at me, then touched my cheeks. She began to sob. I held her in my arms. She was speaking Portuguese. "What is she saying?" I asked Adolpho. "That you are the same face as her late husband. He was Mazursky just like you. From Kiev!" The sister spoke no English, so I tried some Yiddish, the international language of Jews. She smiled at me; she spoke Yiddish perfectly. Mine was not very good, but we were able to communicate.

I was caught in a strange dilemma. Was this sobbing woman really related to me? Would I blow the Bloch connection if I denied their claim? Was I indeed related in some distant way to her dead Russian husband? I was by now pretty loaded. I told them that my mother's father, Sam, was from Kiev. The sister doubled her weeping. "We are from Kiev," said Bloch, teary-eyed. "Yes. But my name comes from my father's side. Mazursky is more Polish, from the Pale of Settlement where the Russians sent the Jews." This didn't mean a thing to him. "My sister says you are the same face exactly as her late husband. You are Mazursky." It was settled.

I learned that Adolpho Bloch had come to Brazil in the 1920s from Kiev. He'd been a linotype operator. Within a decade he became a printer and finally a world-class publisher. He left us for a moment to speak to an admiral. Pato, exhausted, was slumped in a chair at the dining table.

In my makeshift Yiddish I explained to the sister that I was a movie director. Her eyes lit up. She told me that she had studied acting with Stanislavsky himself! And she had appeared at the Moscow Art Theater. Amazing! Adolpho returned with another caiparinha. I downed it in two gulps, the ice stabbing at my eyeballs. Uncertain of my Yiddish, I asked Adolpho to retranslate. "She was actress in Moscow with Stanislavsky," he told me. This was too weird. I had studied the Stanislavsky method with Paul

Mann and Lee Strasberg. I had even spent three months in Mexico City studying alone with a Japanese-Mexican teacher named Seiki Sano who had been a student of the great Stanislavsky. I decided that the sister was somehow a blood relative. I was close to tears and really drunk. I held the little sister close. The diners applauded as we sat down to eat. Adolpho Bloch toasted me. Pato was barely awake. (The meal was perfect: borscht, potatoes, sour cream, blintzes, and a variety of Brazilian specialties.)

Later, when we got ready to leave, Adolpho said to me, "Whatever you need, you have from Adolpho Bloch. You need money, you have it, Mazursky." I told him that I had plenty of money to make the movie. "But maybe I'll need some help down the line, Mr. Bloch." "Then call me. It is yours." I promised him that I would.

〜

Richard Dreyfuss played both the dictator and the New York actor who is forced to act the dictator when the real dictator dies of cirrhosis of the liver. Raul Julia, his hair bleached white-blond, played the Naziish minister. Sonia Braga, the splendidly sexual Brazilian actress, was the dictator's mistress. (In *Parador* she then becomes the actor's mistress.) I liked the script a lot. I felt that it was potentially commercial as well as smart. In Dreyfuss, Julia, and Braga I had three great actors. To complete the major roles I cast Jonathan Winters as a flaky CIA man, Fernando Rey as the dictator's ever-stoic valet, Sammy Davis, Jr., as Sammy Davis, Jr., Charo as the dictator's buxom maid, and Judith Malina (cofounder of the Living Theatre) as the dictator's elderly, forgetful, and near-sighted mother. The rehearsals were held in the Copacabana Hotel in Rio de Janeiro (the same Copacabana that Orson Welles had stayed at in the forties while, back in Hollywood, R.K.O. was re-cutting *Magnificent Ambersons*).

The rehearsals were hilarious. Raul had been brilliant in *Tempest* as Kalibanos, the goatherd. Now, as the evil power behind the dictator, he was frighteningly malevolent and outrageously funny at the same time. (When Dreyfuss as the dictator is apparently assassinated, the crowd turns on Raul Julia. He falls to the cobblestones, dying, and mutters "I hate actors.") Sonia Braga is a very smart actress who uses her sexuality with deceptive ease; she is also a woman of no pretense. She's hot without being girlishly cute. Richard Dreyfuss again proved to me that he is one of our great actors, possessed of a range usually reserved for the Brits. Winters and Rey were perfect.

Fernando Rey was the suave Spanish actor who had starred in several wonderful Luis Buñuel films and also in *The French Connection.* I stood in awe of Fernando. He immediately caught the essence of the joke of *Parador.* I treated him with kid gloves. Then one morning he asked if he could speak with me. "Of course," I told him, worried. He smiled. "Paul. I know you have great respect for me so you say very little to me. But, please, I beg of you, treat me like the dog-actor that I am! Help me! Please! I am only an actor!" He was an irresistible man.

My only real problem at rehearsals came because I had cast Rene Kohldehoff in the role of Gunther, the dictator's barber. Kohldehoff was a German actor whom I had seen in prominent roles in several films. His English was excellent (I had spoken to him earlier on the phone). His large weathered face was perfect, hawk-nosed and elegant, easily at home as a Nazi in hiding.

Albert Wolsky, the costume designer who has been with me for twenty years, approached me with a puzzled look on his face. "Paul. Have you met your 'Gunther' yet?" I sensed something odd in Albert's voice. "No. He got in from Berlin last night." Albert smiled weakly. "Oh, so you haven't met him?" "No. What's the matter, Albert?" "Had you planned on him playing Gunther as a man who has just had a stroke?" "Stroke! What are you talking about?" No matter how turbulent the air ever got, Albert always remained poised. "The man has clearly had a stroke. He can barely walk. I was taking some waist measurements, and I asked him to turn around. Paul, he couldn't turn around." I was speechless. Albert continued, "And I don't think he can speak very well."

I raced down the corridors of the Copacabana Hotel. I found Rene Kohldehoff standing in our production office. He looked absolutely perfect. I introduced myself, my heart pounding.

"It . . . is . . . a . . . great pleasure . . . to . . . meet . . . you, Mr. . . . Mr.—" I said, "Mazursky." "Ya! Mazursky!"

Rene didn't sound at all like the man I'd spoken to on the phone months before. "Are you all right, Rene?" I asked him. "Oh, yes. . . . - It's just . . . that I had a . . . little setback . . . but, please . . . I . . . can do . . . the film. . . . Please—"

I told him I'd see him later at rehearsals, but I knew I had to make a quick decision. Should I get another actor, which could take a week or two and really fuck up the schedule, or bite the bullet and risk all with Rene, who was perfect except for the fact that he could barely walk and talk? I decided to gamble. The shooting was a nightmare. Many of Rene's lines were to the valet played by Fernando Rey. Rene never said two lines in a row correctly. It wasn't his fault. He was clearly suffering from something physical. His line readings when he managed to get them out were brilliant. Fernando never once betrayed the slightest impatience or anger at his fellow actor. Always the perfect gentleman, just like the valet he was playing, Fernando helped guide poor Rene through take after take, even to the point of an incredulous look every time Rene blew a line, a look that somehow seemed absolutely appropriate. Thank you, Fernando!

Only Sammy Davis, Jr., and Judith Malina were not present for rehearsals. They were due to arrive two days before they were scheduled to shoot their scenes. We managed to rent the lobby of the Rio Opera House for three days. It was an almost exact replica of the Paris Opera House. There we would shoot the great ball of Parador and then the scene where the actor (playing the dictator) meets his mother who has just returned from a shopping spree in Paris. Our production manager, John Broderick, made the routine phone call to Los Angeles to make sure that Miss Malina had her plane tickets. He was astounded to learn from her agent that Judith Malina was in Germany directing an opera. "How the hell is that possible?" I shouted at Broderick. "The agent fucked up," he told me. "Well, let's call her in Germany. We still have two days!" I was in shock. Judith was perfect for the part. Geoff Taylor, one of my coproducers, offered to speak to the Germans in German.

While they were trying to locate Malina, I began to think about who else could play the mother. There was the great Zoe Caldwell, but could I get her on one day's notice? And we had to shoot the scene that week because after that I'd lose the opera house.

"I've got her, Paul," shouted Geoff. "She's crying. She says it's all a big mistake."

I grabbed the phone, and a weeping Malina begged me to get her German boss to let her go for several days so she could fly to Brazil. Judith sounded perfect even on the phone. "I'm directing a student opera, for Christ's sake. We have plenty of time."

We got the opera manager's number from Judith, and Geoff called him. Geoff's German was good but not good enough to sway this anal asshole. Judith Malina was a memory, and I had to quickly replace her.

Ellen Chenoweth, the casting director, soon told me that Zoe Caldwell was on a motoring trip in the States and couldn't be found. We tried another couple of names but had no luck. They were either already working or just not around. In one of those moments that are never clear as to why they occur, I asked Ellen if she thought I could play the mother. "I'll wear a hat and veil and a dress, and do it in a high voice." I improvised the voice—sort of like my mother's voice.

Ellen regarded me with suspicion. I was famous for putting people on. "Well," she said, "I'm not crazy about the Brazilian actresses we met. . . . I don't know." She took a long swig from her ever-present bottle of Evian. "I'm going to ask Dreyfuss," I said. Ellen agreed that this was a good idea.

On the way to meet Richard I passed Pato and told him that I might play the mother. Pato laughed. "Why not, Pablito? This is Parador!" I found Richard, and he regarded me with total seriousness. He suggested I read with him. After all, the scene was between the dictator (actor) and his mother.

I found myself in the curious position of auditioning for a role in my own movie and as a woman. I read with Dreyfuss. He never cracked a smile. "You've got the part. You're perfect," he said. "Just make sure they give you a nice dress." I hugged Richard, "Thank you, my son."

I soon found Albert Wolsky and told him about Judith Malina and Zoe Caldwell. Albert shrugged with deep resignation. "So what will you do, Paul?" "I'm going to play the mother." Albert smiled weakly. "And I suppose you get to keep the dress." This in reference to my habit of always keeping the clothes of the roles I acted in. I told Albert that I was serious. Without losing a beat he asked me what size shoe I wore. "I'm a nine in a man's shoe. I don't know what it is for women." Albert's color was fading fast. "The shoes are a big problem. Let's get your measurements right now for the dress. I think something in basic black, eh?" said the implacable Albert.

Two days later I found myself tottering on high heels up the steps of the opera house, my silk-stockinged legs bowed in my black knee-length frock and a large black chapeau on my head with a veil covering my face. I wore red lipstick, too much rouge, and a beauty mark on my cheek. Playing the mother was the highlight of my acting career. Now I knew just how far an actor would go to get a part.

⁂

A week later we stopped our work in Rio and moved the company to Ouro Preto, where we found our hotel to be quite modest. It was the best hotel in town, but that wasn't saying much. It was clean, however, and ideally located. Sammy Davis had requested the biggest suite the hotel had, plus a couple of rooms for his assistant and his bodyguard. We were also informed that Sammy traveled with twenty-two pieces of luggage. Geoff Taylor told me, though, that the biggest suite they had wouldn't hold all that luggage—it was a room just slightly larger than the others.

Pato and I had met Sammy in Las Vegas months before. He was outrageously wonderful. Huge glass bowls of Pall Mall cigarettes and candy bars were all over Sammy's monster suite at the Sands. I promised him that we would take good care of him in Ouro Preto, but now, as I walked down the corridor of the hotel, I felt a certain trepidation. As Pato, Geoff, and I approached the suite I noticed a dozen or so large trunks in the hallway. Seated nearby were two beefy Brazilian security men. Geoff explained, "They couldn't fit all his trunks in the room, so we put them in the hall." Pato and I laughed. We knew we were in for a rough time.

I knocked at the door. Sammy's right-hand man, a guy of about sixty-five, told me right off that "the boss ain't none too happy with his accommodations." Then a tallish younger man with a British accent introduced himself as Sammy's security. "Sammy's a bit peeved," he whispered. "Rather smallish room."

We stepped further into the room. There were trunks everywhere, their goods displayed for all to see: dress shirts, cuff links, trousers, cigarettes, videos, shoes, stockings, cans of strawberry soda—all of the paraphernalia someone on the road might deem necessary. Then I saw Sammy—in the middle of the king-sized bed. He seemed tiny. I began to worry. I knew that he was having severe hip problems, and now he had to deal with this room.

"Hi, Sammy. It's great to have you here in Ouro Preto."

Sammy sat up and propped a large pillow behind his head. "I feel like shit," he said. "First, the flight from Vegas to Miami. Endless. Then Miami to Rio. The food was like cardboard. The trip must've taken a couple of days. Then Rio to a town called Belo Horizonte. That miserable flight near killed me. But best of all was the limo that took us from Belo whatever to Ouro Preto. Limo, my ass! It was a Chevy with springs coming out of the seats and shooting straight up into your ass. My hips are destroyed. I know I can't walk. So, yes, Paul Mazursky, it's great to be here in Brazil with you and yours!"

I couldn't stop laughing. Sammy got out of bed and gave me a big hug, but I knew that he meant every word he'd uttered. Jonathan Winters had just arrived and was in the same hotel. He kept complaining about the low per diem. There was a horrible inflation in Brazil, so the weekly per diem came in huge bundles of cruzados. Winters was pissed. "Takes two million cruzados, or whatever the hell you call this dough, to buy a lollipop."

Jonathan and Sammy soon bonded. Each night they would treat us to an impromptu show in the hotel dining room. Most of the patrons spoke no English, so they had no idea what Winters was saying, but that didn't stop the great Jonathan. He did riffs for any Brazilian who would stand still. He even did his act on street corners for smiling but confused Ouro Pretans. Raul Julia sang Latin songs for us. It was more like a party than a movie location.

My only real concern was Sammy's hips. He used a cane most of the time, and it was obvious that he was in great pain. I was worried about his big scene coming up in a few days. In the midst of thousands of Paradorians in the great plaza, Sammy would sing the Paradorian national anthem. We parodied "Besame Mucho," and Sammy promised it would be wonderful. He had learned the new lyrics and felt fine. I just hoped that he could make it onto the samba float to do the number.

Two nights later, as the plaza filled up with seven thousand samba dancers, I went around the corner to say hello to Sammy. He was in the smallest trailer I'd ever seen. His tuxedo shirt was open to the fourth button. He smiled at me, looking about as tired as a man could be. "Welcome to my trailer. Fit for a munchkin, eh?" I told him I was sorry, but that was the biggest trailer we could fit into these small side streets. "Kid, just give me an idea how much longer it will be. I'll just take a nap." I told him it would take another couple of hours to get the crowd organized and the lighting ready. Sammy curled up on the small bed. Outside I asked his British security man if Sammy was okay. "You'll get a performance, all right, but the sooner the better is all I can say, sir."

About three hours later I knocked at the door to Sammy's trailer. He opened the door, yawning, "Ready, kid?" "Yes, Sammy. But let me prepare you. There are about seven thousand dancing Brazilians out there." Sammy chuckled. "I've played bigger rooms." He was noticeably limping as we turned the corner, but then he saw the vast, colorful crowd. Right in front of my eyes I saw Sammy Davis, Jr., get magically younger. He handed his cane to his man, straightened up, and tied his big bow tie. He was excited. "Where do you want me?" he asked. I steered him to one of the floats and said I wanted him to stand in between half a dozen gorgeous women with perfectly formed Amazonian bodies. He practically hopped onto the float.

For the next three hours Sammy sang perfect renditions of "Besame Mucho," Parador style, never off a beat. He had the body language of a man of thirty. The crowd went wild. It was impossible to get them quiet. They were here, after all, to party as much as to earn a few cruzados. When I finally called a wrap about five in the morning, I saw Sammy's body sag. They helped him off the float and handed him his cane. He was limping again, badly, and suddenly an old man.

"Thank you, Sammy." I put my arms around him. "I know you're in a lot of pain." He smiled wearily. "Just tell me one thing, kid. Did I do good for your movie?" I told him yes. "You were magnificent." "Great," said Sammy. "But, kid, there is no way I'll ever make this trip again." He waved at me and disappeared into his tiny trailer.

A few days later the company moved to Salvador, to Bahia, one of the most intense cities I've ever been in—humid, torrid, and where the jungle and the sea meet. We shot in a hotel that was once a monastery. I managed to get Betsy into a scene. She had one line to speak, and as usual she was perfect. As an American tourist standing on the buffet line she asks, "*Por favor*, but do you think the food is safe here?" Betsy was completely natural. Cassevetes would have loved her.

We returned to Rio for the last weeks of shooting. I managed to see Adolpho Bloch and his family several times while there. Indeed, it felt like a visit with relatives. I spent a weekend at Adolpho's country house in Petropolous and went with his son to a soccer match in Rio—130,000 screaming Brazilians shooting off fireworks and waving flags. So far I had not asked Adolpho for anything. Then Pato told me that he needed some classy contemporary art to decorate the walls of the minister's office. "Pablito, you remember all that good stuff at the Manchete building?" I called Gita and told her about my plan to call Adolpho Bloch. She laughed at me. "You may be his relative, Paul, but Senhor Bloch will never permit one of his paintings to leave the building. These paintings are for museums only."

I had nothing to lose. I got right through to Bloch. "I'm calling for a favor, Adolpho. A big favor." "It is yours whatever it is," he said. "I will still be your friend if you say no," I told him. "What is your favor, Mazursky?" I told him about the scene in Raul Julia's office. I told him what a boon his paintings would be for us. He paused for a second or two, then asked me where I wanted the paintings delivered. It was a done deal.

I gave Gita the news. She was shocked. "I cannot believe this! My God, you are really lucky to have such a *mishpucheh* in Brazil."

Marriage,
Yiddish Style

I had been interested in Isaac Bashevis Singer's novel *Enemies, A Love Story*, a darkly funny tale of Holocaust survivors living in New York in the forties. Since it was published in the early seventies I learned that the book was available, but I knew it would be easier to raise money for a film with a star attached. I sent a copy of the book to Dustin Hoffman, figuring he would be a perfect Herman Broder. I never heard from him. I forgot about *Enemies* and went on to write *Next Stop, Greenwich Village*. After every film I made for the next fifteen years, I would always return to the story of Herman Broder and his three wives.

I loved all of Singer's works—nonsentimental, funny, filled with marvelous detail and, ultimately, a biting portrait of Singer himself. In many of his novels and stories the hero is a man who cannot remain faithful to one woman. It smacked of something very personal. In *Enemies*, Herman has married the shiksa Yadwiga who saved his life in Poland by hiding him from the Nazis in a barn. Yadwiga and Herman live in a small apartment in Coney Island. The gullible Yadwiga knows nothing about Masha, Herman's mistress in the Bronx. The beautiful Masha is a concentration camp survivor. She is profoundly sad and profoundly sexual. One day Herman learns that a relative of his wants him to make contact. He does and soon discovers to his dismay that his "dead" wife Tamara is alive. She survived the awful days and nights of the camps. Left for dead in a mass grave, she escaped.

Singer's novel is a thing of beauty. By juxtaposing the three stories, we see that the hapless Herman is the true victim. I wanted desperately to make this film. After the success of *Down and Out in Beverly Hills*, I found an unexpected patron in Disney. They agreed to finance a script written by Roger Simon and me. (Perhaps this was a payoff for the large grosses of *Down and Out*. I remembered getting a large gift box from Michael Eisner after the film was clearly a hit. Inside was a white tennis shirt with Mickey Mouse on it. I ripped the cardboard box apart and searched through the wrapping paper. It just wasn't possible that all I'd get was a Mickey Mouse shirt. I figured there must be a check or keys to a Mercedes. I called my agents, who informed me that I was lucky to get the shirt.) I loved the concept of Disney doing the Holocaust! I was giddy! Maybe we could animate the rabbis and the Nazis.

The writing went well. Simon, who was already known for his Moses Wine mystery novels, was passionate about *Enemies*. In less than three months we had a script. We cut a lot of the book, but we felt that we had kept the power and the dark humor. We turned in the script to Michael Eisner and Jeff Katzenberg. "Do you think they really read the novel?" I asked Roger. "No. They must have read coverage," he said, smiling.

A few days later an inquiry was made as to what I thought the budget for the film would be. I ran it through my mind. It was a period piece, which means more money. I knew our chances of actually getting the project approved were slim to begin with, so I gave the lowest possible number. At the end of a week I was summoned to Katzenberg's office at Disney. Eisner, a tall, friendly-looking man, stood up to greet us. Everybody was very cordial. They liked the script but had some concerns. Was it all too Jewish? I reminded them that Singer had won the Nobel Prize, that the film would become universal by its specificity. I asked Jeff Katzenberg to play my cassette of Yiddish Klezmer music, and as the jazzy, haunted melodies played, I acted out scenes.

"How much will this cost?" asked Eisner.

"I'm not sure, Michael. I think I can do it for under ten."

Eisner was not happy. "Ten million is risky for this story. Can't you do it for less?"

"Shoot it in Canada," suggested Katzenberg.

I explained that because this was a period story, it would be difficult to do it for much less. "I mean," I told them, "it takes place in 1949."

Eisner thought for a moment. Katzenberg turned off the Klezmer music. "Why don't you update it?" said Eisner.

I saw Katzenberg's jaw drop. Update the Holocaust? What next? I thought. "Well," I said, "I suppose I could make Herman a Cambodian and have him married to three Cambodian women."

Eisner immediately understood his gaffe. "No, no," he said. "That won't do."

A few days later we entered the dreaded land of "turn-around," an elephant graveyard for film projects where many writers and directors go but few return. Sam Cohn and Jeff Berg, my agents, loved the script. They took it everywhere, but with no success. Nobody saw any bucks in this Yiddish tale. I had been in this position before with *Harry and Tonto*, *Tempest*, *An Unmarried Woman*, and even *Down and Out*. As Freddie Fields once told me, "You only need one 'yes,' kid." I kept repeating this splendid adage to Roger Simon.

Then I sent the script to Richard Dreyfuss, thinking he'd make a great Herman. Richard's response was quick: He agreed to do it. By some wonderful synchronicity, Irby Smith, who had been my first assistant director on several of my films, called me from New Mexico. Irby told me he'd heard through the grapevine that I was looking for financing for *Enemies*. "You know, Paul, I read the script. It's very beautiful." I thanked Irby. He told me that he was working on a western for Morgan Creek, a new company, and that Joe Roth, the copartner, was a big Mazursky fan. I didn't take it very seriously, but I gave Irby the okay to show Roth the script.

Two days later Irby called. "Joe loves it. He'll give you the money." I was shocked. "Joe Roth will give me ten million to make *Enemies?*" Irby said yes and that Joe himself would call within a day if that was okay with me. I was deeply touched by Irby's passion. Moreover, he asked for nothing. The next day Roth called and told me that Morgan Creek would back *Enemies.* I told him I had Richard Dreyfuss for "Herman" and probably Anjelica Huston for "Tamara." "She'll help us for foreign," said Joe.

I told him about my desire to use Lena Olin. I hadn't yet met her, but I'd seen her brilliant performance in *The Unbearable Lightness of Being,* a splendid film directed by Phil Kaufman. Lena was a great actress with an equally great body! I flew to London to meet with her, and she in turn flew in from Sweden. Over a two-hour breakfast I knew. She was "Masha"!

Back in L.A., Dreyfuss called and said he had a question for me.

"Shoot," I told him.

"I want to come to dailies? Your dailies, I mean." "Richard, you know my policy. No actors at dailies. I never feel free to say everything to the crew in front of the cast. I want to be free to say what takes I like or don't like. I want to tell the cameraman that it's too dark or too light. . . . and on and on." I could hear Dreyfuss's impatience. "But I'm not an ordinary actor, Paul. I'm your partner. For Christ's sake, I'm your Jew!"

I refused to budge, and a day later Richard withdrew from *Enemies.* A few days after that I flew to New York and saw Ron Silver in David Mamet's play *Speed the Plow.* Sam Cohn had recommended Ron for "Herman." I thought he was first-rate in the play. That night we had dinner after the show. Ron seemed perfect—his Lower East Side background, his knowledge of Judaism and the Holocaust, his ever-present irony. The next day I offered him the part. He accepted. I called Joe Roth and told him that Dreyfuss was out. Without a beat, Joe asked me, "Who do you have in mind?" I told him about Ron Silver. "I like Ron. That's fine with me." I was relieved. Joe Roth was a producer from heaven.

I soon completed casting. Margaret Sophie Stein would play "Yadwiga," Herman's shiksa wife. Alan King was the rabbi that Herman ghostwrote for; Judith Malina was Lena Olin's sickly mother (she'd better not be in Germany directing an opera). I would play Leon Tortshiner, Masha's jealous ex-husband.

As we were getting close to shooting, I met with Jim Robinson, Joe Roth's partner and the real money behind Morgan Creek. He reminded me of Brian Donlevy in Preston Sturges' *The Great McGinty*, a tough, confident guy with no frills. (Robinson is one of a kind in Hollywood. He gets right to the point. I like him.) Jim wished me luck and said he knew that I would be "fiscally responsible," and I was.

At the last moment, a week or so before rehearsals were due to begin, I decided to meet Isaac Singer, who was wintering in Miami Beach, Florida. I spoke on the telephone with Alma, Singer's wife: "Oh, Mr. Mazursky. Isaac will be happy to meet with you, but he is always a little tired." I assured Alma that I would fly to Florida, spend only an hour or two with her husband, and be on my way. All I wanted, I explained, was a few minutes. Maybe Singer would say something that would further illuminate his great novel.

A few days later I found myself in a taxi cruising down Collins Avenue in Miami. It was very hot; I arrived at a very tall beach-front apartment building. Alma greeted me in the air-conditioned lobby. "You are so much better looking than your pictures!" she told me in her Yiddish accent. "But you are much younger!" I assured her that I wasn't that young. "So," she said, "where would you like to meet Isaac? Out by the pool where he's sitting? Or upstairs in the apartment?" "It's probably easier to just go out to the pool," I said.

Alma was a very neat-looking seventy-plus woman—her hair and makeup were good, and she dressed simply and with excellent taste. "We have, *kinnahora*, a beautiful swimming pool. Olympic

size! Come, Mr. Mazursky, I'll take you." I urged her to call me
Paul, but she never did.

When we stepped outside to the pool area, I was almost
blinded by the sun. The blue Atlantic shimmered in the distance.
It was almost a David Hockney L.A. scene. There sitting in a chair
next to the pool, I saw Isaac Singer. He wore a seersucker jacket
and a pair of slacks that didn't match. On his head he wore a small
straw Panama hat. He was fast asleep. A Latina nurse wearing a
white uniform sat next to him. "I don't want to wake up your husband, Alma," I whispered.

"Listen, Mr. Mazursky, if you don't wake him up, then how
can you talk to him? *Nu?*" That made a lot of sense. She dragged
me over to Singer and said to him in a loud voice, "Isaac. Isaac!
This is Paul Mazursky, the boy who is going to make a moving
picture from *Enemies.*

Singer opened his blue eyes and looked up at me. He took
my hand in his and gripped it tightly. He spoke with surprising energy: "I didn't like vat Barbra Streisand did mit *Yentl!*" "Mr. Singer,
I can promise you that there will be no songs in *Enemies.*" He gave
me a weak smile. "You're a good boy," he told me. I chatted with
him about Coney Island, about the two pet birds Herman kept in
his Coney Island apartment, about where he got the story for *Enemies.* "I got the story from the cafeteria. What do you think, I
made it up?"

Alma nodded. "In New York City, Isaac always goes to the
same cafeteria," she said. "And everybody has some kind of story."

Singer told me that he had dozens of unpublished tales underneath his bed in their New York apartment. He seemed to drift
in and out—sometimes alert and sharp, and other times vague and
distant. The Latina nurse smiled at me. She was happy to see
Singer chatting.

"I'd like to show you photos of the cast, Mr. Singer," I said,
hoping I was doing the smart thing. What if Singer hated the pictures? Should I recast? I swallowed my paranoia and showed him a
glossy eight-by-ten of Ron Silver. "This is Ron Silver. He will play
Herman Broder." Singer looked at the picture and nodded. "He'll

make a good Herman," he said. I was relieved. I unfurled a photo of Margaret Stein. "This is Yadwiga, Mr. Singer, a Polish actress named Margaret Stein. She's a real shiksa." Once again Singer was positive. "A good Yadwiga." He seemed to be tiring, so I quickly went to Anjelica Huston. She was stunning even in her photo. "Here's your Tamara, Mr. Singer. A great actress. The daughter of John Huston" (as if Singer knew who the hell John Huston was). I felt as if I was pitching a studio head who was falling asleep on me. Singer nodded with approval. "She'll make a good Tamara," he said, stifling a yawn.

Now I brought out my pièce de résistance, a photo of the luscious Lena Olin. She stared right out at you, her intelligence and her sexuality indelibly there for one to see. Singer took this photo in his hands. He looked at it with more intensity than the others. He sighed and looked up at me. "You will make a good picture. A nice picture!" The old guy still knew a beautiful dame when he saw one.

W

We shot *Enemies* in eleven days in New York and about forty days in Montreal. The year 1949 was not easy to duplicate. The streets were now filled with parking meters. Television antennas dotted the skyline, cars were different, clothes were different—and we had very little money. In New York we shot in Coney Island, in the subways, at the Prospect Park Zoo in Brooklyn, on Riverside Drive and the Lower East Side. We filled the streets with pushcart peddlers, horses and wagons. A teeming crowd of extras fit right in. In Montreal, Pato built amazing sets for the three main apartments. We had researched everything and also tapped into my memory. I remembered my grandparents' apartment. It seemed so large to me when I was five years old, but when I left Brooklyn to move to the Village, their apartment shrank to its real size.

Everything about *Enemies* worked: Fred Murphy's camera, Pato's sets, Albert Wolsky's perfect period costumes. The actors were inspired. I was blessed. Stuart Pappe's first cut of the film gave me goose bumps.

About six weeks later we showed the film to Roger Simon, Joe Roth, Jim Robinson, Sam Cohn, Jeff Berg, and Jack Brodsky, the publicist. No matter what any filmmaker tells you, you are always terrified at this first screening. It's difficult to stay involved because you are terribly aware of every cut, of the bad sound, the temporary music, the black crayon marks on the film. You've told the assembled few about all these problems, but what the hell do they know? But this time I found myself deeply involved in the movie. There was a bit of appropriate laughter now and then, but nothing else that revealed a real reaction. As the movie was about to end, Anjelica holds up the baby, Masha, named after Lena Olin's character "Masha" who has committed suicide. Roger Simon gasped and fought back tears. So did I. It was a moment I've had only once or twice in my career. The last shot in the movie was the ever-spinning Coney Island Wonder Wheel.

The lights came up. Joe Roth came over and hugged me. James Robinson was very complimentary. Jack Brodsky, the cautious publicist, looked spent. "It's a great movie, Paul." Roger dried his eyes. Jeff Berg hugged me.

"I think Isaac would be happy," I said.

Roth told me that he wanted to test the film before an audience. "It's a classic," he said. I didn't know whether this was good or bad. Classics, like satire, usually die at the box office. To make big bucks in Hollywood you usually need one-syllable words and lots of sex and violence. *Enemies* had plenty of sex, but with a Holocaust accent. Just the thought of a preview caused my stomach to growl.

Stuart Pappé and I made a few changes, fixed the sound track a bit, and delivered the film for a preview at Fox. This was not an easy film to read. The audience laughed a bit, but not enough to satisfy me. At the end there was some applause, but not what I had hoped for. I wanted cheers, ovations! We waited outside for the dreaded cards. The audience would give you their verdict, and a special focus group of fourteen men and women would get very specific. I was nervous. Joe Roth seemed strangely calm. Robinson suggested I lose the shot of the Wonder Wheel at the end, but he said he loved the movie. Stuart and I had been through the preview mill many times. We knew that only a high score would satisfy the studio.

Jack Brodsky came out of the theater looking as if he'd been hit by a truck. "The numbers are not too nice," he said, handing the scores to Roth and Robinson. "Thirty-six percent 'Very Good' or better," said Joe. I sighed, "I'm going to give up the business!" Joe urged me to relax. "Paul, all this means is that thirty-six percent of the public will want to see this picture. Do you know how big thirty-six per cent is?" Everyone agreed with Joe's interpretation. "I want to release this picture just as it is. It's a classic. Congratulations!" He embraced me and his wife hugged me.

My head was reeling. Hit! Bomb! Only thirty-six percent like it! Classic, schmassic!

Two months later we began the critics' screenings. We knew from the start that *Enemies* was going to be a critical success, that there might be some Academy Award nominations, and that it might even make money.

There was a special screening in Miami for Isaac and Alma. Alma sent me a note stating that this was the first time Isaac had liked a movie made from one of his stories.

In a P.S. to the note, Alma asked me if there was any more money coming to them. I laughed. It was a line right out of a Singer story.

Lena Olin, Anjelica Huston, and Simon and Mazursky were nominated for Oscars. I hoped I would win so that I could thank Isaac. But I didn't win, and a few months later the great Nobel Prize–winning author died. Sad ending? No. I think Singer would have been amused at all the Oscar brouhaha.

18

The Ones
I Never Made

Since I've written many scripts with both Roger and Leon, we often commiserate about the ones that never got made. Why were some produced and others not? This is the eternal question in Hollywood. So many of the films that get made are not only dumb but destined to fail. The price tags are way too high, and shooting begins on scripts not close to being ready—but there is a release date to be met, and they have a big star in place. "We need a big Christmas picture!" "We need a big summer picture!" "Your picture is too small! We need something that can gross a hundred million!" (I hate the term "small"—it sounds as if a piece of junk is "big" and Fellini or Bergman is "small.") But just when you think all is lost, the studios surprise you with taste and daring, coming out with a *Cuckoo's Nest* or an *Amadeus*.

H-BOMB BEACH PARTY!

The first script that never got made was *H-Bomb Beach Party!* Larry Tucker and I wrote it in 1965 while we were toiling for Danny Kaye. It was based on a true story about two American H-bombs that were lost off the coast of Spain. Larry and I flew to Spain for research. By the time we returned to the States, we had developed a story. "Marapalo" is an island so poor they don't even have money for a red light outside the local house of prostitution. There is no economy except for the rare capture of a whale. There is no tourism on Marapalo. Get the picture? U.S. Intelligence can't find the second bomb. One night in Marapalo a whale washes ashore, a parachute sticking out of its mouth. The whale has swallowed the bomb! At a hastily assembled meeting the townspeople, led by their priest, decide to keep the truth from the U.S. Army. They know that troops will pour into Marapalo in an attempt to find the bomb. Tourism will flourish, and Marapalo will once again be a jewel of the Mediterranean. It was an outrageously broad farce.

We sent the script to the great George Stevens who was about to direct *The Greatest Story Ever Told*. We knew he loved comedy—after all, Stevens had directed W. C. Fields! Mr. Stevens shocked us one afternoon by calling us at our CBS office. He told us that we were gifted, that *H-Bomb* was funny. He encouraged us, but he couldn't do the film. I'll never forget that call.

A few weeks later a producer named Hunt Stromberg, Jr., optioned the script. We were elated. A meeting was arranged with Larry, me, and Laurence Harvey, the elegant British actor. We dined at the Bistro, a really "in" joint. Harvey was smart and very enthusiastic about the script. He had no airs, and he made a lot of sense. He agreed to star in the film. I would direct, and Larry would produce under the auspices of Hunt Stromberg, Jr. We left the Bistro in a state of exhilaration. By the next morning the deal had evaporated. We were on the mad seesaw of Hollywood. You're in! You're out! Up! Down! Always ready to believe any morsel of hope thrown your way! But that was that. We never really learned what happened. It took a while for us to accept the fact that *H-Bomb Beach Party!* might never get made. I reread the script last week. Thirty years later it's still funny. Maybe with a polish and a bit of updating . . .

UNCLE SAM'S WILD WEST SHOW

Uncle Sam's Wild West Show was a script Larry and I commissioned Venable Herndon to write. We were hot enough (post *Bob & Carol . . .*) to get money from United Artists to pay Venable who was just coming off *Alice's Restaurant.* I originally got the idea from Pirandello's play *Enrico IV.* A medieval king holds court, but when he leaves the stage, we learn that he is a modern man whose courtiers are paid professional actors. Enrico is nuts. It seems he fell off a horse in a pageant and lost his memory. But is he really crazy? My idea was to switch it to the Old West. A once-great American film director has fallen off a horse and lost his grip on reality. His estate pays for a group of actors to pretend to be cowboys in an old western town.

We bought the rights only to learn that the Pirandello estate would not permit us to use the central device of Enrico pretending to be mad. I was thus thrust into my own Pirandellian nightmare. Larry and I came up with a new story. The last of the great Hollywood tycoons is about to lose control of his studio to a conglomerate (circa 1972). The producer is making a film about an Indian called *Uncle Sam's Wild West Show.* The aging producer slowly begins to identify with the Indian. He even participates in peyote ceremonies. He begins to run the studio wearing buckskins. He takes meetings on the floor of his office and passes the peace pipe. It all ends tragically. In reading what I've just written, even I am confused. Did I ever think I'd get this one made?

PICTURES OF FIDELMAN

Pictures of Fidelman was adapted from the novel by Bernard Malamud. A New York artist is bombed by the critics and flees to

Italy to find the "answer to art," but all he gets into is trouble. It's a funny, picaresque book that Roger Simon and I adapted. Of all the scripts I have sitting on the shelf, *Fidelman* is the one I still want to do the most. We've come close many times: money from Italy if we can get so-and-so to star; money from the States if we can cut the budget in half; money from here, money from there, but finally no money—a familiar Hollywood tale.

For many years now, raising money for *Fidelman* has been my main occupation. Once, during a visit to Rome to see Fellini, the Maestro himself called Vittorio Cecchi-Gori to arrange a meeting. Cecchi-Gori is a well-known Italian producer with tons of lire, but most of his hits have been gangster movies and broad comedies. Just listening to Fellini trying to explain *Fidelman*, the story of a Jewish painter, to Cecchi-Gori over the phone was reward enough. Fellini urged me to take the meeting. "Who knows, *carino*, what these animals will like? I personally always have trouble finding money."

Fidelman sits on my desk, patiently waiting for a buyer. For some magical reason I still have hope.

MOSCOW ON THE ROCKS

Moscow on the Rocks was a sequel to *Moscow on the Hudson*. Leon and I wrote the script. In this story we meet the Robin Williams character, Vladimir, ten years later. Vlad now lives the life of a successful New York yuppie. Although he has a great pad in Soho and plenty of money, he has lost his Russian soul and replaced it with a superficial existence. Vlad gets a call from his mother in Moscow informing him that his younger sister is getting married and that he must come to Moscow for the wedding. Vlad, who defected ten years earlier, is terrified of what awaits him in Russia, but off he goes. It's a new Moscow filled with fancy cars and gangsters. In the hurly-burly of his first few days, Vlad is simultaneously touched, frightened, and skeptical. Then he falls in love! The ultimate dilemma of whether he should stay in Russia with this fabulous female or go back to New York is the meat of the movie. After Robin Williams read it, he sadly told me that he just didn't think it was safe to work in Russia at the present time. (There were many violent incidents reported in the press.) I tried my best but to no avail. *Moscow on the Rocks* is still on the rocks.

POOR

I wrote the script for *Poor* on spec and then quickly sold it to my old friend Jim Robinson at Morgan Creek. *Poor* is about a fortyish Santa Monica banker who loses his job, his house, and his dignity. Robinson wanted a big star. I sent the script to Warren Beatty. As usual, Warren procrastinated.

Two weeks went by. I got a phone call from Robert Redford. "Hi, Paul. How come I never got to read *Poor?*" I'd met Redford— or Bob, as he is usually called—at the Sundance Institute. (Sundance is Bob's creation, and it is a marvel. Nobody has done more than Redford to help new cinema.) When I got the call, I got very excited. "Well, Bob, that's very flattering, but I thought you were busy." "I'm not too busy to read a script of yours," said Bob. " What's this about Warren?" he tossed in. I told Bob the truth and assured him that we had no commitment to Warren. I was sitting pretty. If I didn't get Beatty, I'd probably get Redford, or vice versa. Two weeks later Beatty passed, and Redford's agent called to tell me that Robert didn't want to do *Poor.* I was back on the seesaw!

Jeff Bridges passed, but at least he had the courtesy to tell me himself. I met with Christopher Reeve, who wanted to play the part. He would have been very good, but Morgan Creek felt he was not a big enough star. "But he's Superman!" I shouted to my agent. Jimmy Woods came by—an extremely bright actor; he wanted to play the part. No soap. Not big enough. Soon, *Poor* began to fade away.

BROKE

Poor was Betsy's favorite script of mine. One day she suggested that I turn the idea of *Poor* into a sequel to *Down and Out in*

Beverly Hills. Richard Dreyfuss loses his hanger factory, his money, and his house. Bette Midler is forced to get a job. And Nick Nolte falls for the high-powered Beverly Hills real estate lady who sells the house. I pitched the idea to Joe Roth at Disney, and soon Leon and I were writing the sequel to *Down and Out.* We called it *Broke.* Four months later Joe turned down the script. We were devastated. Dreyfuss, Midler, and Nolte all wanted to do it. Maybe one of these days another studio will go for *Broke.*

MY FRIEND, THE MESSIAH

Carol Reed's great film *The Third Man* is a favorite of mine. The script by Graham Green and the performances of Orson Welles, Joseph Cotten, Trevor Howard, and Alida Valli were perfect. I got the idea to do a movie that used the same central device as *Third Man.* A mystery writer arrives in postwar Vienna to attend his best friend's funeral. It doesn't take long for him to discover that his friend, Harry Lime, was up to no good. Then, to his great surprise, he finds out that his friend is alive and well.

My take was to switch it all to Jerusalem. In *My Friend, the Messiah* a Jewish mystery writer from New York arrives in Jerusalem to attend his Catholic friend's funeral. He begins to investigate the mysterious death of his best pal and discovers that he is alive! Moreover, he's become messianic.

Roger Simon and I went to Jerusalem and Qumran to research the script. Qumran is where the Dead Sea scrolls were discovered. With the help of a brilliant American archaeologist, Robert Eisenman, we got into the caves where the scrolls were actually found. We were beginning to understand the life of the Essenes, a pre-Christian cult that sometimes spoke in the language of Christ. It was an inspiring trip. We were taken by a Palestinian merchant named Fouad to the markets of Jerusalem at the height of the Palestinian troubles. Although it was considered a dangerous thing to do, we drove to the town of Ramallah with Fouad, a deeply religious and intelligent man.

While he was driving the old Volvo through the desert, he

told us, "If Allah will be kind to me, he will let me kill two men." We asked him who the men were. "First, Arafat. Yasser Arafat."

We were shocked. "But Arafat is your leader. Arafat is your friend."

Fouad shook his head. "Arafat is only for Arafat!"

"I see."

"Who's the other man?" asked Roger."

Without missing a beat, Fouad said, "Salman Rushdie. He deserves to die for what he has written. The blasphemy!" I asked him if he'd actually read Rushdie's novel. "Of course I have read this terrible book! If only Allah would be kind to Fouad, he will let me be the one to kill this man."

We told him that his position was intolerable, that we were both writers. "Why not kill us?"

"Ah, but you have not blasphemed my religion," he said.

Despite our disagreement, we found Fouad to be a very warm and interesting man.

When we returned to L.A., we wrote *My Friend, the Messiah.* That was about six years ago. Columbia passed on the script, and there have been no buyers. The story is more pertinent than ever. It's unlike any movie I ever made. Action! Intrigue! Romance! Humor! Commercial! Dustin Hoffman or Richard Dreyfuss as the Jewish mystery writer, and Warren Beatty or Jack Nicholson as the Catholic messiah! Or should we go younger with Ben Stiller or Matt Damon? Boffo box office! . . . I'm still available.

HEART OF A DOG

Ilya Baskin, the Russian actor who played the clown in *Moscow on the Hudson*, put me onto a splendid novel by the wondrous Russian writer Mikhail Bulgakov. *Heart of a Dog* was set in Moscow in the twenties. A doctor experiments with a dog, and one day the dog becomes a man. Pandemonium! Bulgakov wrote this comic parable to ventilate his feelings about the dog's life that Russians were living. I decided to switch the idea to modern-day New York City. A Russian émigré doctor performs the experiment, which goes haywire. The climax of the film takes place when the doctor, having finally civilized the wild dog/man, takes him to a Broadway show. Unfortunately, it's *Cats*. When the dog/man sees all the cats onstage, he flips and reverts to his wild animal ways.

I wrote the script for Disney with my daughter Jill, a writer who has had two films made. Disney liked the idea of my working with a younger writer—the first real sign that you're getting old. My daughter is super-fast with the computer, and she wears a pager. I was afraid it would be a difficult job, but it turned out to be a delight. Jill pushed me to work faster. The script quickly fell into shape, and I deluded myself into thinking that we would soon get a green light. The first sign of trouble came when the new head executive of Hollywood Pictures, Michael Lynton, failed to call us back. A week or so passed. My agents finally told me that Lynton had read the script and wanted to talk to me about it. Furthermore, he wanted to come to my office. That sounded promising (oh, what crumbs we hang on to when we're desperate), so we set a time. Jill and I prepared our strategy. I told her I'd even read scenes aloud for Lynton. We were shocked when he told us he didn't "get" the script. "It's not really funny, is it?"

I began to act out whole scenes. As the dog/man, I barked and yelped and threw myself on the floor of my office, holding up my arms the way a dog holds up his paws. Lynton could not stop laughing! "That's funny!" he cried. I looked at Jill. She was laughing, too.

Two days later Lynton officially passed on *Heart of a Dog*. I've since tried to get Robin Williams, Eddie Murphy, and Bill Murray involved with the project. I toyed with the idea of making the lead a female pooch. How about Whoopi Goldberg or Ellen DeGeneres? Maybe Julia Roberts as a saucy cocker spaniel? So far there have been no takers, but I'm a very patient man. However, one of the problems with turndowns is you often learn that someone else has come up with pretty much the same idea and it's a go picture.

FREDDY FAUST

My last collaboration with Roger L. Simon was *Freddy Faust.*
We pitched the idea to Disney and got a quick yes. Freddy Faust is
a once great Hollywood comedy writer now fallen on hard times.
His old buddies who meet him regularly at the Farmer's Market in
L.A. wonder what happened to Freddy. We learn that after experiencing several bleak turndowns, he finds himself talking to the
Devil on his computer screen. The Devil is a bit like Bill Gates.
He promises Freddy ten great years—success, money, women, the
works. Freddy accepts. *Freddy Faust* is one of my favorites. When
the studio passed, I was bewildered. Roger and I had had previous
turndowns, but *Faust* seemed a shoo-in. It was funny and it was
emotional. It took advantage of all the new computer image possibilities. I wonder what I would do if the Devil offered me the
money to make *Freddy Faust.*

19

A Place in My Heart

I had a four-way bypass in May 1996. The operation was successful, but I now view myself with different eyes. Every morning when I wake up, it takes me a few minutes to remember that I'm sixty-eight years old. I stumble into the bathroom, do my morning toilette, and look in the mirror. The man I see doesn't look like me. He has bags under his eyes and a bit of a double chin. The "me" I best remember has a crew cut and is waiting tables in the Catskills, or he has a pompadour and is onstage at some New York nightclub. He's somewhere between sixteen and thirty. This fellow in the mirror can't be me, except for his hair: His hair is still black.

Many of my friends think I dye my hair. In fact, they're so insistent about this that I've invented a woman in San Diego who specializes in "star dying." I tell them that she used "to do Danny Kaye." The story is so convincing that I'm beginning to believe in this myself. The truth is, my dark hair comes from my father, Dave, and his father, Charlie Mazursky. Charlie drank a lot and made mattresses in Perth Amboy, New Jersey, for a living. Even that didn't turn his hair white. And Dave, even though he suffered through the Great Depression and fought with Jean every day, died with black hair. My mother's father, Sam Gerson, my *zeda*, was totally bald.

I've never really thought much about all these things, but four-way bypasses tend, I suppose, to make you reassess your life. All sorts of weird stuff floats into the mind: the high-topped black shoes I wore when I was six years old and went to school for the first time (at P.S. 144); sex, as it happened or didn't as the case may be; and hair. How could I have black hair and need a bypass? Dead friends visit your hospital room, friends like Pato Guzman and Fellini and Raul Julia, my Latin amigos. You wonder if you're go-ing to join them soon. Your successes and your failures loom large in newspaper headlines: MAZURSKY BOMBS IN DALLAS! MAZURSKY SELLS NEW SCRIPT! *Mazursky Has Open Heart Surgery!* You swear yourself to a new, calm, meditative life, even though you fear that would be intolerable. You even consider becoming a disciple of Deepak Chopra! You realize how wonderful your family is, how much you love your friends, and how much you've taken them for granted. You make a promise to really *listen*, not to be so self-in-volved.

When Betsy, Meg, Jill, and Jill's husband, Steve, came to my room at Cedars-Sinai, I was grateful to be alive. There hadn't been much time to think about the operation. I had gone to my cardiol-ogist, an intense Israeli named Dr. Yitzhak Charuzi, for my yearly treadmill test. I have been overweight for the past ten years, so I made it a point to take annual stress tests. I lead an active life. I had trekked in Nepal and was a daily tennis player. I never had trouble. But this time the EKG showed odd lines. The following morning I had an angiogram, and Dr. Charuzi saw four blocked arteries. I was soon introduced to Dr. Alfredo Trento, the eminent heart sur-geon. He reminded me of Marcello Mastroianni. Trento told me that all would go well. "Is more dangerous to take out the appendix," Trento assured me. After he left I spoke to my internist, Dr. Norman Lavet. Norman has been both my friend and my doctor for thirty-five years. He told me that Trento was first-rate. "He's the best! He did me last year," he added. I'd forgotten that Norman had had a bypass. That was good enough for me. Not only that, but I soon learned that Trento had done Michael Eisner's bypass. I was in luck!

Three days later I checked into Cedars-Sinai at five in the morning. Betsy came with me, doing her best to hide her fears. We knew that Meg and Jill were frightened. Meg, my older daughter, is a beautiful woman with a Mother Teresa complex. If there's something wrong, Meg will be there for you. Jill is more of a jokester, like her father. But this time she had no jokes. They had said good-bye to me the night before, and I could see the fear in their eyes. "Relax," I told them. "It's less dangerous than taking out the appendix." I said good-bye to my grandchildren, Carly and Katie. They didn't seem too concerned, and of course I played it the same way. Katie at nine was already a performer; she danced and sang a number for me in her munchkin-like voice. Carly embraced me. She was twelve years old. "I love you, Poppa. I love you," she said. Jill had even brought her dogs to say their farewells—Snowball, a white Samoyed, and Manza, a large black-and-white Husky. The dogs are best friends and seem to understand everything anyone says to them. I love these dogs, and I could tell that they were worried. The whole thing felt like a scene from a soap opera, only it was my life.

At about 7:00 A.M. I was told that the operation wouldn't begin until 9:30. I told Betsy to go home and get a couple of hours' rest. Oddly, I really did not feel fear. If anything, the entire affair was like a dream. I had faith. If Trento did Michael Eisner, he must be pretty good. Then the anesthesiologist came into the room. "Are you allergic to anything, Mr. Mazursky?" he asked. I assured him I wasn't. He smiled and said, "I wonder if I could ask a favor of you." "Sure," I told him. "Well, I'm a very big fan, and my favorite movie of yours is *Enemies, A Love Story.*" I smiled weakly. The tranquilizer they had given me was working. "Thank you. What's the favor?" I asked. "I have a laser disc of *Enemies.* I wonder if you'd sign it for me." I almost did a double take. "Do you want me to sign it right now, or can we do it after the operation?" He blushed and told me he'd be only too happy to wait.

It was at that moment that I understood the nature of fear. By God, this guy figured I might kick the bucket during the operation, and he'd end up with an unsigned laser disc! Fortunately, I was so groggy that I soon fell asleep.

When I woke up, I was in the recovery room. I was very tired but also elated. I was alive! There was a tube down my throat that caused some discomfort. I nodded to the Filippino nurse that I wanted something. I felt very dry. It was impossible to speak clearly with a tube in my throat. I muttered the word "water," but it must have sounded like "wawa." "You want to make 'wawa'?" the nurse asked me, picking up a bedpan. I shook my head. "Nahhh! Wawa! Wawa!" I tried to indicate the act of drinking, but I was too weak. The nurse summoned a doctor. He looked at me: "You need something, Mr. Mazursky?" "Wawa," I said. "Wawa." He turned to the nurse. "Give the man some water—but only a few drops."

In a few minutes Betsy arrived. She looked just like the girl I had picked up in Greenwich Village more than forty years ago. Or was I dreaming? "They gave you a pig valve!" she blurted out. She was almost crying. "That man, that Dr. Trento, came out during the operation and said you needed a new valve—a metal one or a pig valve. Dr. Lavet was there and said do the pig valve." I could tell that Betsy was afraid that I might not want a pig valve. I smiled. So did she. "I know it's not kosher," she said.

Being unable to talk was especially difficult. I had a million jokes in my head: "I'm glad I have a pig valve. Oink! Oink!" "I'll have a B.L.T. on rye toast. On second thought, save the bacon!"

Within hours of recovery, heart bypass patients are asked to start walking, to move. Have they no pity? No, and for good reason. A friendly volunteer came to see me and told me that I'd be depressed and subject to sudden bouts of tears. "I don't cry easily," I said. She left the room and I began to sob. Then my daughters showed up. I was back from the dead! I wanted to be alone so that I could cry. It's an emotional seesaw. On the second day I was moved from the recovery room to a normal room. They helped me sit in a wheelchair and pushed me down several corridors. As we passed a large window, I saw trees—tall green trees in the sunshine. This set off a profound feeling of awe. "How amazing to see a tree!" I thought. "Why was I such an ungrateful bastard?" I wiped my eyes and swore eternal goodness—not just to my family and my friends, but to trees and plants and fishes.

Warren Beatty called me almost every day for two weeks. "How are you?" My voice was still hoarse. "Warren?" "Yeah. You sound hoarse." "I am. But I'm fine." Warren talks in a very low phone voice. "You're fine?" "Yes. I feel great." Actually, I was still exhausted. "Did they cut you open?" asked Warren anxiously. "Yeah. They saw your chest open." Warren wanted all the details. I urged him to do a lot of exercise. "I do! I do!" he said. "Every day?" I asked him. He sounded worried. "Do they tell you to exercise every day?" "As soon as I begin rehab." He was talking to me as if I were a doctor. Warren's concern touched me deeply. He had taken the time to call me again and again. So why the hell hadn't he ever done one of my projects? I wondered. I was still confusing art with real life.

One day Mel Brooks called: "What happened? What happened?" I explained the entire heart bit to Mel and assured him I was fine. "I want to see you. I've got to see you!" He sounded desperate. But I admit I loved it. Warren Beatty on the phone and Mel Brooks coming over. I was star-fucking post-bypass! Mel rang the bell to my front door. Slowly I shuffled to the door and opened it. I was wearing a jogging suit and could only move with careful steps. Mel took one look and embraced me. "You can't go yet, Mazursky! You're a national treasure!" He had tears in his eyes. "I'm not going!" I assured Mel. I remembered the Peter Sellers incident when Peter screened *The Producers* (Mel's masterpiece) the night that I'd failed to order Fellini's *Vitteloni*. Mel can really make you laugh. I remembered going once to Junior's Delicatessen in Westwood to have lunch with Mel. They reserved a table for him by writing his name on a paper napkin. His visit lifted my spirits.

Two and a half years have passed. I go to rehab three times a week. I do the treadmill, the bicycle, the rowing machine, and I lift weights. Last year I climbed Mount Sinai in Egypt. I am stronger than ever. I am a lucky man. I think I'm calmer, but then again, who knows? When I'm driving my car and some moron in front of me makes a sudden right turn from the left lane, I still fervently wish I had a ray gun to kill the jerk!

20

Buddies

Growing up in Brownsville is probably the reason I still try to live a street life. Ironically, you have to be poor to have a street life in Los Angeles. Action, games, fights, gossip—these were normal on my block in Brooklyn. The block was our playground. There was punchball, tag, ring-a-levio, hide-and-seek, incessant debates about "Joltin' Joe" DiMaggio versus "Stan the Man" Musial. I still try to operate that way, which is not easy in Beverly Hills where you can be searched by a cop just for taking a walk. So I find my action in a variety of other places. For more than twenty years I've played poker every Wednesday night, gone to the Farmer's Market most weekday mornings for coffee and a cinnamon bun, and ridden my bicycle in Venice every Sunday. These activities keep me grounded. It's more like real life, whatever that is. The poker players are not in show business, except for Jason who once played "Flesh" Gordon in a soft-core porno. Jason is the only non-Jew in the game; he puts mayonnaise on his corned beef on rye. (My wife, Betsy, drinks milk with her pastrami sandwich, a typical shiksa habit.) The other poker players (eight of whom have passed on to the Big Casino in the sky) sell mobile homes, lawn furniture, imitation watches, and engage in other "real" occupations. One is a psychologist with a nasty temper. All in all, especially if I win, it's a lot of laughs. It's also a bit masochistic, since the screaming and the shouting at the game leaves one exhausted for the next two days.

Plummer Park in West Hollywood is where I've played tennis for thirty-odd years. It's a public park that became for me a New York–type melting pot. The players are from Iran, Israel, England, Germany, Mexico, India, Sumatra, and West Hollywood. The park is a wonderful place to kibitz, and the tennis is surprisingly good. But for my group, the kibitzing is as important as the tennis. The crueler the banter gets, the more you know the other person cares about you. Today, Plummer Park is little Moscow. Russians are everywhere, including Russian senior citizens. When I pass an elderly couple sitting on a bench chatting in Russian, I sometimes imagine that Sam and Ida, my grandparents, are still alive. I think they'd like Plummer Park.

The Farmer's Market is located on Fairfax Avenue and Third Street. It's Los Angeles' version of a large French cafe. It is surrounded by fruit and vegetable stalls, a newspaper stand, a post office, a key maker, and a shoeshine man, and it's populated by a steady parade of all types of people: beautiful women in shorts; odd-looking regulars who wear raincoats in the heat of summer; eighty-year-old guys with white ponytails; Israelis who smoke like chimneys; German tourists looking for some schnitzel; the Latina beauty who hurries upstairs to the office, wiggling her ass as she goes; the folks who seem somehow to resemble famous figures of the past, now resurrected by our motley crew. "There's Marc Chagall! I love your stained-glass windows at the Paris Opera House, Marc!"—this directed at a handsome fellow of about ninety who always wears a Greek fisherman's cap and a dandy sports coat. The combo and his longish white hair mark him as an artist; actually, he is a retired tailor.

Sometimes only one or two regulars show up at our table, but usually there are six or seven. There is Leon Capetanos, my long-time cowriter who shows up with a pot of tea, three daily newspapers, and two bagels. Some days his beautiful young Swedish wife, Lisa, and his adorable four-year-old son, John, join him. We all love the kid who looks just like Leon. Leon is something of a poet, but he is also an obsessive college basketball fan. (Could T. S. Eliot have written "The Wasteland" while watching the Tar Heels of North Carolina on the dish?) Roger Simon is a less frequent visitor. We've written four scripts together. Roger is one of the brightest men I know and a splendid writer, but patience is not one of his virtues. As soon as Roger sits down, he looks at his wristwatch to see if it's time to go. Roger hates to waste time. But then why come to the market? Is the coffee that good? No. Then what is it? It's the energy of the table. The New York juice. The laughs. The put-downs. The vulgarity. The opinions. And, once in a while, the compassion.

Marty Elfand produced *An Officer and a Gentleman*. He's smart and has good taste, two qualities that bode badly in La-la Land. He's an incredible golfer and he loves children. Right now his career is on hold. But then again, so is mine. My money is still on Marty.

David Freeman is a novelist, a critic, and a journalist as well as a screenwriter. David is often on the verge of never writing another screenplay. "You don't get paid enough to make up for the endless dreary meetings, and then the damned thing doesn't get made," David will tell you. There is hearty approval from Leon, Roger, and me. David puts his money where his mouth is by writing novels that get published. He is a rather small man with a big heart who wears an old straw hat. He is a compulsive analyzer, perhaps because he is a critic. David can tell you why he didn't like a certain film, but he can also tell you why *you* didn't like it.

Charley Bragg is an artist, a painter, a balding man with a white goatee. He is a funny fellow who constantly chuckles. Somehow I have his number. If I so much as sneeze, he falls into a paroxysm of laughter. I told him once that he suffered from "hebrophenia," a disease that makes people laugh without cause. (Many cartoonists have hebrophenia.) Charley told me he couldn't find the word in the dictionary. I told him I probably made it up. That produced a three-minute chuckle. His paintings are somewhat in the style of Hieronymus Bosch—grotesque comic exaggerations of our foibles, drawn with superb technique. He has never had a drawing lesson. Most of the characters he paints look suspiciously like Charley, who wears loose-fitting jogging pants and Hawaiian shirts. His best friend Gene comes to the market about one week a month. Gene lives in Manhattan but loves L.A. His wife, however, loves Manhattan, so he's worked out this compromise. Gene, who had been an ace art director for a New York publisher, decided to retire after thirty-five years of deadlines. He probably shouldn't have retired. Now all he has to worry about is his cholesterol, which weighs in at about 450 no matter what Gene eats.

Phyllis Smith used to be my assistant. Before that she ran a boutique in Manhattan's West Village. Her New York accent is a thing of beauty, and to her credit she has made no attempt to Californiaize it. Phyllis loves foreign films and brunches. "Yeah, yeah," she'll say about something she agrees with, "Yeah, yeah..." Brooklyn on the Pacific.

Len Klady is a Canadian who writes articles and reviews for *Daily Variety*, our show business journal. He shows up on Mondays, always dropping a sheet of white paper on the table. It's the weekend grosses. In a few minutes the table analyzes the results: This piece of crap made a fortune, that piece of utter slime did well, this moronic shoot-em-up is going to be a monster hit! Where are the good old days? we mourn. Where are Fellini, Truffaut, De Sica, Ernst Lubitsch, Billy Wilder, Hitchcock, John Ford, Preston Sturges, and their likes?

"Kubrick's coming out with a new picture," someone offers. "Yeah, but he only makes one movie a decade," says Len as he lights yet another Rothman cigarette. We all wave our hands in the air to clear away the dreaded smoke. "Woody is doing good things," offers another regular. "Yeah, but he gets private money," another retorts. "So what? He makes grownup movies!"

One of our regulars was Allan Malamud, the sportswriter. Allan—or Mud, as he liked to be called—was a Runyonesque type. He loved to play the horses. He was perennially overweight. (Who isn't?) He knew a lot about sports, but deep down I think Mud wanted to be an actor. (I used him as a caterer in *Down and Out.* Richard Brooks cast him in a small role in *Fever,* and his good buddy Ron Shelton used him in several films.) Most of the market regulars love sports, and Allan gave us the inside dope. It's through Allan that Leon and I had lunch with Tommy LaSorda at a downtown Chinese restaurant, a memorable afternoon for me. When Allan died, the Farmer's Market did something very special. They put a permanent plaque on our table honoring Mud. There was a touching morning ceremony complete with free coffee and doughnuts. We toasted Mud with our cappuccinos and lattés. Sometimes we wonder if Mud is worried about the latest Dodger slump.

At the market we dissect films, TV shows, news events, novels, deals. We offer advice on health, exercise, penile implants, the Middle East, new restaurants, used cars, and feta cheese. For about an hour every morning we rate the world, ogle the girls, and eye the types. We are sometimes brutal, finding the jugular veins of each other's lives, but almost always there is affection and concern. While I'm there, my life as a boy in Brooklyn doesn't seem so far away. I'm still trying to make the guys laugh. I still have the camaraderie of the streets. For an hour each morning, life still seems spontaneous. Our Farmer's Market antics have been recorded in British and French documentaries. While both films were excellent, they didn't quite capture the wild life of our species. I'm afraid the real quality of the table has to be experienced in the flesh. So join us one morning if you will. We're the noisy group sitting near the magazines and the doughnuts. Come in around eight-thirty. We'll probably be staring at you.

Index